BUDDHIST ETHICS

WORKS OF THE SAME AUTHOR

Saral-Pāli-Śikṣā
Mahabodhi Society, Sarnath, Banaras, 1948

Upāsakajanālaṅkāra
A Critical Edition and Study
Pali Text Society, London, 1965

Pāli Tipiṭaka Concordance
Volume III Parts II, III,
Pali Text Society, London, 1968–69

BUDDHIST ETHICS

Essence of Buddhism

BY

H. SADDHATISSA, M.A., Ph.D.

Tripiṭakācārya, Paṇḍita

FOREWORD BY M. O'C. WALSHE, M.A.

Vice-President, The Buddhist Society

GEORGE BRAZILLER

NEW YORK

For information address the publisher:

George Braziller, Inc.
One Park Avenue
New York, New York 10016

Standard Book Number: 0-8076-0597-2 (Paperbound)
0-8076-0598-0 (Hardbound)
Library of Congress Catalog Card Number: 75-141044

Printed in the United States of America

FOREWORD

BY M. O'C. WALSHE, M.A.

The Ven. Dr H. Saddhātissa was born in Ceylon and is now living in London, head of the London Buddhist Vihāra. Having graduated from the Vidyodaya Pirivena (now University), he was ordained in the Order in Ceylon in 1926, and has now reached the highest rank—Mahāthera. Continuing his studies at Banaras Hindu University, he received a BA. Honours Degree, and for being placed first in the Order of Merit, he was awarded first prize while obtaining his MA degree there. He was a research scholar at London University and received his PHD from the University of Edinburgh for his erudite thesis on Buddhist Philosophy. He is proficient in Pali, Sanskrit, Sinhalese and Hindi, and is conversant with several other oriental as well as occidental languages. He has taught Buddhism to scholars and laymen in Ceylon, India, England and America for many years, and held the post of a Professor of Buddhism and Pali at Banaras University and the University of Toronto. Among his works, the *Upāsakajanālankāra*, published by the Pali Text Society, London, is well known among Pali scholars; he has also contributed numerous articles to various scholarly journals. Currently he serves on the Executive Council of the Pali Text Society, and as President of the British Mahabodhi Society and the Sangha Council of Great Britain.

The Ven. Dr Saddhātissa has written a most important book which, strange as it may seem, fills a considerable gap. The only book at all comparable is Tachibana's *Ethics of Buddhism* which is far less comprehensive.

It is sometimes thought in the West that Buddhism is 'a magnificent system of ethics' and little more. This is of course a gross misapprehension based on a superficial or biased view of the Buddhist teaching as a whole. It is one of the great merits of the Ven. Dr Saddhātissa's book that it makes clear what is the rightful position of ethics within the whole system of Buddhist thought and practice. In doing so he draws not only on the scriptures of the ancient Buddhist school which he represents—he is in fact its senior representative in London at the present time—but also on the schools of Mahāyāna or 'developed Buddhism'.

Though ethics is far from being the whole of Buddhism, its scope within the Buddhist system is very wide, and in consequence this book contains a great deal of information about general Buddhism;

and since all Buddhist practice is oriented towards the goal of Nirvāṇa it is fitting that the last chapter should deal with this.

Some particular points should perhaps be emphasized here. The Buddhist ethic is autonomous. The five basic precepts for the layman, and the greater number of precepts or rules observed by monks or by lay people on particular occasions, are not arbitrarily decreed 'commandments' but 'rules of training' which are voluntarily observed because one is aware of the purpose they serve. They do not include any purely ritual obligations. It is therefore relevant to point out, for instance, that the practice of prostration before the Buddha image, and the offering of flowers and incense, is an expression of reverence and respect but not of worship, and may be dispensed with, which does not mean that it is necessarily without value.

Again, the practice of virtue is difficult. Buddhists are particularly well aware of the proneness of the mind to wander into unwholesome thought-patterns from which various forms of misconduct take rise. The proper practice of Buddhist meditation helps here, whether it takes the form of *samādhi* or the so-called *Jhāna* states developed by mental concentration, or that of the practice of mindfulness leading to insight (*vipassanā*) into the true nature of things. In particular, the author explains in some detail how the systematic cultivation of *mettā* or loving-kindness can be used to overcome anger and ill-will.

The Ven. Dr Saddhātissa has not only collected together all the material on his theme scattered throughout the early Buddhist scriptures, but he has also drawn extensively on his profound knowledge of Vedic and Upanishadic thought to supply the necessary background, besides making some interesting comparisons with Greek thought.

This book will be of great value to all serious students of Buddhism, or of comparative religion and morals. Its exhaustive collection of material makes it a scholarly contribution of permanent value, while its lucid presentation makes it a pleasure to read, and its wide range makes it also in many ways suitable as a general introduction to the study—and practice—of Buddhism. It is particularly welcome at the present time for several reasons. There is a growing interest in Buddhism in the West which often takes on forms that are at best dilettante and sometimes positively harmful in circles where the ethical aspects are ignored or relativized. This book should serve as a useful corrective to such tendencies, as well as being a source of authoritative information for the serious enquirer.

PREFACE

There is much truth in the belief that those who follow a religion or teaching by conviction, who adjust and improve their lives through self-conversion are generally speaking more conscious and sincere in their actions than those who have merely been born into that religion. The latter may often adhere to its tenets due to social pressure or force of habit.

Of course strictly speaking Buddhism is not a religion in the generally accepted sense of the word, and it would be more accurate to describe it as an ethico-philosophy to be practised by each follower. And it is only by practice, by an uphill spiritual struggle, that happiness in life either present of future, as well as the goal of Nibbāna, can possibly be obtained.

Music and similar arts are enjoyed in order to gratify one's *emotional* desire. Morality (*sīla*) on the other hand, is indispensible to the spiritual life which cannot conceivably be fulfilled by sense pleasures, and is therefore an essential factor by which we may determine a truly cultured individual.

To be a good Buddhist implies that one is ethical, that one lives according to a minimum of five moral precepts or rules (*sikkhāpada*). These train the mind so as to lessen the grip of sense desire upon it. Formal ceremony in accepting them is considered quite unnecessary, the prime object being that, through their influence one may become one's own master, and be able to examine one's state of inner life. Moreover one will be able to direct one's thoughts and aspirations so as to fulfil a rational meaningful existence. Meditation is the chief means whereby one may gain mastery over oneself, leading inevitably to wisdom (*paññā*). The Buddha categorically points out how one should tread the path, as follows: 'By confidence, by morality, by energy, by meditation, by the investigation of the Truth, by being endowed with knowledge and good conduct, and by being mindful, put aside this great suffering.' (Dh. v. 144)

The approach to the Buddha's path, therefore, does not require prayers or worship, nor does the path contain anything of an esoteric nature, but consists simply in a day-to-day life of love and sympathy with all that breathes.

The object of the present work is to treat comprehensively the study of the ethical principles as depicted in the Buddhist literature. The world's current difficulties show clearly that there has never been a greater need than now for the widest possible understanding and practise of such principles. For this reason an attempt has been made to write in such a way as to make the material understandable to the intelligent layman and the student as well as acceptable to the scholar and expert. Likewise no special attention has been paid to any particular Buddhist sect or sects, but rather the emphasis is on basic ethical concepts which are accepted by all schools; namely the teachings of the Buddha as recorded in the Sanskrit and Pali scriptures, the earliest written accounts. This then is the aim of the writing; only the reader can judge how successful it is.

Whilst writing this book, I was deeply appreciative of the help provided by my friends and colleagues, amongst whom I would like especially to thank Ven. Dr W. Rāhula, Mrs A. A. G. Bennett, Miss (Dr) I. B. Horner, Professor D. Malvania and Mr M. O'C. Walshe.

London, 1969 H. SADDHATISSA

ABBREVIATIONS

(PTS indicates issues of the Pali Text Society)

A. *Aṅguttaranikāya*, vol. I, ed. R. Morris, 2nd edn., 1961, vol. II, ed. R. Morris, reprint, 1956, vol. III, IV. V, ed. E. Hardy, reprint, 1959, PTS.

Ap. *Apadāna*, vol. I, ed. M. E. Lilley, 1925, vol. II, ed. M. E. Lilley, 1927, PTS.

Ndii. *Cūlaniddesa*, ed. W. Stede, 1918, PTS.

Dh. *Dhammapada*, ed. Sūriyagoḍa Sumangala, 1914, PTS.

DhsA. *Dhammasaṅganī Aṭṭhakathā* = Atthasālinī, ed. E. Müller, 1897, PTS.

D. *Dīghanikāya*, vol. I, ed. T. W. Rhys Davids, J. E. Carpenter, reprint, 1947, vol. III, ed. Carpenter, 1960, PTS.

Dvy. *Divyāvadāna*, ed. E. B. Cowell and R. A. Neil, Cambridge, 1886.

J. *Jātaka*, vol. I, ed. V. Fausböll, reprint, 1962, vols. II, III, ed. Fausböll, reprint, 1963, vols. IV, V, VI, ed. Fausböll, reprint, 1964, PTS.

Kkvt. *Kaṅkhāvitaranī*, ed. D. A. L. Maskell (née Stede), 1956, PTS.

Kvu. *Kathāvatthu*, vol. I, II, ed. A. C. Taylor, 1894, 1897, PTS.

Khp. *Khuddakapāṭha*, ed. Helmer Smith, reprint, 1959, PTS.

Lal. *Lalitavistara*, ed. S. Lefmann, Halle, 1902.

Ndi. *Mahāniddesa*, vols. I, II, ed. L. de la Vallée Poussin, E. J. Thomas, 1916, 1917, PTS.

Mtu. *Mahāvastu*, ed. É. Senart, 3 vols., Paris, 1882–97.

M. *Majjhimanikāya*, vol. I, ed. V. Trenckner, reprint, 1964, vols. II, III, ed. R. Chalmers, reprint, 1960, PTS.

Miln. *Milindapañha*, ed. V. Trenckner, reprint, 1963, PTS.

Ps. *Paṭisambhidāmagga*, vols. I, II, ed. A. C. Taylor, 1905, 1907, PTS.

Pv. *Petavatthu*, ed. J. Minayeff, 1889, PTS.

Sdhp. *Saddhammopāyana*, ed. Richard Morris, JPTS, 1887.

S. *Saṃyuttanikāya*, vols. I–V, ed. L. Feer, reprint, 1960, PTS.

Su. *Suttāgame*, ed. Puppha Bhikkhu, Sūtrāgamaprakāśaka Samiti, Gurgaon Cantt. East Punjab, vol. I, 1953, vol. II, 1954

Sn.	*Suttanipāta*, ed. Dines Andersen, Helmer Smith, reprint, 1948.
Tkg.	*Telakaṭāhagāthā*, ed. E. R. Gooneratne, JPTS, 1884.
Thag.	*Theragāthā*, ed. H. Oldenberg, R. Pischel, 1883, PTS.
Ud.	*Udāna*, ed. P. Steinthal, reprint, 1948, PTS.
Uv.	*Udānavarga* (= Skt. Dharmapada), ed. N. P. Chakravarti, Paris, 1930.
Uj.	*Upāsakajanālaṅkāra*, ed. H. Saddhatissa, 1965, PTS.

CONTENTS

BUDDHIST ETHICS

CHAPTER I

DEFINITIONS AND HISTORICAL BACKGROUND

(*a*) *Scope of the Study of Ethics*

The term 'Ethics' derives from the Greek *ethikos*, that which pertains to *ethos*, character. It is also called 'Moral Philosophy', from the Latin custom. Popularly, 'ethics' is described as 'the science treating of morals'[1] but since precise definition of the term is lacking it is necessary to state the ground which a consideration of 'Ethics' is intended to cover. G. E. Moore, in his *Principia Ethica*,[2] refusing to take as adequate a definition of 'Ethics' as dealing with 'the question what is good or bad in human conduct', proceeds to declare: 'I may say that I intend to use "Ethics" to cover more than this—a usage for which there is, I think, quite sufficient authority. I am using it to cover the general enquiry into what is good.'

A more detailed description is given by Rev. H. H. Williams: 'In its widest sense, the term "ethics" would imply an examination into the general character and habits of mankind, and would even involve a description or history of the habits of men in particular societies living at different periods of time.' Observing the exceptionally wide field that would be so covered, the author concludes: 'Ethics then is usually confined to the particular field of human character and conduct so far as they depend upon or exhibit certain general principles commonly known as moral principles. Men in general characterize their own conduct and character and that of other men by such general adjectives as good, bad, right and wrong, and it is the meaning and scope of these adjectives, primarily in their relation to human conduct, and ultimately in their final and absolute sense, that ethics investigates.'[3]

[1] *Odhams Dictionary of the English Language Illustrated*, Odhams Ltd, 1946; The *Elements of Ethics*, H. John Muirhead, London, 1910, p. 4; *A Manual of Ethics*, S. John Mackenzie, London, 1929, p. 1.

[2] *Principia Ethica*, G. E. Moore, Cambridge University Press; Reprint 1954, p. 2.

[3] *Encyclopaedia Britannica*, 1926 ed., Vol. 9, p. 809. Article: *Ethics*. Rev. H. H. Williams (Fellow, Tutor and Lecturer in Philosophy, Hertford College, Oxford).

We are therefore concerned with a consideration of certain terms as used in a particular connection and also with their meaning in the absolute sense. In conjunction with these aspects the opinion of Professor Muirhead may also be borne in mind: 'We have two kinds of sciences . . . those concerning themselves with the description of things as they are, and those which concern themselves with our judgments upon them. The former class have sometimes been called "natural", the latter "normative", or, as is better, "critical" sciences. Ethics is critical in the sense explained. Its subject-matter is human conduct and character, not as natural facts with a history and causal connections with other facts, but as possessing value in view of a standard or idea.'[1]

The various ethical systems are therefore more likely to show divergence when one comes to consider the standard or ideal which furnishes the value of human conduct rather than with the prescriptions for the conduct itself. For example, killing, thieving, lying are in general considered to be evils, though whether they are at any time justifiable will depend on the terms of the ideal; on the other hand, happiness is invariably associated with good.

The study of Ethics as a particular discipline contributing to philosophical enquiry as a whole was due originally to Aristotle, since he distinguished between 'first principles', or the investigation of the ultimate nature of existence as such, and the subsidiary disciplines which, though having the same purpose, were of themselves able to deal with only a particular approach to it. Ethics constituted one such approach, and, of the many hundreds of Aristotelian writings, three major works on Ethics have come down to us. Aristotle maintained throughout the fundamental doctrine of Socrates and Plato that 'Virtue is Happiness', a doctrine with which Buddhist thought would, in general, be in agreement,[2] and on two occasions was inspired to poetry concerning this tenet. In the Elegy to Eudemus of Cyprus he praised the man who first showed clearly that a good

[1] *Encyclopaedia of Religion and Ethics*, ed. James Hastings, Edinburgh. T. and T. Clark; New York, Charles Scribner's Sons, 1908–26. Vol. 5, p. 414. Article on *Ethics:* by J. H. Muirhead (Professor of Philosophy in University of Birmingham; author of *Elements of Ethics, The Service of the State*, etc.).

[2] Dh. v. 118: *sukho puññassa uccayo*—Happiness is the accumulation of merit.

man and a happy man are the same, and in the Hymn in memory of Hermias he begins: 'Virtue, difficult to the human race, noblest pursuit in life.'[1] Two of the successors of Plato at the Academy showed the same belief in the necessity of virtue, division of opinion occurring only with the view as to what good is. Some two centuries earlier, a learned and eminent brāhman, having expounded his teaching as to what qualities are essential to the character of a 'true' brāhman—'brahman' here representing the ideal—and having reduced them to morality and wisdom, was asked by the Buddha what that morality and wisdom are. The brāhman answered: 'That is the farthest we have advanced, Gotama. It would indeed be well if the esteemed Gotama would clarify with regard to these words.'[2] The lengthy exposition with which the Buddha replied[3] constituted a standard basis for development of his teaching and will be referred to in detail in the course of the present text.

Returning to Aristotle, the theory that Happiness is Activity is contained in two of his most authoritative works, the *Metaphysica* and the *De Anima*, as well as in the three ethical treatises, the *Nicomachean Ethics*, the *Eudemian Ethics*, and the *Magna Moralia*, these three proceeding on similar lines up to this point. The *Nicomachean* then continues to the theory 'that the highest happiness is the speculative life of the intellect . . . but that happiness as human also includes the practical life of combining prudence and moral virtue; and that, while both lives need external goods as necessaries, the practical life also requires them as instruments of moral action. The treatise concludes with the means of making men virtuous; contending that virtue requires habituation, habituation law, law legislative art, and legislative art politics. Ethics thus passes into Politics'.[4] The *Eudemian Ethics* and *Magna Moralia* continue to considerations of good fortune and gentlemanliness, the latter being regarded as perfect virtue, containing all particular virtues.

Herein lie no indications of an ultimate or transcendental

[1] *Encyclopaedia Britannica*, 1926 ed., Vol. 2, p. 512, Article on *Aristotle* by Thomas Case, President, Corpus Christi College, Oxford, etc.

[2] D. I. 124.

[3] *Ibid.* I. 124 and substantially in all *Dīgha suttas*.

[4] *Encyclopaedia Britannica*, 1926 ed., Vol. 2, p. 513; Article on Aristotle by Thomas Case. (See p. 17, note 1.)

state, and for these one must look to later developments of the science of ethics, whether they arise in logical continuity or exist merely as arbitrary attachments introduced for the sake of convenience. Only the former condition would provide justification for considering ethics as a genuine contribution to the science of philosophy proper. In his article on Ethics in *Encyclopaedia Britannica*, 1951 edition, Professor Wolf has this to say of the study:[1] 'ethics is not a positive science but a *normative* science—it is not primarily occupied with the actual character of human conduct but with the ideal. Many moral philosophers, indeed, have stated explicitly that the business of ethics merely consists in clearing up current moral conceptions and unfolding the ultimate presuppositions involved in them, and that it is not its function to discover any new moral ideas. It may be remarked that even the ethics of Aristotle attempted no more, although he was not bound by anything like this authority, and the traditions of the Christian Church.' Professor Wolf then states that the main problems of ethics 'turn chiefly on the following conceptions: (i) The highest good of human conduct, or its ultimate ideal aim, which may serve as the ultimate standard of right conduct; (ii) the origin or source of our knowledge of the highest good or of right or wrong; (iii) the sanctions of moral conduct; (iv) the motives which prompt right conduct. Another problem discussed by moral philosophers is that of Freedom of the Will. . . .'

In a consideration of Buddhist ethics these problems may be rearranged with advantage for two reasons. In the first place, according to Buddhist and other Indian thought the highest state is one which lies beyond good and evil. In the second place, according to Buddhism there is no break between the moral teaching and that which pertains directly to the ideal state; humanity, sufficiently advanced in the practice of the moralities, rises and continues to rise above the common limitations of time and space whether these terms are interpreted from the point of view of the physical sciences or with reference to historical and geographical location. The first of the main problems set forth by Professor Wolf, namely, the ultimate

[1] *Encyclopaedia Britannica*, 1951 ed., Vol. 8, p. 757. Article on *Ethics:* Abraham Wolf. Former Head of the Department of the History and Method of Science at University College, University of London, etc.

ideal aim which may serve as the ultimate standard of right conduct, relates, according to Buddhist thought, to the supramundane or *lokuttara* state, and the connection between the moralities of everyday life and this *lokuttara* state is one which is entirely covered by the Buddha's teaching. It is, in fact, that which is known to Buddhists as *mārga, magga*, the Path, the Road, along which each person must travel for himself beginning with the practice of the common moralities up to the supramundane state beyond good and evil. From this point of view Buddhism can be said to provide the complete ethical study.

Following on certain introductory remarks which should serve to clarify the position taken up by Buddhist thought, the present consideration will be made under four main headings: (I) Origin and Source of Knowledge of the Highest, (II) The Sanctions of Moral Conduct: The Three Refuges; The Precepts, (III) Moral Principles as possessing Value in View of a standard or Ideal, (IV) The Ultimate Ideal Aim which may serve as the Ultimate Standard, namely: The Realization of the Four Noble Truths.

(*b*) *Indian Thought in the Sixth Century BC*

It must be emphasized at the outset that recognition of a state beyond good and evil in no way implies that a person who has performed a number of 'good' deeds may then relax morally and do anything he pleases; it merely hints at a state described by the Buddha when he was asked: 'Where do the four primary elements, earth, water, fire and air, entirely cease?'[1] He replied that it was not so that the question should have been put. It should have been thus:

'Where do water, earth, fire, air, find no place?
Where do "long and short", "fine and coarse",
"Pleasant and unpleasant", not occur?
Where are mind and body, mental and physical states,
entirely stopped?'[2]

And the answer to this is:

'Where the consciousness that makes endless comparisons is
entirely abandoned,

[1] D. I. 222. [2] *Ibid.* I. 223.

Here "long and short", "pleasant and unpleasant" do not occur.

Here are stopped name and form, mental and physical states.
Here with the dying away of consciousness these things have no place.'[1]

In this description the terms 'long and short', 'fine and coarse', 'pleasant and unpleasant', carry their customary meaning; the significance of 'name and form, mental and physical states' is less obvious since the expression *nāmañ ca rūpañ ca* has a variety of associations. In the early *Upaniṣads*, 'Brahman' was the Absolute Reality, while the term *nāma-rūpa* stood for the things of common experience. According to the *niṣprapañca*[2] ideal of Brahman, the things of common experience represent phenomena with Absolute Brahman as the noumenon; Brahman is here the mere ground of subject and object. According to the *saprapañca*[3] ideal, the things of common experience emerge from Brahman and are later re-absorbed into it. So far Brahman was not personified, but in early Buddhistic literature it is the personification that comes under discussion, sometimes as 'Brahma', though also on occasion as 'Brahman', while 'Brahmā' appears also in the early portions of the epic *Mahābhārata*. In the latter case, however, 'Brahmā' is frequently identified with *Prajāpati*,[4] a much older concept than Brahmā, but who at one time represented the creative power of nature. Confusion arose since both *Prajāpati* and Brahmā were considered, at different times to be the ultimate sources of all. But in whatever form Absolute Brahman is presented, it is distinguished from the things of common experience which are *nāma-rūpa*. *Rūpa* is the specific form and nature of a phenomenon, while *nāma* is the word or name serving as its sign; taking the terms together, *nāma-rūpa* should be understood as the particularity

[1] D. I. 223; M. I. 329.

[2] *niṣprapañca:* from *niṣ* plus *prapañca; niṣ*, free from; *pra* plus *pañc*, to spread out, i.e. 'expansion, diffusion, manifoldness'. Therefore, *niṣprapañca:* free from diffusion.

[3] *saprapañca: sa* plus *pra* plus *pañc*. Therefore, *saprapañca:* with diffusion, with manifoldness, etc.

[4] *prathama-ja*, the 'first-embodied'. Prajā-pati occupies the first place in the Brāhmaṇas. *Śatapatha Brāhmaṇa v.i.* 2, 10 *and* 13 state that there are thirty-three gods and that Prajā-pati is the thirty-fourth including them all.

or determinate character of individual things. A further connection between *nāma* and *rūpa* is indicated in *Bṛhadāranyaka Upaniṣad*[1] where a triad is mentioned consisting of *nāma, rūpa* and *karma* (action), the implications of which are very considerable; consideration of them is therefore deferred. Excluding karma for the moment, in Buddhist teaching *nāma* is also a metaphysical term used as comprising the four mental groups, or khandhas, of feeling, perception, mental formations and consciousness.[2] These, together with the material principle *rūpa*,[3] make up the 'individual person' as distinguished from other 'individuals'. *Nāma-rūpa* thus becomes 'individual being' or 'individuality'. In the above quotation from the *Kevaḍḍha Sutta* we understand for *nāma-rūpa* 'mental and physical states',[4] so that when these cease without remainder the consciousness that makes endless comparisons will also cease and the supramundane state be attained.

Still one point remains which may have been present in the first linking-up of *nāma* and *rūpa* and which is again prominent in present-day thought: this concerns the singling-out of any one phenomenon from the whole mass of phenomena, which act is in general called a 'discovery'. With *nāma* closely associated with *rūpa*, the singling-out is not entirely disconnected with those parts of the mentality of the discoverer which could hardly be classified as 'perception'; therefore he may look to recognize a closer union between *nāma* and *rūpa* than it has so far been possible to demonstrate.

If however Indian thought looked towards an ultimate state in which pairs of opposites did not figure, considerable distinction has always been drawn between the conventional 'right' and 'wrong' of the present existence. The idea of a fixed physical

[1] *Bṛhadāraṇyaka Upaniṣad. I. vi. I.* 'Verily this is a triad, name, form, and work'. *The Upaniṣads.* Tr. by F. Max Muller, Oxford, 1900. Part II, p. 99. (The Sanskrit term here translated as 'work' is 'karma'.)

[2] *vedanā, saññā, saṅkhāra, viññāṇa*, respectively.

[3] The *rūpakkhandha* consists of the four *mahābhūtas*, or 'great' elements, namely, earth, water, fire, and air. A similar classification of 'elements' was made in ancient Greece.

[4] Modern Pali-English dictionaries are quite clear on this point, but standard translations of Buddhist texts, many of which were made in the closing decades of the nineteenth century, use *nāma-rūpa* only for 'name and form', thereby imposing an unwarranted limitation which often obscures the meaning of the text.

law, as of uniformity of nature or the ordered course of things such as the alternation of day and night, was formed at a very early date, probably well before the separation of the Aryan migrants into Indian and Iranian contingents. In the *Ṛgveda* it was known as *ṛta*, but the word occurs in Persian proper names as early as 1600 BC in the form *arta*, and in the *Avesta* as *asha*. By the time of the Mantras *ṛta* had also taken on the significance of a moral order, and expressions such as *gopā ṛtasya*,[1] guardians of *ṛta*, and *ṛtāyu*, practisers of *ṛta*, are frequently met with. The Vedic gods were therefore both maintainers of cosmic order as well as upholders of moral law. In course of time other views appeared, but the main line of development of Indian thought did not lie in a unity of godhead, to the reduction of many gods to one who would be assumed to make and guide the world; rather it lay in a monism which traces the whole of existence to a single source. In the meantime, though performance of sacrifices was often dominant, since they were taken to be essential to the satisfying of man's desires, the idea of morality was never superseded. There existed a triad of obligations (*ṛṇa-traya*) for the fulfilment of which sacrifice was only the first; the second lay in indebtedness for the culture inherited, this to be discharged by handing on the traditions to the rising generation, and the third lay in continuing the race. The ideal includes the practice of adherence to the truth, of self-restraint and kindness. Benevolence was particularly praised and meanness deplored. 'He who eats by himself will keep his sin to himself,'[2] says the *Ṛgveda*.

The earlier gods were upholders of the moral order to the extent of rewarding virtue with happiness in heaven in their company. There is no explicit reference to 'hell' in the *Ṛgveda*, though it is clear in the *Atharvaveda* and in the *Brāhmaṇas* where it is a place of eternal darkness from which there is no escape. The idea of *iṣṭāpūrta*, however, occurs in the *Ṛgveda*, *iṣṭa* standing for the sacrifice to the gods and *pūrta* the gifts made to the priests, the merit accruing from these acts preceding a person into the next world where it secured him happiness. This merit is not entirely ethical but may become so if the reference to sacrifice is excluded and if the results

[1] *Ṛgveda*, VII. 64. 2. [2] *Ṛgveda*, X. 117. 6: *sa kevalāgho bhavati kevalādi.*

of both good and bad deeds are assumed to pass on to determine the circumstances and conditions of the next existence. In that case we have an elementary idea of karma. Moreover, in the scale of rewards and punishments corresponding to the good and evil deeds of the present life, the Brāhmaṇas include amongst their serious punishments *punar-mṛtyu,* repeated dying, this is to take place in some other world; there is no mention of repeated births though obviously these must occur if there are to be repeated deaths. In the early Upaniṣads the whole conception was clarified by recognition of a series of births and deaths as taking place either in this world or in a realm of better or worse conditions according to one's record here. Concern was then principally with the natural fruits of good and evil deeds maturing either in the present life or in some future life, irrespective of deities. What, then, was the position of a 'god'?

The word *deva,* from *div,* to shine, in Sanskrit means 'god'; it is cognate with the Latin *deus.* It points to an era preceding that of the settlement of the Aryans in India in which the conception of god was associated with the luminous powers of nature. The spirit of veneration with which the early Aryans regarded such powers is also indicated by *yaj,* worship, a root found in many European languages. We have the association with the Vedic *yaj,* to sacrifice, as in the title '*Yajurveda*'. But with the development of the idea of karma and consequent lack of authority of the deities over man, the value of *deva* is modified.

In Buddhism the rendering of *deva* as 'god' is acceptable only in the sense that the being indicated is of a type superior to the average human, and whereas the gods of mythology resemble largely the creations of poetic fancy, taking their status more or less in accordance with the importance of the natural phenomena with which they are associated, the *devas* exist in definite grades according to their condition of mental development. In the *kāmaloka,* or world of desire, there exist six grades of *devas;* in the *rūpaloka* or fine-material world there are four, and in the *arūpaloka* or immaterial world there are also four grades. Beings attain to these spheres in accordance with the doctrine of karma, the spheres corresponding to the degrees of mental concentration and one-pointedness of mind (*cittass'ekaggatā*) which, from time to time, have been experienced temporarily in the present existence. In the Indian religions these mental states are known as the *Jhānas*, or *Jhānic* states. They are described frequently in the Buddhist texts, notably in the *Poṭṭhapāda Sutta*, the ninth of the *Long Discourses of the Buddha*, otherwise, *Dīgha Nikāya*, where the sequence is complete, the theme being that with study and discipline states of consciousness arise and with study and discipline they pass away. The substance of the account is as follows.

Being well-practised in the Moralities, having attained to a state of mindfulness and awareness, and being accustomed to simplicity of life, the meditator retires to a solitary place. He must overcome, at least temporarily, sensual desire (*kāmacchanda*), ill-will and anger (*vyāpāda*), sloth and torpor (*thīna-middha*), restlessness and worry (*uddhacca-kukkucca*), and doubt (*vicikicchā*). These are the Five Hindrances (*pañca nīvaraṇa*) to mental development and vision, and, having subdued them, he feels extremely happy. So is born joy, a calming of the body, ease, and the ability to achieve much concentration of mind. He separates himself from sensuous enjoyment but, continuing to apply and sustain his thoughts with regard to objects, external and ideational, attains to and remains in the joy and ease resulting from his detachment. This is the first Jhānic state. The second is attained by his withdrawing his thought from the object, thereby attaining to the serenity of mind and singleness of purpose consequent thereon. Withdrawing his thought from joy he observes his mental states with equanimity (*upekkhā*), but always remains alert; this is the third Jhānic state. For the fourth he withdraws from all ease and dis-ease, so retaining only his equanimity and one-pointedness of mind. These four Jhānic states concern the consciousness of the world or sphere of form, *rūpaloka* or *rūpāvacara*. The meditator may now proceed to the Consciousness of the Formless, *Arūpāvacara Citta*, of which there are four states. In this case there is no gradual suppression of the factors of consciousness, these having already been reduced to the two mentioned. There is, however, progressive change of the plane of thought, and the meditator is always directing his own mind. The first stage is the Jhāna-consciousness dwelling on the

Infinity of Space (*ākāsānañcāyatana*) or Non-Collision of Objects, the second on the Infinity of Consciousness (*viññāṇañcāyatana*) or Non-Collision of Ideas, the third on Nothingness (*ākiñcaññāyatana*), and the fourth that wherein cognition is so extremely subtle that it cannot be said whether it exists or not (*nevasaññānāsaññāyatana*).

Of the whole succession of Jhānic states, the first two may be wrongly assumed from causes producing a temporary joy and ease which have no moral foundation whatever; if from such a state of mind it is not possible to proceed to the equanimity and alertness of the Third Jhānic state then the assumption that the joy and ease had any connection with *Jhāna* is entirely wrong and harmful in the extreme. With regard to the *Arūpāvacara Jhāna* consciousness, the third, 'Nothingness' has been reached, if one may judge by their descriptions, by practised meditators of a variety of theological beliefs, Christian Mystics included, so that the progress through the Jhānas is genuinely one of increasing mental concentration and is independent of creed. But whatever values are attached to the Jhānic states, to the Indian mind they are connected with the general structure of their cosmology. The deva realms, for example, represented states or types of existence into which were born beings who in the present existence had attained to various of the Jhānic states. The five physical senses do not necessarily persist through all the grades of devas since presumably they are replaced by finer perceptions, the *Ābhassara* devas, for example, who correspond to beings with experience of Second *Jhāna*, retaining only sight and hearing. However, all devas are subject to birth and death. Therefore for Buddhism the highest state, which constitutes complete emancipation, is beyond any of the devas; it is that of the Buddhas who are for ever tranquil and stable and who see all things *yathābhūtaṃ*, according to Absolute Truth. This view has been expressed in the following verse: 'There is no track in the sky, externally there is no recluse. Conditioned things are not eternal; there is no instability in the Buddhas.'[1] At the other extreme, below the level of mankind, are the denizens of the Demon World (*asuranikāya*), of the Ghost Realm (*petaloka*), the Animal Creation (*tiracchānayoni*), and Hell

[1] Dh. v. 255.

(*niraya*). The whole range represents, therefore, a structure of grades of intelligence extending one side and the other of the human state as we know it at present, the higher being dependent, in the final instance, on the putting away of the Five Hindrances to mental development and vision, which is to say, dependent on the Moralities. Over this mental development and vision of man the devas have no control; they merely represent states to which man may aspire with increasing morality and developing intelligence but they can be no more than incidental, and to a person intent on the Final Goal are of little interest.

That the doctrine of karma was not known to the Vedas,[1] but it was accepted in principle and had been so for some time before the Buddha's day is clear enough from the *Bṛhadāraṇyaka* and *Chāndogya Upaniṣads*, and since, according to much modern scholarship, these are the only two pre-Buddhistic *Upaniṣads*, further development of the karma concept may be due to either Brahman or Buddhist influence. Common to both, however, is the clear distinction between karma and karmic effects, for 'karma' literally means 'action' in the abstract, while karmic effects are effects of particular actions. In fact, the doctrine of karma was elaborated and developed by non-vedic traditions such as Jainism and Buddhism. Buddhism briefly defines meritorious and demeritorious volition (*cetanā*) as karma. The Buddha said: 'It is mental volition, O monks, that I call karma. Having willed, one acts through body, speech or mind!'[2] The expressions 'good karma' and 'bad karma', used frequently in the West, have therefore no logical significance, though obviously karmic effects may be either good or bad. Nor has karma anything whatever to do with 'Fate'. The outstanding karmic effect for all Indian

[1] According to Louis Renou some material was taken over from Dravidian (or pre-Davidian) religion into Vedic religion. The doctrine of rebirth or *saṃsāra* were fully formulated in the earliest *Upaniṣads*. Even the word *saṃsāra* does not appear before the *Kaṭhopaniṣad*. Referring to karma he says: 'The doctrine did not attain acceptance, however, without the influence of its ethical element: reward and punishment for merit and sin. The same word, *karman*, which meant "ritual act" now receives the meaning of moral act and the result of action.' *Vedic India* (Classical India Volume Three) Louis Renou, Calcutta, 1957, see pp. 37, 57 and 89.

[2] A III. 415: *Cetanā 'haṃ bhikkhave kammaṃ vadāmi. Cetayitvā kammaṃ karoti kāyena, vācā, manasā.*

thought lay in the round of rebirths, and with the postulated means of breaking these rounds were associated the various developments of religious and philosophic thought. If for the Brahmans the ideal came to be realization of the union of Ātman, the 'inner self' of man, with Brahman, the Absolute Reality or its personification, this as representing the impossibility of further rebirths, then stress would be laid on theories involving a transmigrating essence of the 'soul' nature, in other words the *jīva*, to take effect while the ideal remained unrealized. Buddhism, on the contrary, though recognizing the karmic effect of the round of rebirths, developed the doctrine of karma in conjunction with the *anatta* doctrine, or absence of a permanent in-dwelling 'self', and so presented life and the series of lives as a stream of consciousness. The form of this presentation may be seen by study of the following *gāthās* taken from the anthology of the earliest Buddhist literature or teaching, the *Dhammapada*.

The most elementary Buddhist exposition of karma reads as follows: 'He who speaks or acts from a mind defiled, that one suffering follows as a wheel the foot that leads it,'[1] and: 'He who speaks or acts from a pure mind, that one happiness follows as his shadow that never leaves him.'[2]

Many passages exist in the Buddhist texts to the effect that for an evil-doer 'when his body is destroyed the fool arises in hell',[3] but the statement is merely a generalization in respect of worlds inferior to that of the present and indicates the nature of the relationship between action and the results of actions. More precise indication is given in the *Dhammapada* chapter on 'Pleasant Things'[4] 'Just as a traveller who has been long absent and comes back safe and sound is greeted on his return by his kinsfolk, friends and comrades, in the same way when a man passes from this world to another after a life of merit, so his good deeds welcome him as dear kinsmen on his return.'[5] Further: 'Therefore amass good deeds for the other world; for men, everything in the other world rests on merits.'[6] Corre-

[1] Dh. v. 1. [2] *Ibid.* v. 2. [3] *Ibid.* v. 140.

[4] *Piyavagga:* This is the ch. XVI which contains 12 verses from 209–20.

[5] Dh. vv. 219, 220.

[6] S. I. 72; Uv. v. v. 22:

Tasmāt kuruta puṇyānām nicayaṃ sāmparāyikam
puṇyāni paraḷoke hi praitiṣthā prāṇināṃ hi sā.

spondingly we have: 'If in committing evil acts the fool does not awake to understanding, he is burnt by his own actions as by fire.[1] These quotations represent the more specific attitude of Buddhism towards action and the results of actions, the indication being more a running-on of the deeds themselves than a distinct break as might be inferred from specifying an act and its results to the performer. The idea is expressed, in particular reference to hatred, in the early verses of the *Dhammapada:* Surely in this world enmities at no time cease through hatred; they cease through lack of hatred. This is the primeval law. Not having formerly perceived "In this matter we touch the realm of death", those who perceive this connection thereupon cease from strife.'[2] Sanskrit *Dharmapada* and Rockhill's translation from the Tibetan *Udānavarga* contain the first sentence of this; the second is peculiar to the Pali. Here we have the suggestion of the running-on of the action, the effect being continuity of that particular action.

The quotations immediately preceding represent, however, only the latter part of the chain of events relating to an act, and for its whole history the origin of the act must also be taken into account. Regarding this origin we have the first lines of the two *Dhammapada* verses just quoted in part. They are identical in both cases: 'Mind precedes all things; all things have mind foremost, are mind-made.'[3] Here we have the key to Buddhist Ethics and, in fact, to the whole Buddhist teaching, for Buddhism is essentially a mind-culture. Any improvement or retrograde step must occur initially in the mind of the person concerned whether it proceeds to external manifestation immediately or at a later date, so that the importance of being aware of, and of controlling, one's thoughts is continually stressed. Each of the *Dhammapadas* has its chapter on Mind, and each deals at length with the difficulty of achieving control. We have, for example, 'Just as the arrow-maker straightens his arrow, so does a wise man make straight his mind, which is agitated, fickle, difficult to keep guard on, difficult to hold back.'[4] The simile is a very old one in Indian literature and furnishes the

[1] Dh. v. 136; Uv. IX. v. 12. [2] *Ibid.* vv. 5, 6; see also Uv. XIV. v. 11.
[3] *Ibid.* vv. 1, 2.
[4] *Ibid.* v. 33; Uv. XXI, i; *Gāndhārī Dharmapada*, ed. J. Brough, London 1962. VIII. v. 136.

subject of a bas-relief at Bharhut.[1] Here is shown an arrow-maker seated at the door of his house; he has heated an arrow in a pan of coals and has made it wet with sour rice-gruel; closing one eye he is looking down the length of the arrow and is making it straight. Standing by are a mendicant, the ex-king Janaka of Banaras, and his former queen, Sīvalī, who has followed him contrary to his will. The ex-king asks the arrow-maker why he closes one eye, and is told that with both eyes open the vision is distracted whereas with one eye open the vision is true. The moral is that one's mind should be made pliable, subject to control, with the vision kept clear and concentrated on the main aim.[2]

The Bharhut inscription and its theme of the king turned mendicant draws attention to another basic difference between the line of Indian thought and that of the later Greek ethics from Aristotle onwards, for where the *Nicomachean Ethics* allows external goods to be necessary in the practical life of combining prudence and moral virtue as instruments of moral action, and in the highest life of the intellect as a means of physical subsistence, Indian thought offered nothing so accommodating. Though the value of the present life is emphasized as providing essential opportunities for realization of the ultimate truth—it is, in fact, a stage of development through which one is obliged to pass—it was taken by Indian thought that this truth lies beyond the present state and its not to be considered as merely an improvement on present conditions with those conditions persisting in principle. The renunciation of one's social status, as in the case of King Janaka of Banaras, was a natural preliminary step to the renunciation of the whole round of rebirths. From early days, even when the *Brāhmaṇas* were in process of compilation, certain people had left their homes to live in the forests; vivid pictures of the life are given in the *Rāmāyana* and other facts concerning the hermits are found in the *Dharma Sūtras*. By the time of the early *Upaniṣads* there were several classes of people who had adopted the homeless life, some because they objected to the authority of the *Vedas*, some because they wished to conduct their enquiries for the Truth with as little disturbance from the outside world

[1] Cunningham's Bharhut Plates, XLIV. 2.

[2] See *Mahājanaka Jātaka*, J. (No. 539), Vol. VI, pp. 30–68.

as possible, and others who were said to have already attained to the Truth. Originally the hermits were known as *vaikhānasas*, from *Vikhanas* the traditional originator of the Rule, but later the term *vānaprastha*, forest-dweller, came into use. In course of time the leaders of the homeless life were wanderers (*parivrājakas*), wearers of matted hair (*jaṭilas*) or finders of subsistence (*ājīvikas*). Extreme forms of asceticism were often resorted to, but the Buddha, from his own experience of them, considered them to be useless or even harmful unless they were accompanied by, or came as the result of, a very high degree of mental development. Still, detachment from the things of the present life formed an essential part of his teaching.

Returning to the question of breaking the round of rebirth, if for Buddhism there was to be no Brahman, no god, no inherent 'self', did the whole spell complete annihilation? This the Buddha repudiated entirely, classing a doctrine of annihilationism along with other speculations concerning the future, happy or otherwise. The Goal is completely unconditioned, and to attempt a description of it in terms of the conditioned state which we know at present is as futile as to attempt a description of a 'happy' state. The point is illustrated in a conversation held by the Buddha with the well-known wandering mendicant of the day, *Poṭṭhapāda*.[1]

'There are, Poṭṭhapāda, some samaṇas and brahmans who hold and expound the view: Certainly the self is completely happy and healthy after death. I went to them and said: "Venerable Sirs, I have heard that you teach the certainty of a happy and healthy self after death. Is this so?" They acknowledged that it was so. I asked: "Is the world, as you know it and see it, completely happy?" "No," they said. I asked them: "Have you produced for yourselves complete happiness for one night or one day, or even for half a night or half a day?" They replied, "No." Then I asked: "Do you, Venerable Sirs, know a path or a method by which a realm of complete happiness may be reached?" They replied that they did not. "Have you heard of gods, who have arisen in a completely happy world, saying: 'There is a path, O Sirs, which, entered on and followed thoroughly and exactly, will lead to this world of

[1] D. I. 187–93.

complete happiness? We, Sirs, by following this path, have been reborn in a completely happy world.' They replied: "No." ' The Buddha compared this state of affairs to that of a man who declared himself in love with a beautiful woman whom he had never seen and whose appearance and lineage he knew nothing whatever about; alternatively he likened it to that of a man building a flight of steps to a palace whose location and details of construction he did not know.

If then we have no details of the state of happiness, other than that it is 'happy', it remains only to consider what things give rise to unhappiness and to avoid them. Hence the Buddha's teaching of the Four Noble Truths: 'Suffering, the Origin of Suffering, the Cessation of Suffering, and the Way to the Cessation of Suffering.'[1] Beginning with the seemingly simple practice of the ordinary moralities of everyday life, the teaching continues unbroken to the transcendental state known generally as '*Nirvāṇa*'. There is no modification for any particular person or class of persons, lay or otherwise, and, if the progress is sufficient, Nirvāṇa is obtainable in the present life. 'Cut out the love of self as you would an autumn water-lily with the hand; develop the way to peace, to Nirvāṇa, taught by the Happy One (the Buddha).'[2] There is no other training for the attainment.

[1] D. II, 33. [2] Dh. v. 285; Uv. XVIII. v. 5; J. I. 183.

CHAPTER 2

ORIGIN AND SOURCE OF KNOWLEDGE OF THE HIGHEST STATE

(a) *The Enlightenment of the Buddhas*

To the Buddhist the origin of the knowledge of the Highest State lies in the Enlightenment of the Buddhas, and the Buddhist's knowledge concerning this is derived from the teachings of Gotama Buddha. That these should be sufficient, if followed sincerely, is evident from the declaration made by Gotama Buddha to his devoted attendant Ānanda shortly before his passing away (*Parinibbāna*): 'I have expounded my doctrine throughout, in its entirety, Ānanda; the Tathāgata[1] has not the closed fist of a teacher who holds back something of his Doctrine.'[2]

Enlightenment consists essentially in knowing things in accordance with reality (*yathābhūtaṃ*). In seeing thus there are no misconceptions or mental projections regarding the appearance of a thing or a course of events; the seeing is entirely clear and according to absolute reality. Gotama Buddha describes the climax of the Buddhist's training thus: 'He comes to know what, in absolute truth, are the influxes

[1] *Tathāgata:* The name used by the Buddha when referring to himself. No satisfactory derivation of the word has been established and the commentaries, suggesting a variety of definitions, are obviously uncertain about its meaning. Since, however, the accepted meaning of *Tathāgata* is 'One who is Enlightened' or 'One who has attained to the Truth', it seems the derivation of the word might be from '*tathā*', 'reality', 'truth', and '*gata*', 'gone', 'arrived at', 'having come to'. Thus *Tathāgata* means 'One who arrived at Truth' or 'One who discovered Truth'.

[2] D. II. 100: *Desito Ānanda mayā dhammo anantaraṃ abāhiraṃ karitvā; na tatth' Ānanda Tathāgatassa dhammesu ācariyamuṭṭhi*. Rhys Davis has translated the first sentence: 'I have preached the truth without making any distinction between exoteric and esoteric doctrine' (*Dialogues of the Buddha*, Part II, p. 107); but there is no justification for the terms 'exoteric' and 'esoteric'. Rather the sense would be 'having made not-inside and not-outside'. The only esoteric school claiming to be Buddhist is the Shingon, which dates from about the seventh century CE, over a thousand years after the *Parinibbāna* of the Buddha. But '*Shingon*' is a Japanese translation of the Skt. term '*mantra*'; hence, perhaps, the confusion with '*antaraṃ*'. See *Essentials of Buddhist Philosophy*, J. Takakusu, University of Hawaii, 2nd ed. 1949, reprint, 1956, pp. 142–8.

(*āsavas*) (see p. 83), their origin, their cessation, and the way to their cessation. From knowing thus and seeing thus, his mind is freed from the influxes and he knows "I am free." He knows: "Exhausted is birth; the Higher Life has come to perfection; that which should be done has been done; there will be no more of the present state." '[1]

(*b*) *Life of Gotama Buddha*

The historic personage known to Buddhists as 'the Buddha' is Gotama Śākyamuni. He was born about the middle of the sixth century BC, probably in the year 566, in Lumbini Park in the neighbourhood of Kapilavastu in the north of the Gorakpur district. A pillar, erected in 239 BC by the emperor Asoka, marks the place of his birth. Both his parents belonged to the Śākya clan, his father being a Chief. Astrologers had foretold that Gotama would become either a world-monarch or a great spiritual leader, and since it was taken for granted that in the latter case he would adopt the homeless life, his parent took every precaution to prevent his coming into contact with any form of unhappiness, surrounding him always with those things which, to them, seemed the best that life could offer. However, at the age of fourteen, one day in his father's garden, he did experience a state of mind in which he became aloof from his surroundings though still maintaining his faculties of observation and application of them.[2] Many years elapsed before further developments occurred; Gotama married, had a son, and, to all appearances, led an existence suitable to a man of his rank. Then, in spite of all the precautions he encountered an aged man, a sick man, a corpse, and a man wearing the yellow robe of the wandering mendicant. Appreciating that old age, sickness and death are the lot of mankind, and that there existed persons who aspired to an existence where these did not figure, he resolved that he too would devote himself to finding the truth about life and the cause of all the suffering it entailed.

According to tradition, Gotama was twenty-nine years old when he left his father's house, his wife and child. One night he rode out with a single attendant beyond the city, dis-

[1] D. I. 84. [2] See M. I. 91 f.; J. I. 57.

mounted, sent his horse back, and himself took to the homeless life of the forest. For some time he studied under famous teachers of the day but always found their doctrines deficient;[1] the best of them could offer only a temporary, self-induced state of cessation of consciousness, and many relied merely on theorizing. Practising strenuous asceticisms he became so weak that he was hardly able to stand; then, finding that these served only to dull his thought, he abandoned them. With returning health he came to remember his early experience in his father's garden and to see that the only means of arriving at a solution of man's sufferings lay in his own meditation. One night he took up his position under the Bodhi tree (*Ficus religiosa*), determined to remain there until he had reached complete understanding.

(*c*) *The Paṭiccasamuppāda*

Canonical texts vary as to the hour at which Gotama reached this understanding and so became 'enlightened'; the *Udāna* gives in each of its first suttas of the Bodhivagga[2] accounts of the process of reasoning connected with the Enlightenment, identical in every respect except that the first, second and third watches of the night, respectively, are stated as the time of attainment. However, the main importance lies in the facts that the process of reasoning did immediately precede the Enlightenment, and that all the Buddhas attained to their respective Englightenments by this process. It is known as the *Paṭiccasamuppāda*,[3] or, more popularly, as the Nidāna[4] Chain or Chain of Dependent Origination.

[1] The two generally mentioned in the Buddhist texts are: Ārāda Kālāma and Udraka Rāmaputra. According to *Lalitavistara* (Ch. XVI, XVII) the former could not teach beyond the third *arūpāvacara jhāna* nor the latter beyond the fourth. Gotama, having soon absorbed all that Ārāda Kālāma could teach him, went to Pāṇḍava Hill close to Rājagṛha where King Bimbisāra saw him on an alms round. Struck with the brilliance of his appearance the King made offers which Gotama refused; he did, however, promise that if he ever attained to the Highest Truth he would teach it to Bimbisāra. Under Udraka Rāmaputra Gotama soon attained to the fourth *arūpāvacara jhāna*, then lacking a teacher who could teach him anything more, he set out on his own wanderings, pursuing the course of asceticism.

[2] Ud. pp. 1–3.

[3] *Paṭiccasamuppāda:* 'paṭicca'—on account of, because of, concerning; '*samuppāda*': *saṃ* and *uppāda*—coming into existence, appearance, rising. *saṃ*, Skt. *sama*, even the same, *samā*, in the same way. *sa* (Pāli and Skt.)

The *Mahānidāna Suttanta*[1] contains an account of the *Paṭiccasamuppāda* as delivered by the Buddha, and he goes over it as in the *Mahāpadāna Suttanta.*[2] As recorded in the latter, the occasion is given as that on which Venerable Ānanda remarked that the *Paṭiccasamuppāda* was easy to understand, the Buddha replying: 'Do not say so, Ānanda; do not speak like that. Deep, indeed, Ānanda, is this *Paṭiccasamuppāda,* and it appears deep too. It is through not understanding this doctrine, through not penetrating it, these beings have become entangled like a matted ball of thread, like a matted bird's nest, like *mūñja* grass and rushes, subject to the round of rebirths (*saṃsāra*) in a state of suffering.'[3]

Nāgārjuna opens the *Mādhyamika-kārikā,* the textbook of the Mādhyamika school by the following dedication:

'The Perfect Buddha.
The foremost of all Teachers I salute;
He has proclaimed
The Principle of Universal Relativity.'[4]

Indeed, so revered is this doctrine, that the well known Indian Mahāyanist scholar Śāntarakṣita offers his adoration to the Buddha in one of his treatises, the *Tatvasaṃgraha* as the 'Great Sage who taught the doctrine of *Paṭiccasamuppāda*'.[5]

It must be remembered that unlike the majority of other religious philosophies, Buddhism has never given importance to the idea of the first cause, nor indeed to any form of cosmology. Theology did not develop in Buddhism as practical realization is expected of the Bhikkhu and not abstruse disputation. In any case, Buddhism does not recognize a conflict between

together. *Visuddhimagga* (p. 521) gives *sammā* or *saha uppajjati* as equivalent to *samuppāda. sammā* (Skt. *samyak*) correctly or towards one point. Therefore, *paṭicca* or *pratītya,* together *samuppāda* or *samutpāda* appearance means coming into existence together, in the same way, and to one end. The expression *hetuppaccayasāmaggī* has precise and direct reference to the causal relation of things as explained by *Paṭiccasamuppāda.* See UJ. p. 23.

[4] *nidāna:* source, cause, origin.

[1] D. II. 55–71. [2] *Ibid.* II. 31–5. [3] *Ibid.* II. 55.

[4] *Conception of Buddhist Nirvāṇa* by Th. Stcherbatsky, Leningrad, 1927, p. 91.

[5] *Tatvasaṃgraha,* Vol. I, ed. Embar Krishnamacharya, General Library, Baroda, 1926, p. 1.

religion and science as the former is, properly speaking, a practical spiritual application of the principles of the latter.

As the universe comprises the sum total of sentient life, there are, as one would expect, a multiplicity of causes which brought this entity into being. And in this connection, the doctrine of *Paṭiccasamuppāda* recognizes twelve distinct phases, links or divisions (*nidānas*) in cycle of causation, which, being interdependent, the whole doctrine can be termed that of 'dependent production'.

The abstract formula of the whole sequence of the doctrine has been schematized, showing the logic of it without the contents, as follows:

'Imasmiṃ sati idaṃ hoti;
imass' uppādā idaṃ uppajjati;
imasmiṃ asati, idaṃ na hoti;
imassa nirodhā imaṃ nirujjhati.'[1]

'That being thus this comes to be;
from the coming to be of that, this arises;
that being absent, this does not happen;
from the cessation of that, this ceases.'

There is law in this process of causal sequence in which cycle it is impossible to point out a First Cause, simply because it forms a circle—the 'Wheel of Life' (*Bhavacakka*). Most people are accustomed to regard time as a line stretching from a finite past to a finite future. Buddhism, however, views life as a circle and life, reflected as such, is repeated over and over again, an endless continuum. Moreover, the whole series of phases must be taken in their entirety, the conception of the 'Wheel of Life' being in relation to space and time.

As recorded in the scriptures it is customary to begin the exposition of *Paṭiccasamuppāda* with the factor of (i) Ignorance (*Avijjā*). This ensures the continuation of death and remains a crystallization of the acts one performed during life. Ignorance, therefore, as an antonym of knowledge (*vijjā*) or (*ñāṇa*), leads inevitably to (ii) volitional activities or forces (*saṅkhārā*) good and bad, or rather wholesome and unwholesome (*kusala akusala*), the effect of which leads to the motive for, or will

[1] M. II. p. 32.

to, life. These two factors were regarded as the causes of the past.

In the present life, the first stage is (iii) consciousness (*viññāṇa*) of mind or will towards life. When this takes upon itself (iv) material form or mind and body (*nāma-rūpa*), this action constitutes the second step. The third phase soon manifests itself as (v) the six sense organs (*saḷāyatana*), of which (vi) the sense of touch (*phassa*) predominates. The consciousness of the living being rears itself, followed quickly by (vii) feelings (*vedanā*) pleasurable (*sukha*), painful (*dukkha*) or neutral (*adukkham asukha*) associated with seeing, hearing, smelling, tasting, bodily and mental impressions.

In these stages, the individual is formed, but he is not entirely responsible for his present condition due to complex past causes. The first of three causes which will ensure a future life for each individual, is (viii) desire (*taṇhā*) which can be neutralized; but if joy, sorrow and the like are experienced, then (ix) attachment (*upādāna*) is produced, which in turn leads to one's clinging to the object of desire. The formation of another, (x) becoming (*bhava*) is ensured; (the latter term is preferable to that of 'existence' as this phase falls midway between this life and the next).

While the individual is enjoying the effects of his past, he is unaware of his creating the conditions for a future life. The whole process may be likened to that of the growth of an ordinary plum-tree: its very existence depends upon fertile soil, a suitable environment and favourable weather; next, after the elapse of a considerable period of time, when at last the tree has reached maturity and is blossoming, the fruit is finally born; but then, in no time at all, the fruit perishes and dies and the stones drop and are scattered, only to become seeds and produce trees in their turn. In the matter under discussion, therefore, (xi) birth (*jāti*), (xii) decay (*jarā*) and death (*maraṇa*) in themselves constitute the causes for renewed life.

In Buddhism, every stage is a cause (*hetu*) when viewed from its effect (*phala*) and there is nothing rigid or unalterable in this theory. The ignorance that remains after death is regarded as *kamma*—a dynamic manifestation of physical and mental energy. This latent energy is potential action, the motivating force behind the cycle of life. A living being determines his own action and as this cycle has been trodden over innumerable years, no beginning can be seen to this process.

Saṃsāra 'Constant Flow' is the sum total of conditioned existence and as such has been likened to an ocean upon which the ripples of the waves denote each life, each one influencing the next. It follows from this analogy, that just as each life can only be influenced by the one preceding, so no outside power, such as a divine being, can possibly trespass and claim property rights!

Before closing the subject, it is noteworthy to recall that there are four kinds of *kamma* with regard to begetting future life: that having immediate effect in this life itself (*diṭṭhadhamma-vedanīya*), that having effect in the next succeeding life (*upapajja-vedanīya*), that having effect in some after life (*aparāpariya-vedanīya*) and that whose effect has completely lost its potential force (*ahosi*).

Finally, to sum up: there is only conditioned existence (*sahetudhamma*) with the necessary causes, the factors of which are considered as belonging to every individual. A fundamental doctrine of Buddhism is to regard everything in the universe as dynamic becoming but it is through this becoming that delusion increases and ignorance is prolonged. This fact, as Chandrakīrti says, is in existence everywhere in the universe:

> 'Nothing at all could we perceive
> In a universe devoid of causes,
> It would be like the colour and the scent
> Of a lotus growing in the sky.'[1]

As associated directly with the Enlightenment of the Buddha the declaration of the *Paṭiccasamuppāda* would end with the actual enumeration of the links of the Nidāna Chain. This and the realization of other noble doctrines (dhammas) would constitute the aspect of the Enlightenment of the Buddha known as his *Mahāprajñā*, or Great Wisdom. However, before considering the bearings of these on the Buddhist's knowledge of the origin and source of knowledge of the Highest State,

[1] *Conception of Buddhist Nirvāṇa, op. cit.*, p. 122; *Prasannapadā*, ed. La Vallée Poussin, Bibliotheca Buddhica, St Petersburg, 1913, p. 38.

there remains, according to the *Mahānidāna Suttanta*, one more corollary declared by Gotama the Buddha in his instruction of Ānanda. This concerns the nature of the 'self'.

(*d*) *The Self and the Anatta Doctrine*

The Buddha gives the current opinions concerning the self to be: (i) My self is small and has material qualities, (ii) My self is limitless and with material qualities, (iii) My self is small[1] and without material qualities, (iv) My self is limitless and without material qualities. Again there were persons who would make no declaration concerning the self.[2]

The Buddha asks in what respects the self is perceived. It is seen thus: 'Feeling is my self'; 'Feeling is not my self, my self does not experience feeling'; 'Feeling is not my self, my self does not lack experience of feeling'; 'By my self are things felt, the thing that feels is my self.' To those who hold these views that feeling is my self, it should be said that feelings may be happy, unhappy or neutral; any one of these three feelings, while it endures, excludes the other two. All of them are impermanent, conditioned, arising from other relations, things of decay, age, destruction, annihilation. If to a person experiencing any one of them it should seem 'This is my self', then with the passing of that feeling it should also seem to him 'Gone is my self'. A person declaring 'Feeling is my self' is taking for the self impermanence, a mixture of happiness and suffering, a thing coming into existence and dying away, here amongst the things of this world. Therefore the statement 'My self is feeling' is not acceptable.[3]

On the other hand, to a person who declares 'My self does not consist in feeling, my self does not experience feeling', it should be said: 'Where there is entirely no feeling, can it be said "I am"?'

Again, whether it is claimed that 'my self does not consist in feeling, my self does not lack experience of feeling', or the converse, it may also be replied that if feeling should cease

[1] In each case the word 'small' refers to the theory that the self is composed of atoms very much finer than those which go to the building-up of material substances such as the body.

[2] D. II. 66. [3] *Ibid.* II. 66.

utterly, in every respect, could it be said there that 'I, this person, am?'

None of these statements concerning feeling and the self is therefore acceptable.[1] The Buddha concludes: 'From the time, Ānanda, that the bhikkhu ceases to regard the self as consisting in feeling, experiencing feeling, and does not maintain "my self experiences feeling, the thing that feels is my self," he grasps at nothing in the world, and, not gripping for support, does not long for anything. Not longing for anything, he attains to his final release for himself.[2] He comes to know: "Exhausted is birth; the higher life has come to perfection; that which should be done has been done; there will be no more of the present state."'

Concerning the existence of the Tathāgata after death, the Buddha said that any statements that he did or did not exist, or both, or neither, were 'foolish theories'. Why? 'As far as the contact of mind and mental objects and the range thereof, as far as language and the range thereof, as far as concepts and the range thereof, as far as intelligence and the roaming of intelligence, so far does there reach the cycle of rebirth and its turnings. Having thoroughly understood that, the bhikkhu is freed, and, being so freed, does not know and does not see in the same way. To him the theories are not intelligent.'[3]

From the direct statements of the *Nidāna* Chain, it is clear that 'life', in the usual interpretation of the term, moves as a vicious circle continuously kept in motion by a drive of anxiety that it should do so. It is necessary to bear in mind that the term 'consciousness', as used in the Chain, refers to the general sense, as one might say that a person is 'conscious' if he knows what is going on around him, 'unconscious' if he does not. Having established contact with an object or event, one registers judgement on it; one may find it pleasant, unpleasant, or one may be indifferent to it. In the first two cases one wishes either to perpetuate the liaison or to destroy it; in the third one is merely not interested. Yet though in the main there are no fixed standards of pleasantness or unpleasantness, there are certain states which man, irrespective of time or place, dislikes, and certain others which he ardently desires. The outstanding example of the first is death, and of the second, life. Only

[1] D. II. 66 ff. [2] *Ibid* II. 68. [3] *Ibid.* II. 68.

the worst agonies to which man has been subjected have made him desire death, while dissertations on happy after-lives, Elysian fields, or whatever their appellation, have never superseded his desire to prolong the present existence. But the present existence has never shown any security of tenure, and to make it continue, or appear to continue, indefinitely, it has always been necessary to provide a support.

Yet in existence as we know it at present, life as followed by death, or a series of lives punctuated by deaths, how much of man has ever 'lived'? What is it of him that 'dies', and what is it of him that is 'reborn'? The sūtra and suttas quoted above supply the answer to the questions, and in the Buddhist teaching, far from living one single isolated life man lives a long series of lives connected with each other by a potential constituted by his previous actions. As one life draws to a close, the characteristics which would previously have been taken to constitute 'unconsciousness'—using the word in the general sense as previously—disappear. There remains a consciousness, sometimes referred to as the sub-consciousness, but which more accurately is the infra-consciousness, which is the potential mentioned above and which leads to a blind activity, the energy or effect of which is the will to live. At the moment of conception the first stage of the individual existence is that of the infra-conscious mind, or the blind will towards life. Its next stage of development lies in that of mental and physical states, the stage of pre-natal growth with the mind and body evolving in combination. From here onwards we have the development of the sense-organs, the making of contact with the outside world, and so on. But throughout these events, and throughout the existence just started, is the undercurrent of potential, the result of past actions, which determines the personality of the individual in question and which is constantly making itself felt.

How far the individual can improve on this undercurrent will decide his circumstances and disposition in future lives, but there is no question of any organ representative of the individual, such as a jīva or soul, experiencing one existence only and fading out into some realm of happiness or misery, or with its potential lost in the general mass of the world's activity. Just as modern biologists tell us that there is no permanent part of the physical organism which sustains, or could possibly sustain, the whole process of life, but, on the contrary, that life consists in the processes of growth, nourishment, renewal, and such like which were once assumed to be the accompaniments to life, so there is no 'self' which stands at the centre of the mentality to which characteristics and events accrue and from which they fall away, leaving it intact, at death. The stream of consciousness, flowing through many lives, is as changing as a stream of water. This is the anatta doctrine of Buddhism as concerning the individual being. Extended to all the phenomena of the universe we have a parallel in the Steady-State Theory, or Theory of Continuous Creation as advanced by present-day astronomers, this in contrast to the former periodical creations as developing from Brahma or a primeval atom, or with the Creation once-and-for-all as put forward by the Zoroastrians and taken over by the Christians and other monotheistic religions.

(*e*) *Three Characteristics of Existence*

The anatta doctrine is counted among the three characteristics of existence as put forward in the Buddha's teaching, the other two being Impermanence, or *anicca*, and Suffering, or *dukkha*. They are essentially present in all teachings claiming to rank as 'Buddhism'. The *Dhammapada* treats of them in a passage not presented identically, though often approximately, elsewhere in the Buddhist scriptures as we know them at present. According to the *Dhammapada* we have:

' "All mental and physical phenomena are impermanent." Whenever through wisdom one perceives this, then one becomes dispassionate towards suffering. This is the road to purity.

' "All mental and physical phenomena are painful." Whenever through wisdom one perceives this, then one becomes dispassionate towards suffering. This is the road to purity.

' "All things are without self." Whenever through wisdom one perceives this, then one becomes dispassionate towards suffering. This is the road to purity.'[1]

[1] Dh. vv. 277, 278, 279.

Two points are of particular note in the translation of these verses. The first, 'is indifferent to suffering', is explained, both here and in the corresponding Sanskrit text, as 'a sense of indifference to suffering arising out of a true knowledge of the real character of existence'. The meaning is due to Buddhaghosa and is also borne out in the Tibetan version. R. C. Childers, in an early translation of the Pali *Dhammapada*, gave the sense correctly as 'only does he conceive disgust for (existence which is nothing but) pain'.

The second point consists in the employment in the third verse of the word 'things' as contrasted with the 'mental and physical phenomena' of the first and second. The coresponding Pali terms are *saṅkhāra* and *dhamma*. The meaning of *saṅkhāra* is more comprehensive here than in the previous case mentioned[1] and now extends to all mental and physical phenomena which are *saṅkhata* (i.e. put together, compounded, conditioned). *Dhamma*, of which the corresponding Sanskrit form is *dharma*, carries a yet more extensive meaning. 'Dharma' derives from *dhṛ*, to hold, bear, so that the noun *dharma* would be 'that which is held to', therefore, figuratively, the 'ideal'. This to the Buddhas would be their Enlightenment, the Supreme Wisdom, *sambodhi*. To their followers it would be 'that to be realised', the seeing *yathābhūtaṃ*; expressed in words dharma would be the Buddhas' teaching, the Moralities, Precepts, and general discipline of *magga*, the Road. But these meanings of dharma are not here applicable and are not intended, and dharmas in the everyday world as 'that which is held to' are the things, material or otherwise, of everyday life. Used in this connection it is better not to translate 'dharma', but if translation is imperative 'thing' is the only possibility since it has no pretensions to being a scientific term. The rendering made by Stcherbatsky, 'elements of existence' is merely an aggrandisement which does nothing to clarify the meaning, for, as will be seen by the forthcoming classifications of dharmas, the word 'element' as used in the strict sense is not here applicable, while that which qualifies for 'existence' from one point of view is 'non-existent' from another. The term does not seem to have met with Stcherbatsky's entire satisfaction for we have from him shortly after: 'A Buddhist element is always a separate

[1] See p. 21 note 2.

entity, it is neither "compound" nor "phenomenon", but is an element (*dharma*).'[1] The confusion becomes even greater when one finds 'entity' to mean 'A thing complete in itself, its actual existence as opposed to qualities and attributes; something with a real existence of its own.'[2] Rhys Davids was nearer the mark when he translated *diṭṭhe va dhamme* as 'in this very world', the context being to the following effect.[3] An enquirer having observed that craftsmen such as mahouts, horsemen, high-ranking military officers, cooks, bath attendants, confectioners, garland makers, accountants—many others were mentioned—were able, from the proceeds of their occupation, to support their families and enjoy themselves generally *diṭṭhe va dhamme,* asked if there accrues to a person who becomes a recluse any comparable result *diṭṭhe va dhamme.* Taking *diṭṭhe* as 'seen, perceived, understood', and *va* for *iva,* 'like, as', with *dhamma* 'that which is held to', we have for the whole expression 'that which is held to in everyday life'. Again, Rhys Davids and William Stede in their Dictionary give for *diṭṭhe va dhamme* 'in the phenomenal world', as contrasted with *samparāyika dhamma,* 'the world beyond'.[4] A. C. Banerjee, in his *Sarvāstivāda Literature,* gives for *dhamma* 'existent things', and for *dhammas* 'things'.[5]

Taking the classifications of dharmas according to the Buddhist philosophical systems, *Sarvāstivāda*[6] and *Vijñaptimātravāda*[7] enumerate seventy-five and a hundred dharmas respectively. These divide into five groups entitled Mind, Mental Concomitants, Forms, Things not associated with Mind, and Things which are not put together. The first four groups are *saṃskṛta* dharmas, *saṃskṛta* corresponding to the Pali term *saṅkhata,* otherwise dharmas that are formed, prepared, put together, etc., while the fifth group contains the *asaṃskṛta* dharmas, things which are not formed, prepared,

[1] *The Central Conception of Buddhism and the Meaning of the Word 'Dharma'* Th. Stcherbatsky, publ. Royal Asiatic Society, London, 1923, p. 30.

[2] *Odhams Dictionary of the English Language Illustrated.*

[3] D. I. 51.

[4] *Pali Text Society's Pali-English Dictionary,* p. 336.

[5] *Sarvāstivāda Literature,* Anukul Chandra Banerjee. Publ. D. Banerjee, Calcutta, 1957, pp. 52, 65.

[6] *Sarvāstivāda:* The most extensive of the early Buddhist Schools.

[7] *Vijñaptimātravāda:* The School holding that nothing exists apart from consciousness. It is also known as *Vijñānavāda* or *Yogācāra.*

etc. The *saṃskṛta* dharmas, which include the body and the four sense-organs of eye, ear, nose and tongue, include also the corresponding touch, form, sound, smell and taste, as well as the eye-consciousness, ear-consciousness, and so on. Amongst the mental concomitants which all systems treat with great respect, are feeling (*vedanā*), will (*cetanā*), vigilance (*appamāda*), while the class 'Things not associated with Mind' contain such various dharmas as birth (*jāti*), number (*saṅkyā*), region (*deṣa*), time (*kāla*). The *asaṃskṛta* dharmas comprise space, modes of exhausting the life-process, and, in the *Vijñaptimātra*, that which transcends all specific character and conditions, namely, *Tathatā* (Thusness, i.e. Truth, reality). Pali Abhidhamma condenses to four categories: Mind, Mental Concomitants, Form and the *Lokuttara* (supramundane).

According to the *Dhammapada* verses 277–9 quoted above, then, one turns away from, or becomes dispassionate towards an existence which by reason of the transitoriness of the phenomena brings only sufferings; further we are reminded of the lack of stability of all things.

Dukkha, here translated as suffering, may also represent misery, unsatisfactoriness, or evil. '*Dukkha*' is the first of the Four Noble Truths, and figures in 'Feelings' to the extent that these may be painful or unpleasant as regards the physical and mental senses. 'Birth is painful, old age is painful, disease is painful, death is painful, grief, lamentation, suffering, misery and despair are painful, not to get what one wishes for is painful; in short, the clinging to the Five Khandhas is painful.'[1] Yet these five sensorial aggregates condition the appearance of life in any form, and in an existence that is essentially conditioned, even to the extent that it itself 'exists', we cannot know from our present standpoint anything that is unconditioned. Therefore we follow the Path pointed out by the Buddha, the Way to the Cessation of Suffering, so coming to a position from which, or in which, we may gauge that which is greater than happiness.

(*f*) *Mahākaruṇā of the Buddha*

From the foregoing account of the Buddha's Enlightenment it is clear that the enlightening consisted primarily in the

[1] D. II. 305; Vin I. 10.

perceiving of the real nature of life as experienced in the present existence and the beings living it. Further there were the expectations of future more or less similar existences and the means of bringing about cessation of the conditioning of them all. But if the Buddha's teaching had been confined to these matters regardless of their application, though no doubt he would have drawn a considerable following of learned people throughout the ages, he would have come down in history as a great thinker and philosopher but as a theorist only. That this was not his intention, and that he took into consideration the estimate of the ordinary person as concerning himself, is clear from his exposition in the Pali *Brahmajāla Sutta* where, at the outset of this very comprehensive and profound discourse he remarks: 'An average worldling appraising the Tathāgata would speak of relatively small things, the things of this world, the Moralities. What would he say?'[1] The text continues to the effect that the average worldling would say that the Samaṇa Gotama does not take life, does not take that which is not given, and so on, enumerating the Moralities. Therefore, though he would not appreciate in detail the high attainments of the Buddha with regard to perfect wisdom and understanding, he could not fail to see the reflection of this in the Buddha's daily life of the present existence. Could the average person establish any connection between the supreme understanding and the ordinary moralities?

Many recent western writers have adopted the stand that original Buddhism consisted entirely in a reformatory movement amongst recluses, and that the laity were considered only in so far as they were necessary to the physical maintenance of the bhikkhus. 'Buddha's Church is a Church of monks and nuns, . . . He who cannot or will not gain this freedom (*i.e. leaving the home*) is not a member of the Church,' says Oldenberg, and continues: 'But while there was framed from the beginning for the monastic Church an organization, clothed with strict forms of spiritual procedure, there was no attempt made at creations of a similar kind for the quasi-Church of lay-brothers and lay-sisters.'[2] Quotations adduced in support of these

[1] D. I. 3.

[2] *Buddha: His Life, His Doctrine, His Order,* Hermann Oldenberg, Edinburgh, 1882, p. 381.

statements and other similar ones are drawn almost exclusively from Vinaya texts which, of course, deal essentially with the Rules of the Order. But making due allowance for the facts that Oldenberg published his work over eighty years ago, that the western nations had many centuries of strict Christian tradition behind them from which they were hardly beginning to get themselves free, and that such a term as 'Church' pertained strictly to their own terminology, the idea that Buddhism was entirely the property of monks and nuns, or bhikkhus and bhikkhunis, still persists. That the Saṅgha should form the nucleus wherefrom the Buddha's teachings should be perpetuated is reasonable enough; for if with the vicissitudes of time the laity became estranged from Buddhist teachings, provided the Saṅgha remained true to its trust the populace could reform around it. History has shown that such vicissitudes did occur on more than one occasion and that the laity did so reform. If it is contended that the laity might have been more rigorously controlled so as to have been more independent of the Saṅgha, then it must be recalled that the strict control, religious or political, which has been such a feature of Western religions, was entirely contrary to the whole spirit of the Buddha's teaching. It cannot be argued that the laity was not adequately provided for at the outset of the teaching of the Buddha-Dhamma, or that Buddhism represented merely a new doctrine for the consideration of recluses. That these and kindred notions are grossly incorrect is evident from a study of the events immediately following the Enlightenment itself.

It is a matter of extreme importance that the account of the Enlightenment of Vipassi Buddha as given by Gotama Buddha ends, not with an exposition of the *Paṭiccasamuppāda*, but with the conversation with the Great Brahmā. If the Enlightenment of the Buddha constituted his *Mahāprajñā*, the first result of this was his *Mahākaruṇā*, or Great Compassion. *Mahāpadāna Suttanta* gives: 'Then there occurred to Vipassi, the Exalted One, Arahat, and All-Knowing One: "What if I should now teach the Doctrine, the Truth?" But there also occurred to him: "I attained to this Truth, profound, difficult to discern, difficult to understand, of peaceful and excellent import, not of the order of logical deduction, subtle, which only the wise can appreciate. Yet this generation is attached to pleasure and delights in the attachment, and because of this it is difficult for it to understand the matters, namely, this causation and the Law of "This arises depending on That". These, too, are matters difficult to understand, namely: the calming of all mental concomitants, the forsaking of all substrata of rebirth, the destruction of craving, dispassion, quietude of heart, nibbāna. If I should teach the Dhamma and others did not understand it from me, that would be wearisome to me; that would be a vexation to me." '[1]

At that point, the Great Brahmā appeared to him, asking him to preach the Dhamma, for the reason that there existed beings with few defilements who, without knowledge of the Dhamma, would dwindle away. Vipassi replied that he had considered preaching the Dhamma and gave his reasons for deciding against doing so. The Great Brahmā asked him a second time and received a similar reply. On the request being made a third time, 'Vipassi felt compassion for all beings, and with his Buddha's vision, saw beings of various degrees of defilement, of sharpness and faculties, of various dispositions, of different capacities for learning, living in evil and fear, with small appreciation of a world beyond'.[2]

Two gāthās follow this description, the first, due to the Great Brahmā, enlarges on this previous reason as to why the Buddha should preach the Dhamma.

> 'As a man who has climbed to the hill-top
> Looks down on the people below,
> So the Sage having reached to All-Vision
> Sees men as afflicted with woe.
> He considers their birth and decaying,
> And attaining to victory himself,
> A Leader, a man free from Grasping
> Who has broken the rounds of rebirth,
> Sees others possessed of ability—
> May he teach them the Dhamma himself!'

To this Vipassi replied:

> 'The doors of the deathless state are open wide.

[1] D. II. 35 f. [2] *Ibid.* II. 39.

> Let those who have ears abandon blind beliefs!
> Brahmā! Perceiving vexation in teaching,
> I did not declare my Dhamma to mankind.[1]

Vipassi immediately set about his task of teaching the Dhamma, and, under similar circumstances, Gotama Buddha did likewise.

Though the incident may seem familiar to Buddhist readers, it contains one point which is often passed unstressed, namely, that as long as the prospect lay in teaching a few people in comparatively advanced states the Buddha refused to teach; but when he considered the whole heterogeneous mass of mankind and its sufferings he decided without hesitation that he would teach his Dhamma. Therefore, any statement to the effect that the Buddha Dhamma was intended for a select few only, of whatever nature that few might be assumed to be, is not in accord with the statement made by Gotama. Remembering the *Mahāprajñā* of the Buddhas, it is incumbent on one to remember their *Mahākaruṇā*. One may consider, in passing, the import of the presence of the Great Brahmā. Should it be taken that this super-being did present himself to the ocular vision of the Buddha? Or may one take it that the Buddha became conscious of that which the *Mahā-Brahmā* was popularly assumed to represent, namely, the Creator of the world and the living creatures in it? *Mahā-Brahmā* was not Absolute Reality; technically he was a *Rūpāvacara deva*. However exalted he may have been in his own particular realm, he still created in terms of form and was still subject to birth and death. The question 'Where do earth, water, fire and air entirely cease?' has already been referred to in the present work[2] as being put to the Buddha; it has been put immediately before to the *Mahā-Brahmā* who admitted that he did not know the answer and referred the question to the Buddha. From the Buddha's reply that the question should have been stated: 'Where do earth, water, fire and air not occur?' it is clear that the raising of the world from its present condition must be a matter for someone or something greater than its Creator. Hence the *Mahā-Brahmā's* request to the Buddha to preach his Dhamma here.

Therefore, in our consideration of the Origin and Source of

[1] D. II. 39. [2] See p. 19, note 1.

Knowledge of the Highest State, we have to bear in mind the Great Compassion of the Buddha as inseparable from it. If after Enlightenment the doors of the deathless state were open wide, the Buddha, with the profound knowledge of mankind and its needs which his Compassion brought him, was ready to show the way in.

CHAPTER 3

THE SIGNIFICANCE OF THE REFUGES

The Threefold Refuges

In Buddhism there is no formal code of prohibitions. A follower of the Buddha lives according to the Buddha's teaching and declares his intention to do so in using the following formula called '*Tisaraṇa*', or '*Three Refuges*'.

Since the full implication cannot be conveyed in short English phrases, it is necessary to consider the Pali words. They are: *Buddhaṃ saraṇaṃ gacchāmi. Dhammaṃ saraṇaṃ gacchāmi. Saṅghaṃ saraṇaṃ gacchāmi.* They may be translated, word for word, as: To the Buddha as a refuge I go; to the Dhamma as a refuge I go; to the Saṅgha as a refuge I go.

'*Saraṇaṃ*', however, does not denote exclusively 'refuge', and in the comprehensive sense in which it should be taken lies the relationship of the 'Buddhist' to the Buddha which will eventually determine his whole attitude towards life. '*Saraṇa*' is common to both the Sanskrit and Pali languages, and for the Sanskrit Monier Williams gives:[1] '*Śaraṇa*: protecting preserving. (Vedic. *say rakkhake, Ṛgveda* VI. 47. 8); one who protects or preserves; a protector, preserver, defender. (*a*) n. help, defence; a refuge, place of refuge, sanctuary, asylum (sometimes applied to a person); a private apartment, closet; a house, habitation, abode, lair, resting-place (of an animal).' Regarding the Pali we have from Rhys Davids and Stede: '*Saraṇa*: (Cp. Vedic.) . . . shelter, house, refuge, protection, etc.'[2] Buddhadatta Mahāthera gives: 'Protection, help, refuge, a shelter.'[3]

'Refuge' is therefore the most acceptable short-form translation of *saraṇaṃ*, but in no sense can the declaration of taking the Three Refuges be interpreted as an undertaking to comply with blind, unreasoning obedience to a series of orders or commandments. In contrast to the monotheistic religions

[1] Monier Williams: *Sanskrit-English Dictionary*, p. 994.

[2] *Pail Text Society's Pali-English Dictionary.*

[3] *Concise Pali-English Dictionary.* A. P. Buddhadatta Mahāthera. U. Chandradasa de Silva, Ahangama, Ceylon, 1949; See UJ., pp. 6 f., 124 ff.

which depend entirely on faith, and to the systems which have developed *bhakti*, devotion, as an end in itself, the Buddha denounced blind faith, pointing out that it is merely a form of ignorance which retards one's purification and therefore development. When consulted by the Kālāmas of Kesaputta as to how they should choose between the various pronouncements of their many visiting teachers, each of whom claimed that his dogma or method was the only one leading to the desired perfection, the Buddha replied: 'Whenever you find out for yourself . . . "these things are bad, reprehensible, condemned by the wise, are not rightly taken upon oneself, lead to harm and suffering", you should abandon them. . . . Whenever you find out for yourself "these things are good, blameless, extolled by the wise, are rightly taken on oneself, lead to welfare and happiness", you, having attained to this, should there remain.'[1] Frequently throughout this address he observed: 'Do not accept anything because of report, tradition, hearsay, the handing on in the sacred texts, or as a result of logic or inference, through indulgent tolerance of views, appearance of likelihood, or as paying respect to a teacher.'[2] Of his own teaching the Buddha said: 'As a wise man uses gold as a touchstone, heating and cutting, so you, bhikkhus, should take my words after investigation and not because of reverence for me.'[3] So is achieved *śraddhā*, confidence, an attitude directly opposed to that of blind faith. Of it the Buddha said: 'Confidence is the greatest wealth of man in the world.'[4]

Concerning *saraṇa* as 'protection', the Buddha has never made any declaration to the effect: 'Abandoning all duties (*dharmāṃ*) come to me as the only shelter. Do not be grieved; I will liberate thee from all evils.'[5] But he does make clear that one will achieve liberation as a result of one's own efforts made in accordance with the refuge described in the following

[1] A. I. 189 f. [2] *Ibid.* 189 f.

[3] *Tattvasaṅgraha*, Vol. II, Gaekward's Oriental Series, No. xxxi, Baroda, 926, v. 3588:
Tāpāc chedāc ca nikaṣāt suvarṇam iva paṇḍitaih
parīkṣya bhikṣavo grāhyam madvaco na tu gauravāt.

[4] Sn. 182; Uv. x. v. 3.

[5] *Bhagavatgītā*, XVIII. v. 66.
Sarvadharmāṃ parityajya māṃ ekaṃ śaraṇaṃ vraja
ahaṃ tvām sarvapāpebhyo mokṣayiṣyāmi mā śucah.

passage: 'Many persons, indeed, driven by fear, move quickly to mountains, forests, the parks and trees of shrines, as a refuge. That is not a safe refuge; it is not the best refuge. Having come to this refuge one is not freed from all suffering. But he who goes for refuge to the Buddha, Dhamma and Saṅgha, by right wisdom and insight perceives the Four Noble Truths: Suffering, the Origin of Suffering, the Passing-Beyond Suffering, and the Way to the Calming of Suffering. This is the safe Refuge, this is the best Refuge. Having come to this Refuge one is freed from all suffering.'[1]

It should be noted that the protection sought is not only from worldly ills but from the whole mass of suffering to which mankind is subject. The true nature of the Refuges was to be understood as follows: '. . . the disciple of the Noble Ones is possessed of this clear confidence in the Buddha; that the Exalted One is rightly named the Fully-Enlightened One, perfect in knowledge and conduct, wise as to the words, an incomparable guide to man's self-mastery, happy, a teacher of devas and men, a Buddha, an Exalted One. The disciple of the Noble Ones is possessed of this clear confidence in the Dhamma: the Dhamma is well-preached by the Exalted One, is evident in this life, is not subject to time, invites every man to come and see for himself, and brings near that which should be known to the wise each for himself. He has this clear confidence in the Saṅgha: that the Saṅgha of the followers of the Exalted One is entered on the direct right path, is walking in the right path, the proper path, namely the four pairs of persons, the eight classes of individuals:[2] that the Saṅgha is worthy of offerings, of hospitality, of gifts, or being honoured; that the Saṅgha is the incomparable source of merit for the world, that it is possessed of the precepts believed in by the wise, in entirety, without defects, continuously, which bring freedom to men, are extolled by the wise, which are uncorrupted, and which lead to *Samādhi*.'[3] It is now quite

[1] Dh. vv. 188–92. Attention is drawn to the slight variation made here in the wording of the Four Noble Truths. These are generally stated as in p. 31, note 1, and the associated text. See also p. 63, note 2.

[2] There are four pairs of saints who realize the paths (*magga*) and fruitions (*phala*) of the following stages: (i) Stream-winning (*Sotāpatti*) (ii) Once-return (*Sakadāgāmi*) (iii) Never-return (*Anāgāmi*), (iv) Perfection (*Arahatta*).

[3] D. II. 93.

clear that the taking of Refuge means resolving to follow the guidance or shining example of the Buddha, Dhamma and Saṅgha.

(*a*) *The First Refuge: The Buddha*

Taking refuge in the Buddha implies no personal guarantee that the Buddha himself will effect the arrival at the Goal of any of his followers. To the contrary he says: 'Surely by oneself is evil done, by oneself one becomes pure. Purity and impurity are of the individual. No one purifies another.'[1] When referring to progress to the Goal he frequently used the expression '*sayaṃ abhiññā sacchikatvā*', having thoroughly understood and experienced for oneself.

According to the doctrine of karma, future happiness is a direct result or continuation of the maintaining of a satisfactory standard of conduct in the present. But there were wrong actions in the past which must produce their effects in the present and in the future. If inevitably one reaps the results of one's actions, good or bad, and there is no means of avoiding the results on the strength of the moral excellence of another person, the best that can be done to gain secure and lasting well-being is to cut down the evil actions and increase the good ones. There is freedom of will in making a choice, but clearly there must be cultivation of vision and discernment to detect when a choice should be made. Of cultivation of will-power and cultivation of discernment the Buddhist teaching stresses the latter more than the former, for, since blind obedience is not encouraged, unless a person is convinced that he is pursuing a wrong course he is unlikely to abandon it if it seems to be attractive. It says in the *Dhammapada*: 'If by renouncing a relatively small happiness one sees a happiness great by comparison, the wise man abandons the small happiness in consideration of the greater happiness.'[2] It is therefore necessary that one should be willing to discern a possible comparison and be able to draw it.

Such matters are not always evident in the devotion and pageantry associated with Buddhism in the Buddhist countries,

[1] Dh. v. 165.
[2] Dh. v. 290; Uv. XXX. v. 30; *Cf. Mahābhārata*, XII. 174. 46; 177. 51; 276.7.

and the mental attitude of persons participating in these must be made clear. Nowadays the central tangible object of a ceremonial display consists, almost invariably, in a Buddha-*pratimā*, or image of the Buddha, but such figures were unknown until the first century BC. When before that date it was desired to reproduce a scene including the Buddha, his presence was indicated by a symbol such as a Bodhi tree, wheel, lotus or feet, these being also employed to represent certain ideas of Buddhism. It is generally considered that non-Indian influences, notably perhaps the Greek, brought about the representation of the Buddha in the manner of a human figure. But a Buddhist goes before an image and offers flowers or incense not to the model but to the Buddha as the perfection; he goes as a mark of gratitude and reflects on the perfection of the Buddha, meditating on the transiency of the fading flowers. As he offers the flowers the Buddhist recites: 'With divers flowers to the Buddha I do homage (*pūjā*), and through this merit may there be release. Even as these flowers must fade, so does my body progress to a stage of dissolution.'[1] This is not a canonical text but is a very old traditional verse.

Though an image or some such symbol is useful to the ordinary person in helping him to concentrate his attention, an intellectual could dispense with it since he would direct his thoughts, probably concentrating on a passage such as the following: 'Such indeed is the Exalted One, Worthy One, Fully Enlightened One, Perfect One in wisdom and virtue, the Happy One, the Knower of the world, an Incomparable Guide to man's self-mastery, a Teacher of gods and men, the Blessed One.'[2]

But genuine reverence for the Buddha is to be measured only by the extent to which one follows his teaching. 'He who, having entered on the course, lives in conformity with the Dhamma, having engaged in practices in conformity with the Dhamma, pays reverence to the Tathāgata.'[3]

[1] *Pūjemi Buddhaṃ kusumen' anena*
puññena-m-etena ca hotu mokkhaṃ
pupphaṃ milāyāti yathā idam me
kāyo thathā yāti vināsabhāvaṃ.

For this and similar verses (*gāthā*) see *Handbook of Buddhists* by H. Saddhatissa publ. Mahabodhi Society of India, Sarnath, Banaras, 1956 (this v. p. 24).

[2] Vin. I. 35, 242, II, 1; D. I. 49, 87, 224, II. 93 and *passim* throughout the scriptures.

[3] D. II. 138.

How does this attitude affect the moral outlook of the Buddhist? In contrast to the theistic religions where man is a subservient creature, for ever below God or the gods until such being or beings should feel inclined to raise his status, the Buddhist has it in his own power to rise as high as he likes provided he is willing to make the effort. The Buddhist's mentality is never enslaved; he does not sacrifice freedom of thought or freedom of will. Here is the advantage of *śraddhā, saddhā,* confidence born of understanding, over blind faith. The Buddhist pilgrim starts out on a worth while journey in happy expectancy, with plenty of equipment and good chance of success; he is never a 'miserable sinner'.

(*b*) *The Second Refuge: The Dhamma*

'He who sees the Dhamma, Vakkali, sees me; he who sees me sees the Dhamma,'[1] said the Buddha to one of his disciples who was anxious to get a glimpse of him.

We have already considered the term 'Dhamma' as 'things in general' and from its derivation can attribute to it a meaning as of duty or duties; we now take 'dhamma' in the sense of 'teaching' or 'doctrine', and here distinguish between the teaching itself and the sacred texts recording that teaching.

Regarding notable pre-Buddhistic doctrines the Brahman-Ātman ideal and the derivatives of the personification of Brahman as Brahmā have been mentioned, but in order to appreciate fully the innovations of the Buddha's teaching we consider in some detail the current opinions with which he had to deal. Many of them have figured in philosophic and religious thought throughout the centuries, and still form subjects of considerable debate.

In one of the oldest records that have come down to us, namely, the *Brahmajāla Sutta,* otherwise Discourse on the 'Net' of Brahmā, *Dīgha Nikaya* I, dating sixth–fifth century BC, the Buddha described various classes of beliefs and gave reasons adduced by holders as support. He dealt first with persons who attempted to reconstruct the ultimate beginnings of things and who deduced the eternality of the world and the

[1] S. III. 120; *Yo Kho Vakkali dhammaṃ passati so maṃ passati, yo maṃ passati so dhammaṃ passati.* Cf. Ap. 467.

self. In this case, by reason of extreme ardour, striving and right attention, a Samaṇa or Brahman is able to call to mind his earlier existences. He recollects: 'In such-and-such a place my name, ancestry, food, happy and sorrowful experiences were thus and thus, coming to an end at such-and-such an age. Then my consciousness died down, arising again in such-and-such a place. There my name, ancestry, appearance, food, happy and sorrowful experiences were thus and thus, coming to an end at such-and-such an age. Then my consciousness died down, arising again in such-and-such a place. There my name, ancestry, appearance, food, happy and sorrowful experiences were thus-and-thus, coming to an end at such-and-such an age; my consciousness died down and arose again here.' In such fashion he calls to mind, point by point, the activities and circumstances of the existences in which he was previously engaged. He says: 'The self is eternal; and the world, producing nothing new, stands out immovable as a strong pillar. Living beings moving continuously through existences, pass away and rise up again; yet it is eternally the same.'[1] With greater application the ascetic or Brahman remembers existences more remote, while a similar conclusion may also be reached by the sophist-logician who is practised in specious argument and is possessed of a ready wit.

The second class comprises the belief that some things are eternal and others are not. Here it is suggested that the sometime inhabitants of the present world have been reborn as devas, in this case in the realm of the radiance (*Ābhassara*). After a lengthy period one of these beings, either because his merit is exhausted or because his duration of life is spent, re-arises in a lower sphere equivalent to that of Brahma. This is still a 'Fine-material' sphere[2] and birth and death still occur. The fallen one is lonely and wishes for companions. These appear, also from the *Ābhassara*, and for similar reasons. To the first arrival in the Brahma-world they seem to have come in accordance with his wish; to them, from his being there first, he is the ruler of the realm. He is therefore the 'Great' Brahmā, 'Overlord', the Unvanquished, to be perceived by others as 'Be-It-So' (*i.e. self-existent*), wielding power, the Master, the Maker by Creation, the Most Excellent to be produced

[1] D. I. 13.

[2] *rūpāvacara*. See Ch. 1, p. 24.

having power, the Father of all produced in the states of existence.'[1] Subsequently one of the Brahma-world re-arises in the present world. Disgusted with the conditions prevailing, he becomes a samana, or homeless wanderer. He recalls his former existence in the Brahma-world, though not elsewhere, and thinks of Brahmā in the terms described above. But to him it seems also: 'We were created by Brahmā because he is permanent, constant, eternal, a changeless thing; he stands eternally the same, the Truth. Moreover, we who were created by Brahmā have come to the present state as being impermanent subject to change, of short life, as things that fall away and die.'[2] Hence, said the Buddha, arises the opinion that some things are eternal and some are not, that the 'self' and the world are partly eternal and partly not eternal.

Other instances of this belief arise from the falling from the state of gods 'blemished by pleasure' (*khiḍḍāpadosikā*), or 'blemished in mind' (*manopadosikā*). These re-arise in the *kāmaloka*, become recluses, and, realising their former existence, come to the conclusion reached by the beings fallen from the Brahma-world. A fourth case cited is that of the sophist-logician accustomed to specious argument and to use of his own ready wit. Such a person holds: 'That which is called eye, ear, nose, tongue, body, that "self" is impermanent, subject to change, non-eternal, a changing thing. That which is called thought, or mind, or consciousness, that "self" is eternal, a changeless thing, standing eternally the same and thus the Truth.'[3]

Other classes of beliefs which confronted the Buddha and on which, together with the two classes just mentioned, he pronounced a verdict, consisted in the following: the belief in limitation or infinite extension of the world in one or more directions, the existence of the world as occurring by chance, the conscious or unconscious existence of the self after death (with variations as to form, duration, modes of perception, states of happiness or misery), the belief in total annihilation, and the highest bliss obtainable in this world. A short dissertation concerning persons who, through lack of understanding, avoid expressing definite opinions is also included. Of these foregoing, the supporters of the theory of limitation, the fortuitous origin of the world, and the conscious or unconscious

[1] D. I. 18. [2] *Ibid* I. 19. [3] *Ibid.* I. 21.

existence of the self after death, rely for their evidence largely on experience of an exalted state of mind which is here not clearly defined. The Annihilationists and the supporters of the particular states of bliss in this world adduce evidence from their experiences of the Jhānic states.

We come now to the verdict passed by the Buddha. Of the ascetics and Brahmans who reconstruct the past and arrange the future, or both, he says: 'These view-points, thus taken up, thus adhered to, will have for result future rebirth. That the Tathāgata knows, and he knows immeasurably beyond. But he is not attached to the knowledge, and from this lack of attachment has found out for himself the final bliss. Having come to know, as they really are according to the Truth, the origin of feelings, their passing away, their satisfaction and disadvantages, and the way of departure from them, the Tathāgata, from not grasping at the world, is freed.'[1]

Of the speculations he says: 'They derive from the lack of knowledge and understanding of the ascetics and brahmans, and from the resulting feeling and cravings with their attendant worry and struggle. They are due to contact (with the senses). They all experience feelings from constant touching in the six fields of contact. To them, with feeling as cause and conditioning factor comes craving; with craving as cause and conditioning factor comes the grasping for support; from grasping for support, the process of life; from the process of life, birth; and from birth as cause and conditioning factor come decay and death, with the arising of grief, lamentation, ill, suffering, and all trouble. From the time the bhikkhu comes to know, as they really are according to the Truth, the origin and passing away, the satisfaction and disadvantages of, and the way of departure from the six fields of contact, he comes to know that which lies beyond them all.'[2]

To the Buddha, then, the individual theories concerning the ultimate beginnings and ends of things were merely unintelligent, and since they were all founded on one basic error the only worth while course to pursue lay in exposing that error. Summing up his own experience he said: 'Repeated birth is suffering. Housebuilder, you are seen! You will not again build the house. The ribs of the hall are broken, the peak of the

[1] D. I. 36. [2] *Ibid.* I. 45.

house is thrown apart. Having come to a condition divested of all phenomena, mind has obtained destruction of craving.'[1] But there remains also for consideration the effect of teachings regarding the ultimate beginnings and ends of things, and, in view of the deficiencies of these teachings, the estimate of the Buddha's reasons for declaring his own teachings was made by him on many occasions. These were enunciated very clearly on the occasion of his visit to the debating-hall in Queen Mallikā's[2] park where Poṭṭhapāda, the wandering mendicant, was staying at the time.[3]

The Buddha having been welcomed he enquired the subject of the debate in progress, but Poṭṭhapāda introduced instead that of cessation of consciousness, a matter on which discussion was frequently held. After exchange of opinions the Buddha remarked: 'It is difficult for you, Poṭṭhapāda, through your other views, other beliefs, inclinations, connections, procedures, to understand either "Consciousness is a man's self" or "Consciousness is one thing and the self another".'[4] Poṭṭhapāda then put the question: '(i) Is the world eternal, or (ii) is it not eternal, (iii) is the universe finite or (iv) is it infinite, (v) is soul the same as body or (vi) is soul one thing and body another thing, (vii) does the Tathāgata exist after death or (viii) does he not exist after death or (ix) does he both (at the same time) exist and not exist and not not exist?'[5] The Buddha replied: 'I have made no declaration with regard to these ten problems.'[5] Then Poṭṭhapāda asked:

'Why has the Exalted One made no declaration concerning these matters?'[6]

'I have made no declaration concerning these matters because they do not lead to that which is connected with welfare, truth, or the leading of the Higher Life, to disenchantment (with the world), to the absence of desire, to calm, to thorough understanding, to the Highest Wisdom, or the Final Bliss (Nibbāna).'

[1] Dh. vv. 153, 154; Uv. XXXI. v. 6, 7; J. I. (*Nidāna*), p. 76; cf. Thag. 78, 183 f.

[2] Queen Mallikā was a wife of Pasenadi, King of Kosala. See J. III. 403; IV. 437. The Hall here mentioned was one of many such, donated, together with parks and resthouses, by the civil authorities or by distinguished persons, for the holding of religious and philosophical discussions.

[3] D. I. 178–89.

[4] *Ibid.* I. 187; M. I. 431.

[5] *Ibid.* I. 187; M. I. 431.

[6] *Ibid.* I. 188; M. I. 431.

'What, then, *does* the Exalted One teach?'

' "Suffering" is my teaching. "The Origin of Suffering" is my teaching. The "Cessation of Suffering" is my teaching. "The Way to the Cessation of Suffering" is my teaching.'[1]

'Why does the Exalted One teach these things?'

'I teach them because they lead to that which is connected with welfare, with truth, with the leading of the Higher Life, to disenchantment (with the world), to the absence of desire, to calm, to thorough understanding, to the Higher Wisdom, and to the Final Bliss (*Nibbāna*). That is why I teach concerning them.'[2] In the same manner the Buddha dismissed those ten questions posed by Māluṅkyaputta, a young monk.[3]

Buddhism, therefore, does not provide an explanation to all the metaphysical problems that interest mankind. The Buddha explained whatever he thought was necessary in order to get rid of *dukkha* and not in order to satisfy curiosity. It is a means of deliverance and a doctrine of reality in which every encouragement is given to investigate the riddle of life. It is not necessary to indulge in idle speculation or theorizing: neither is faith demanded with regard to a first cause. This knowledge does not bring us any nearer to the goal; it only gratifies childish curiosity. Whatever other religions may teach, Buddhism does not speak about a first cause of life. Nevertheless it stresses the cause and effect with regard to the life continuum according to the doctrine of Dependent Origination (*Paṭicca-samuppāda*). It clearly shows how the cause becomes the effect and the effect becomes the cause. The continuous recurring of birth and death which is called '*saṃsāra*' has been aptly compared to a circling. It is inconceivable to ascertain a beginning in such a circle of cause and effect; therefore, with regard to the ultimate origin of life, the Buddha declares:

'Without cognizable end is this recurrent wandering (*Saṃsāra*), a first beginning of beings who, obstructed by ignorance and fettered by craving, wander to and fro, is not to be perceived.'[4]

One should not worry in vain seeking for a beginning in a beginningless past. Life is a process of becoming, a force, a

[1] D. I. 189; M. I. 431. [2] D. I. 189; M. I. 431 f. [3] M. I. 426–32.
[4] S. II. 178–93 ff., III. 149–51, v. 226, 441; Nd. ii. 273; Kvu. 29.

flux and as such necessitates a beginningless past whether one is ape or man. One should seek the cause of this faring on and live in the present and not in the past. One should utilize one's valuable energy to transform the life stream into the sorrowless, *dukkhaless* state which is *Nibbāna*. As the life span is short one should try to learn only the important things. There is no time to waste: one may live a hundred years or more but this is not sufficient time to study more than a few subjects. A library contains books on many interesting subjects but we must select the most useful subjects and specialize in them. There is no time to devote to metaphysical speculation. Those who pose questions for the mere sake of argument defeat their own ends. One might argue that life had a beginning and a finite past and that the first cause was a Creator-God. In that case there is no reason why one should not question who had created the creator. In other words, no first cause is to be found. Science does not care to investigate into the first cause simply because such an attempt is directly inimical to the advancement of knowledge. The law of *Paṭiccasamuppāda* does not investigate either. Because the very conception of a first cause itself is a complete check in the progress of knowledge.

Sīla, Samādhi, Paññā

The teachings of the Buddha are authoritatively grouped under three headings; *sīla, samādhi,* and *paññā*. A later addition appears to be *vimutti*, deliverance,[1] but the three originals were undoubtedly as stated. To appreciate the authority for the grouping as well as the nature thereof, it is necessary to consider the discourse in the sutta known as 'The Fruits of the Life of a Recluse' (*Sāmaññaphala Sutta*)[2] which, though stated in the text to have been delivered to King Ajātasattu of Magadha, son of Bimbisāra, must have been made originally at a much earlier date. According to modern chronology, Ajātasattu succeeded his father only about seven years before the *Parinibbāna* of the Buddha, whereas the address contained in the 'Fruits' *sutta* was quoted on many occasions some of which date from the very early days of the Buddha's teaching career. It was clearly a standard address which the Buddha

[1] D. II. 122. [2] *Ibid.* I. 47–86.

quoted at length, then referred to in order to emphasize or clarify the particular points under review. Moreover, if anything is to be argued from the order of the arrangement of the suttas in the *Dīgha Nikaya*, and at least the first thirteen of these, perhaps the first sixteen, are amongst the earliest of the Discourses that have come down to us, it appears that they were arranged by the compilers in an order which would produce a cumulative account of the Buddha's teachings. For the first of the sixteen we have the *Brahmajāla*, or 'Net of Brahmā', which contains the lengthy exposition of contemporary views, then the *Sāmaññaphala* which contains the exposition of the Buddha's. While other developments as, for example, the Stages of the Path, the Enunciation of the Goal, the *Paṭiccasamuppāda*, together with dissertations on the nature of true sacrifice, asceticism, and so on, follow in the course of the next sixteen suttas, the sixteenth being the *Mahāparinibbāna Suttanta*. In the meantime, *Sāmaññaphala* traces the development of the prospective Buddhist recluse from the time he decides to adopt the homeless life until he finally attains to realization of the Four Noble Truths. Rhys Davids points out in the Introduction to his translation of the sutta that though the 'fruits' mentioned contain only one that is 'exclusively Buddhist', yet 'the things omitted, the union of the whole of these included into one system, the order in which the ideas are arranged, the way in which they are treated as so many steps of a ladder whose chief value depends on the fact that it leads up to the culminating point of Nirvāṇa in Arahantship—all this is exclusively Buddhist.'[1] In point of fact, the 'fruits', other than the realization of the Four Noble Truths, already existed in Brahman thought in stages varying from the most rudimentary to that of developed growth, so that the enumeration of the whole series formed the ideal basis from which to expound. In the course of the sixteen suttas are introduced the *Brahmavihāra*,[2] also previously

[1] *Dialogues of the Buddha*, Part I, translated by T. W. Rhys Davids from Pali (*Dīgha Nikāya*, I.), London, reprint, 1956, p. 59.

[2] Four sublime states of mental development, i.e. (i) lovingkindness (*mettā*), (ii) compassion (*karuṇā*), (iii) sympathetic joy (*muditā*), (iv) equanimity (*upekkhā*) are called *Brahmavihāra* or boundless states (*appamaññā*). *Brahmavihāra:* Brahma-like (*Brahmasamo*) abodes (*Vihāra*). See D. I. 254; *The Path of Purification* (*Visuddhimagga*) translated by Bhikkhu Ñāṇamoli, Lake House,

known to Brahmanic thought, and, what is far more important, almost the whole of the *Paññā* section is recast.[1] For the present, however, we consider the *Sāmaññaphala* discourse as it stands in the sutta bearing that name.

We have first the recognition of the arising of an Arahat in the present world, the hearing by an ordinary person of his teachings, and the decision of that person to adopt the homeless life. We have then the section on the *Sīlas*, or Moralities, the main ones of which are described in terms of the ordinary man's estimate of the Buddha. The text states that such a person would say:

'Having abandoned the taking of life and continued to abstain therefrom, the Samaṇa Gotama, who has laid the stick and sword aside, feeling shame now shows kindness to all beings; he lives their friend. Having abandoned the taking of that which is not given, and continued to abstain therefrom, the Samaṇa Gotama, taking only what is given, waits for the gift. Committing no theft, he lives as one whose being is pure. Having abandoned the world and become a follower of the religious life, the Samaṇa Gotama lives away from the world and abstains from sexual intercourse. Having abandoned the speaking of falsehood and continued to abstain therefrom, the Samaṇa Gotama is a speaker of truth. Linked to truth he is reliable and trustworthy, never breaking his word to the world. Having abandoned slander and continued to abstain therefrom, the Samaṇa Gotama, having heard a thing in one place does not declare it in another to cause dissension to the people there. Or, having heard a thing elsewhere, he does not repeat it here to cause dissension with the people here. Thus to the disunited he is a conciliator; to the united he is one who strengthens the existing union. He takes delight in peace and his words make for peace. Having abandoned harsh speaking and continued to abstain therefrom, such is the Samaṇa Gotama; whatever words are pure, comforting to the ear, kind, reaching to the heart, gentle, gracious to the people, such is the quality of his words. Having abandoned trivial conversation and continued to abstain therefrom, the Samaṇa Gotama's words are timely, in accordance with the truth, and of things bearing advantage—

Colombo, 1956, Ch. IX; *The Path to Deliverance* by Nyāṇatiloka, Lake House, Colombo, pp. 97–118.

[1] See D. I. 215, 233.

of the Dhamma and the Discipline of the Order. His speech is as a hidden treasure. It is in accordance with the occasion, cumulative and endowed with gain.'[1] Other and minor moralities are recounted, these referring almost entirely to recluses, after which, with the bhikkhu complete in the Moralities, the discourse proceeds to the Samādhi section.[2] Here are described the guarding of the doors of the senses, whereby the bhikkhu is restrained in his faculties; he no longer experiences covetousness, grief and evil things, but experiences 'within himself' an unimpaired ease. Samādhi includes also: mindfulness and awareness, contentment with simplicity, and the destruction of the Five Hindrances to mental development and vision.[3] He now enters on the Jhānic states but the present sutta mentions only the *Rūpāvacara* Jhānas. The third section, *Paññā*, is entered upon with the following realization: 'This is my body, possessing material qualities, formed of the four great elements, produced by mother and father, on accumulation of rice and fluid, a thing by its nature impermanent, fragile, perishable, and subject to total destruction; and this is my consciousness, bound up with and dependent on it.'[4] The meditator then concentrates on the producing of a mind-made body, on acquiring psychic powers such as passing through rocks, walking on water, on attaining to supernormal hearing, on the knowledge of other people's thoughts, recollection of his own previous births, and on the knowledge of other people's previous births. The last concerns the acquiring of the purity of the Celestial Eye. From this point he proceeds to the realization of the destruction of the āsavas and so to the realization of the Four Noble Truths.[5]

Such were the terms in which the Buddha so frequently outlined his teaching. With regard to the amendments mentioned, the possible substitution of the *Brahmavihāras* for the Jhānic states, a much wider use of the term 'samādhi' than is here indicated, and a reconstruction of the *Pañña* section, these will be considered in connection with the Ultimate Ideal Aim. Returning to the authority on which the grouping into the sections of *Sīla*, *Samādhi* and *Paññā* is based, we have the incident recounted in another of the early *Dīgha suttas*, namely, *Subha Sutta*, No. 10.

[1] See D. I. 63 f. [2] *Ibid.* I. 70–6. [3] See *pañca nīvaraṇa*, Ch. 1, p. 24.
[4] D. I. 76. [5] *Ibid.* I. 83.

Shortly after the *Parinibbāna* of the Buddha, Venerable Ānanda was approached by Subha, a young man from Tudi, a village near Sāvatthi and now in the territory of Nepal. Subha said to him: 'You, Ānanda, were for a long time the attendant of the Venerable Gotama, intimate with him, keeping near him. You would know what were the doctrines he extolled, the doctrines with which he aroused people and in which he established them. What are those doctrines?'[1] Venerable Ānanda replied: 'There were three groups of that which the Exalted One extolled: the noble group relating to morality (*sīla*), the noble group relating to *samādhi*, and the noble group relating to *paññā*.' Venerable Ānanda then quoted the Moralities, concluding the section with the remark: 'And after that there is certainly more to be done.'[2] He then described *Samādhi*, concluding with the same remark,[2] but after describing the *Paññā* sections he stated: 'And now there is indeed nothing further to be done.'[3]

The placing of the Moralities as the first section of the Buddha's teaching is not incidental but is essential if the student is to proceed with the mind-culture which is the core of Buddhism. The Buddhist scriptures give frequent warnings regarding the extreme danger of attempting to experience states of mental concentration without thorough grounding in the practice of the Moralities. Any teachings that are issued or that have become extant—and many have done so of recent years—which do not insist on practise of the Moralities before embarking on exercises in mental concentration are fraught with disaster and are to be utterly condemned. At the same time, if the Moralities are to be kept to increasing degrees, then cultivation of *samādhi* and *paññā* are essential; the dictum of Soṇadaṇḍa,[4] endorsed by the Buddha, to the effect that morality is washed round with wisdom and wisdom with morality,[5] that these two together constitute the heights of the world, is incontrovertible. What cannot be maintained is that either morality or wisdom should exist independently of each other.

[1] D. I. 206. [2] *Ibid.* I. 206, 208.
[3] *Ibid.* I. 209. [4] See p. 17, note 2.
[5] D. I. 124; *Sīlaparidhotā hi paññā paññā paridhotā hi sīlaṃ*. Cf. *Viśeṣāvaśyakabhāṣya* on *Āvaśyakaniryukti*, ed. D. Malvania, Lalbhai Dalpatbhai Series, Ahmadabad, 1966, vv. 1127, 1155, 1156, 1162.

However, of the above address in *Sāmaññaphala Sutta*, there is much that might be held to be too advanced for the ordinary layman. The *Dhammapada* tells us: 'The extent to which one is well versed in the Dhamma is not measured by the amount one talks, but if one has heard even only a little and really discerns the Dhamma through the mental body (intelligence), one is, indeed, well versed in the Dhamma who does not neglect it.'[1] The great point is, therefore, that one should understand what one hears or reads of it, and that one should put that into practice. Moreover, of the qualities which the Dhamma texts particularly stress should be cultivated are the two of energy and vigilance. 'Guard your own thoughts. Take delight in a vigilance. From a place difficult of access, pull yourself up as an elephant does out of the mud.'[2] One may quote: 'Vigilance is the way leading to the deathless state; negligence is the road to death. Those who are vigilant do not die; those who are negligent are as if dead already.'[3]

The Noble Eightfold Path

In a very practical sermon known as the 'Discourse of Setting in Motion the Wheel of the Doctrine' (*Dhammacakkappavattana Sutta*)[4]—in fact, it was the first sermon given by the Buddha, at Isipatana near Banaras—he declared that those who wish to lead a pure life should avoid the two extremes of self-indulgence (*kāmasukhallikānuyoga*) and self-torture (*attakilamathānuyoga*).[4] He said: 'Self-indulgence is low, vulgar, ignoble and harmful, and self-mortification is painful, ignoble and harmful—both are profitless.'[4] In fact, the former surely retards one's spiritual progress and the latter weaken's one's intellect.

Both of these erroneous doctrines of extremes were actually propounded by two religious groups at the time: the one, materialist (*Cārvāka*), and supporting hedonism; the other, believing in a transcendental self or soul bound to a material body which should be annihilated by severe ascetic practices in order to release the true self.

[1] Dh. v. 259; Uv. IV. 21. [2] *Ibid.* v. 327; *ibid.* IV. v. 27.

[3] Dh. v. 21; Uv. IV. 1; cf. *Ācārāṅga Sūtra* (in Su. Vol. I, 1953) 1. 3. 1. 165; 1. 5. 2. 277; *Sūyagaḍa*, 1. 8. 3; *Uttarajjhayana* (in Su. Vol. II.), Ch. IV. 6, Ch. XI [4] Vin. I. 10 ff. S. v. 420 ff.

The Buddha himself put into practice both these doctrines before his Enlightenment: the first, when he was a prince in his father's palace before he renounced the world; second, as an ascetic in the Uruvelā forest prior to his Enlightenment. Hence, he realized their futility and discovered that only self-conquest in moderation leads to the ultimate goal—Nibbāna.

Avoiding the two extremes the Buddha, therefore, asked his followers to take the Middle Way (*majjhimāpaṭipadā*) which opens the eyes and bestows understanding, which leads to peace of mind, to the higher wisdom, to full enlightenment.[1] In fact, according to the four Noble Truths, (i) life is subject to sorrow (*dukkha*), (ii) this sorrow is caused by ignorance which results in desire—attachment (*samudaya*), (iii) this sorrow can be eliminated by the elimination of desire—attachment (*nirodha*), (iv) the path to eliminate desire—attachment (*magga*). One can, therefore, put an end to sorrow by adopting and following the path—Middle Way—which to the Buddhist is the philosophy of life itself. This Middle Way of self-conquest, which leads to the ultimate goal is eightfold, namely: (1) Right Understanding (*Sammā-diṭṭhi*), (2) Right Thought (*Sammā-saṅkappa*), (3) Right Speech (*Sammā-vācā*), (4) Right Action (*Sammā-kammanta*), (5) Right Livelihood (*Sammā-ājīva*), (6) Right Effort (*Sammā-vāyāma*), (7) Right Mindfulness (*Sammā-sati*), (8) Right Concentration (*Sammā-samādhi*).

(1) Right Understanding: To begin treading the Path, we must see life as it is, in accord with its three characteristics of impermanence (*anicca*), suffering (*dukkha*), and no-soul (*anattā*); we must possess a clear understanding of the nature of existence, of moral law, of the factors and component elements (*dhammas*) that go to make up this *Saṃsāra* or conditioned realm of life. In short, we must have the clear understanding of Twelve *Nidānas* or the Dependent Production (*paṭiccasamuppāda*) and the Four Noble Truths. We should, therefore, make these the bases of our acceptance of the vicissitudes of life.

(2) Right Thought: This means that our mind should be pure, free from lust (*rāga*), ill-will (*vyāpāda*), cruelty

[1] Vin. I. 10; *ibid.* v. 240.

(*vihiṃsā*) and the like. At the same time, we should be willing to relinquish anything that obstructs our onward march and unselfishly transfer merit obtained to all sentient beings. Three other steps conjoin with and accompany Right Thought, namely: Right Understanding (1st step), Right Effort (6th step), and Right Mindfulness (7th step).

(3) Right Speech: By refraining from lying (*musāvādā*), back-biting (*pisunāvācā*), harsh talk (*pharusāvācā*), and idle gossip (*samphappalāpā*), we create a connecting link between thought and action. One, moreover, which is characterized by wisdom and kindness. Correct speech should not be unduly loud or excitable, not prompted by infatuation, ill-will or selfish interests; it should be free from dogmatic assertations and discrimination; finally, it should not be such as to inflame passions. Three steps are accompanied by Right Speech as in Right Thought.

(4) Right Action: This generally consists in observing the Five Precepts, which can be shown in both their negative and positive aspects: (i) Not to kill, but to practise love and harmlessness to all, (ii) Not to take that which is not given, but to practise charity and generosity, (iii) Not to commit sexual misconduct, but to practise purity and self-control, (iv) Not to indulge in false speech, but to practise sincerity and honesty, (v) Not to partake of intoxicating drinks or drugs which cause heedlessness, but to practise restraint and mindfulness.

It is important to notice that 'sexual misconduct' (*kāmesu micchācāra*) has wrongly been translated as 'adultery' on many occasions, whereas, the original Pali usage '*kāmesu*', being in the plural, denotes that *all* abnormal or illegal practices should be avoided in addition to any other practice or pursuit which tends to overstimulate any of the senses. For the ordinary disciple, moreover, it is essential for him to practise all these injunctions if he wishes to aspire to the higher life.

Particularly abstaining from taking life, from taking that which is not given and from sexual misconduct is Right Action. This is also conjoined with the first, sixth and seventh steps.

(5) Right Livelihood or Vocation: The layman should only pursue an occupation that does not cause harm or injustice to other beings.

To practise deceit, treachery, soothsaying, trickery, usury are regarded as wrong living. The traditional trades from which the layman is debarred are: (i) dealing in arms, (ii) in living beings, (iii) in flesh, (iv) in intoxicating drinks, and (v) in poison.

He should be free from acquisitiveness or any connections with money-making legalized or otherwise, prostitution of any kind and should have a sense of service and duty in life. As the 'homeless life' is the ideal state at which to aim, he should, although encumbered with family and business responsibilities, simplify his needs and devote more time to meditation.

First, sixth and seventh steps are conjoined with Right Livelihood in its practice.

(6) Right Effort: Self-perfection can be achieved by avoiding and rejecting ignoble qualities while acquiring and fostering noble qualities. This stage is, therefore, subdivided into four parts: (i) The effort to prevent the arising of evil which has not yet arisen, (ii) The effort to expel that evil which is already present, (iii) The effort to induce good which has not yet arisen, (iv) The effort to cultivate that good which is already present.[1]

By conscientiously practising the above, the layman will be enabled to more easily cultivate the higher spiritual ideals, the best known formulation of this being termed the Ten Perfections (*Dasapāramitās*): (i) generosity (*dāna*), (ii) morality (*sīla*), (iii) renunciation (*nekkhamma*), (iv) wisdom (*paññā*), (v) energy (*viriya*), (vi) patience (*khanti*), (vii) honesty and truthfulness (*sacca*), (viii) determination (*adhiṭṭhāna*), (ix) loving kindness (*mettā*) and (x) equanimity (*upekkhā*).

(7) Right Mindfulness: This implies a state of constant awareness with regard to the (i) body, (ii) feelings,

[1] A. IV. 14.

(iii) mind and (iv) ideas engendered therein and is, in effect, an additional sense. The development of this type of mindfulness is necessary to prevent the practitioner from being led astray by erroneous views. Thus, it is the culmination of the intellectual process which links up with the intuitive process, namely *vipassanā* or direct insight into things as they truly are. This step marks a further advance from the stage when things were known only by the differing features each displayed, since here all such discrimination is discarded. Although things seem corporeal, good or bad, right or wrong, such attitudes as these only go to prove how the mind views things on an incomplete basis. The process of thoughts are only food for the intellect to enable the mind to diagnose the truth more clearly as such discriminating things first make themselves aware. Hence, we should transcend the intellectual mind if we are to progress further and realize the true significance and relationship of all compound things.

The above four Fundamentals of Mindfulness, practised and developed, bring the seven factors of Enlightenment (*bojjhaṅga*) to full perfection; they are: (i) Mindfulness (*sati*), (ii) Investigation of the Law (*dhammavicaya*), (iii) Energy (*viriya*), (iv) Rapture (*pīti*), (v) Tranquillity (*passaddhi*), (vi) Concentration (*samādhi*), (vii) Equanimity (*upekkhā*).

(8) Right Concentration: At the final stage, we should aim at one-pointedness (*ekaggatā*) of mind directed towards a wholesome object. Through desire and craving, the root of all evil, *kamma* is accumulated making rebirth necessary. To overcome this process, we must understand that everything is impermanent, unsatisfactory and substanceless. True knowledge of this nature is acquired through the practice of meditation, of which there are two aspects: the active of practice, and the passive of realization of truths.

Of these components, the first two constitute *Paññā*, the next three *Sīla*, and the last three *Samādhi*. Clearly the components are not to be accounted as consecutive steps, but even though one takes the Right Speech, Right Action and Right Livelihood components of the *Sīla* group first, in accordance with the order of the three sections *Sīla, Samādhi* and *Paññā*, one remarks immediately that neither Right Speech nor Right Action, much less Right Livelihood, is possible without Right Understanding. The interrelation of the components is inevitable, and recognizing this one comes again to the strength of the Buddhist teaching, namely, that the Moralities are never an end in themselves; they are inextricably bound up with all the other components which form the path to final release from suffering. To what extent, then, is it necessary to study and develop them?

This is the Middle Way, the Buddhist's philosophy of life by which one lives and progresses in accord with the principles of moderation and detachment. Once deliverance is thus obtained from suffering, and the freedom appreciated, it cannot be lost by those who have once won it. The first principle of all Reality is that whatever has a beginning must have an end. The Buddha said: 'Whatever is subject to arising must also be subject to ceasing.' (*Yaṃ kiñci samudayadhammaṃ sabbaṃ taṃ nirodhadhammaṃ*).[1] Suffering is no exception to this law.

The Texts of the Dhamma

The Buddhist scriptures are divided traditionally into three main groups known as 'baskets', '*piṭakas*', the Pali terms being *Vinaya, Sutta, Abhidhamma*, and the Sanskrit *Vinaya, Sūtra, Abhidharma*. Until the early part of the present century it was assumed that the Pali texts represented the only complete Canon, for though the discovery of the Hodgson MSS in Nepal in the 1830's and 1840's did bring to light some Sanskrit texts, it was not until the explorations of the very late nineteenth century and early twentieth that the one-time existence of a Sanskrit Canon became evident. Even so, the Nanjio Catalogue[2] listed 781 *sūtras*, including the *Āgamas*, in addition to 299

[1] D. I. 110, 180; M. III. 280; S. IV. 47, 107, v. 4, 23 *passim*.

[2] *A Catalogue of the Chinese Translation of the Buddhist Tripitaka*, compiled by Bunyiu Nanjio, Oxford, 1882.

other *sūtras* originating between 960 and 1280 CE., 85 *Vinaya* texts, and 131 *Abhidharma* texts; another 342 titles classified as 'Miscellaneous' were also contained. These figures do not include Pali works since Nanjio was dealing largely with Chinese translation, but though some of the Pali texts correspond to some of the Sanskrit originals of the translations sufficiently to make it obvious that the works in question derived from a common source,[1] there is also evidence that some of the Sanskrit texts evolved independently of the Pali though the titles might seem to suggest a parallel.[2] A large quantity of Sanskrit texts have for long been known only in their Chinese and Tibetan translations, but more recent archaelogical research and expert examination have made available the contents of such texts, as for example the *Sarvāstivāda Vinaya*[3] and the *Upatissa* commentary relating to *Vimutti*, or Deliverance (*Vimokṣamārgaśāstra*).[4] However, since all too little information is available concerning the Sanskrit works of dates comparable to those of the Pali, we examine in detail the Pali Canon of which we have a lengthy record, touching only on the texts of Buddhist Schools other than the Pali *Theravāda* or *Sthaviravāda*.

The Vinaya Piṭaka

The *Vinaya Piṭaka* is concerned with the Rules of Discipline governing the Order of Bhikkhus and Bhikkhuṇīs. It is divided into three sections, *Suttavibhaṅga*, *Khandhakas*, and *Parivāra*.

Suttavibhaṅga deals essentially with the rules for bhikkhus and bhikkhuṇīs. The *Bhikkhu-suttavibhaṅga* enumerates 227

[1] Examples of the common origin occur in the cases of the *Āgamas* and *Dharmapadas*.

[2] *Brahmajāla Sutta*, for example, is *Dīgha Nikāya* I in the Pali, *Dirghāgama* 21 in the *Āgamas*, but is also a Sanskrit Vinaya text. The last was trn. into French by J. J. M. de Groot: '*Le Code du Mahayana en Chine*. Publ. Johannes Nuker, Amsterdam, 1893.

[3] See *Sarvāstivāda Literature*. A. C. Banerjee. Publ. D. Banerjee, Calcutta, 1957.

[4] This is a Pali work entitled *Vimuttimagga* written by Arahant Upatissa. See *Vimuttimagga* and *Visuddhimagga*, P. V. Bapat, Poona, 1937, p. 66. *Vimuttimagga*, trn. from Chinese by Rev. N. R. M. Ehara, Soma Thera and Kheminda Thera, Colombo, 1961. The original Pali work was discovered recently in Ceylon, ed. Siri Ratanajoti and Siri Ratanapāla, publ. Department of Cultural Affairs, Government of Ceylon, Colombo, 1963.

rules concerning eight classes of offences the first four of which involve expulsion from the Order. They are: incontinence in sexual intercourse, theft, taking life or inciting to suicide, and false boasting of supernormal attainments. For the other four classes suitable penances are required. The *Bhikkhuṇī-vibhaṅga*, providing similar guidance for bhikkuṇīs, is somewhat longer.

The *Khandhakas* are subdivided into the *Mahāvagga* and *Cullavagga*. The *Mahāvagga* covers the rules of admission to the Order, the *Uposatha* meeting with the recital of the Code of Rules (*Pātimokkha*),[1] residence during the retreat in the rainy season (vassa), the ceremony concluding the retreat (*pavāraṇa*), the rules for articles of dress and furniture, medicine and food, the annual distribution of robes (*kaṭhina*), the rules for sick bhikkhus, sleeping, and the material of robes, the mode of executing proceedings by the Order, and the proceedings in cases of schism. The *Cullavagga* covers the rules for dealing with offences that come before the Order,[2] the re-instatement of bhikkhus, rules for dealing with questions that arise, miscellaneous rules for bathing, dress, etc., dwellings, furniture, lodgings, etc., schisms, classes of bhikkhus and duties of teachers and novices (*sāmaṇeras*), exclusion from the recital of the *Pātimokkha*, the ordination and instruction of bhikkhuṇīs, the account of the First Council at Rājagaha,[3] and the account of the Second Council at Vesāli.[4]

The *Parivāra* consists of summaries and a classification of the Rules of the Vinaya, arranged as a kind of catechism for instruction and examination purposes.

The Sutta Piṭaka

The Pali *Nikāyas* and Sanskrit *Āgamas* are amongst the Buddhist texts which resemble each other sufficiently to point to a common

[1] On the 15th day of the half-month (*Pātimokkha*) bhikkhus are assembled to recite the Code of Rules for the purpose of purge.

[2] These occupy the first two sub-sections of the *Cullavagga*.

[3] The First Council at Rājagaha was convened by Mahā-Kassapa with the assistance of King Ajātasattu shortly after the *Parinibbāna* of the Buddha. It consisted of five hundred of the Buddha's foremost disciples and at it were recited Discourses of the Buddha and the Rules of Discipline.

[4] The Second Council was held at Vesāli, some one hundred years after the Buddha's *Parinibbāna*, with a view to reconciling differences of opinion regarding Vinaya rules.

origin, and wherever they may have been separately compiled the important incidents in the Buddha's teaching career occurring in Magadha are reported in the *Āgamas* no less than in the *Nikāyas*. Only a few discourses are individual to either the *Āgamas* or *Nikāyas*, the main differences between the compilations lying in the order in which the component discourses are arranged. In the Long Discourses of the *Nikāyas* the *suttas* work up from contemporary views and the Buddha's own teaching to the *Parinibbāna* recounted in No. 16, the remaining *suttas* from 17–34 containing varied matter; the Sanskrit Long Discourses begin with a *Nidāna Sūtra* and the *Mahāparinirvāṇa Sūtra*, but the titles corresponding to the first thirteen of the Pali, with the exception of Nos. 6, 7, and 10[1] which are not represented, are consigned to the last places in the Sanskrit. From an editorial point of view, however, it seems clear that the natural development of the line of thought as evident in the Sanskrit compilation must lead to a presentation of Buddhism commonly referred to as 'Mahāyāna' rather than to one with Theravādin characteristics, but such an opinion arises solely from the impression given by the order of the *sūtras* and *suttas* and in no way concerns variation in the matter contained.

Of the remaining *Nikāyas*, *Majjhima*, the Medium-Length Discourses, *Aṅguttara*, the Gradual Discourses, and *Saṃyutta*, the Kindred Discourses, are comparable, respectively, to the *Madhyamāgama*, *Ekottarāgama* and *Samyuktāgama*. The *Khuddaka Nikāya* is not present, as a collection, in the *Āgamas*. Of the *Khuddaka* texts, the *Dhammapada* contains the 'Flower' chapter in which is put the question: 'Who shall conquer this world and the realm of Yama together with that of the gods (*devas*)? Who shall assemble the verses of the Law (*Dhammapada*) well-preached as a skilful person selects a good flower?' The reply to the question is that a disciple in training (*sekho*) will so conquer.[2] Since this text bears the title of *Dhammapada*, or equivalent, and since these are the only verses contained which mention the term '*dhammapada*', it is evident that the simile of selecting flowers is intended to provide evidence that

[1] *Mahāli*, *Jāliya* and *Subha Suttas* respectively.

[2] Dh. vv. 44, 45; Uv. XVIII. vv. 1, 2; *Gāndhārī Dharmapada*, *op. cit.*, vv. 301, 302.

the *Dhammapada* is a genuine anthology which contains the ethical teachings of the Buddha. The value of the *Dhammapada* texts[1] is therefore inestimable. Other components of the *Khuddaka Nikāya*, though in many cases very old and of great interest, can only be of lesser value. They are: *Khuddakapāṭha, Udāna, Itivuttaka, Sutta Nipāta, Vimānavatthu, Petavatthu, Theragāthā, Therīgāthā, Jātaka, Niddesa, Paṭisambhidāmagga, Apadāna, Buddhavaṃsa,* and *Cariyāpiṭaka*.[2]

The Abhidhamma Piṭaka

The *Abhidhamma* literature contains the philosophy of Buddhism in analytical form. It is based on the Discourses of the Buddha, many of which were philosophical treatises, as for example the *Poṭṭhapāda Sutta*,[3] the *Mahā-Nidāna Sutta*,[4] or the *Saṅgīti Sutta*[5] and many other *Suttas*, but which were not necessarily worked out into complete philosophical systems in themselves. Some details of the systems have already been given in connection with the classification of recognizable states (*dharmas*), but a rough indication of the fundamental differences consists in the *Sarvāstivāda* assumption that all things exist, the *Vijñānavāda* that nothing exists apart from mind, and the Pali Abhidhamma that some things exist and others do not. The exact sense of 'exists' is not the same in all three cases, but whatever the differences between the systems they all come under the cover—and as Buddhist philosophies they are obliged to do so—of the three characteristics of Buddhism, *anicca, dukkha* and *anatta*. The sets of philosophical literature were compiled entirely independently of each other, so that it is evident that they belong to a period subsequent to sectarian divisions, the date of the *Vijñānavāda* being already well established.

The Pali Abhidhamma contains seven books, generally

[1] Dh. vv. 44, 45; Uv. XVIII. vv. 1, 2; *Gāndhārī Dharmapada, op. cit.*, vv. 301, 302.

[2] These are described respectively as: Nine short texts for neophytes; A series of stories with maxims; A collection of pieces, many very old; Narratives in verse showing the working of karma (applying to both Vatthus); Poems by Bhikkhus; Poems by Bhikkhuṇīs; Tales of former existences of the Buddha; Commentary on part of Sutta Nipāta; Scholastic notes on the Path of Sacred Knowledge; Biographies and Legends; Versified narrative of previous births of the Buddha. [3] D. I. 178–203. [4] *Ibid.* II. 55–71. [5] *Ibid.* III. 207–71.

known as the seven *Pakaraṇas*, namely: *Dhammasaṅgaṇī*, the enumeration of the dhammas, the *Vibhaṅga*, supplement to the *Dhammasaṅgaṇī*, *Dhātukathā*, the relationship of the dhammas, *Puggalapaññatti*, types of individuals, *Kathāvatthu*, refuting misinterpretations of the Pali Abhidhamma philosophy, *Yamaka*, a treatise of applied logic, and *Paṭṭhāna*, which continues in six volumes from the foregoing *Pakaraṇas* to the Buddhist Philosophy of Relation. Of the seven *Pakaraṇas*, *Puggalapaññatti* and *Kathāvatthu* do not contribute to the development of the main theme.

According to the *Nidānakathā* of the *Atthasālinī*, the commentary on the first of the seven *Pakaraṇas*, the Buddha ascended to the *Tāvatiṃsa* realm to teach the Abhidhamma, his mother being the chief witness, but there is no mention in the *Suttas* of the visit and the highly technical style of the Abhidhamma texts has no parallel in the simple, intimate style of the *Suttas*. Moreover, Mahā-Kassapa, addressing the five hundred Arahants composing the First Buddhist Council said merely: 'Now friends, let us recite the Dhamma and *Vinaya* before the anti-Dhamma (or non-Dhamma) comes to the forefront and the Dhamma is warded off; so with the *Vinaya*.'[1] It is of further interest that the call was made to recite the Dhamma, as containing the material for teaching the ordinary person, before the *Vinaya* which pertained particularly to the Saṅgha.

(c) *The Third Refuge: The Saṅgha*

The Third Refuge taken is in the Saṅgha. In the very early days after the Buddha's Enlightenment, before the formation of the Saṅgha, only two Refuges could be taken; such a declaration was made by two tradesmen, Tapassu and Bhalluka. The circumstances were as follows. For seven weeks after his Enlightenment, the Buddha remained in the neighbourhood of the Bodhi tree experiencing the bliss of Nibbāna; at the close of the seventh week when he was at the foot of the Rājāyatana tree, two merchants passed on the road from Ukkala. A *deva* spoke to them, and, pointing out the tree where the Buddha sat, told them he had recently become enlightened and in-

[1] Vin. II. 285; *handa mayam āvuso dhammaṃ ca vinayaṃ ca saṅgāyāma pure adhammo dippati dhammo paṭibāhīyati avinayo dippati vinayo paṭibāhīyati.*

structed them to offer him rice-cake and honey-comb as a sign of reverence. The Buddha accepted the food, and when he had removed his hands from the bowl they said: 'We take our Refuge, Sir, in the Blessed One and in his Dhamma; may he receive us as lay devotees (*upāsakas*) who from this day on, while our life lasts, have taken their refuge.'[1] Tapassu and Bhalluka were the first lay-disciples of the Buddha, and since they could take only the two Refuges, were known as the *dvevācika upāsakas*.[2]

The formation of the Saṅgha took place at Isipatana after the first declaration of the Dhamma to the five recluses[3] who had previously been companions of the Buddha, but the term '*tevācika*'[4] is used in Pali literature for the first time in connection with the parents of Yasa Thera of Banaras. During the Buddha's stay in that city, his expositions attracted many people by reason of their originality, and one night he was visited by Yasa, the son of a wealthy guild-master. Yasa, tired of the luxury and constant entertainment in which he had been brought up, came to Isipatana where the Buddha was staying, and was instructed by the Buddha who discoursed to him on the evils and vanity attendant on worldly desires, pointing out the path of deliverance. Yasa's father, missing his son from his home, went in search of him; following his track he came to the Buddha. The Buddha comforted him and discoursed to him also, whereupon he took the Three-fold Refuge (*Tisaraṇa*), thereby becoming the first *tevācika upāsaka*, using the three-word formula. In the meantime Yasa, who had heard the instruction given to his father, attained to Arahantship. As he was free from all attachments and could not therefore return to the worldly life, he was ordained and became the seventh member of the Saṅgha. The first women to become lay-disciples (*upāsikās*) were Yasa's mother and wife, both of whom used the *tevācika* formula.[5]

The word 'saṅgha' derives from *saṃ* plus *hṛ*, literally: 'comprising'. In practice it signifies 'multitude' or 'assemblage', but in Buddhist terminology the Saṅgha is one assembly and

[1] Vin. I. 4. [2] *dvevācika*, one who teaches or recites the two-word formula.
[3] 'the group of five bhikkhus' (*pañca vaggiye bhikkhū*). They are: Aññākoṇḍañña, Bhaddiya, Vappa, Mahānāma, Assaji. See Vin. I. 10; S. v. 420 ff.
[4] Three-word formula. [5] Vin. I. 15–18.

one only, namely, the Order of bhikkhus and bhikkhuṇīs, this without distinction of race, nationality, caste or age. Within the Saṅgha the only distinction is that of the *ariyasaṅgha* or *ariyapuggala*, the 'Noble Ones', and the *sammutisaṅgha*. The former are sometimes referred to as 'saints', but correctly described they are those who have 'entered the stream' (*sotāpatti*), otherwise, attained to the supramundane plane.[1] The *ariya-saṅgha* is represented conventionally by the *sammutisaṅgha*, but it is in the *ariyasaṅgha* that the Buddhist takes his Refuge since it consists of those who have realized the Truth and are able to teach it from their own experience.

Here, however, we have something of an anomaly. Of the persons who have 'entered the stream', and who therefore belong to the four pairs of persons and eight classes of individuals described earlier in the present work,[2] it is possible that laymen will be included. Such a layman would therefore be a member of the *ariyasaṅgha* but not of the *sammutisaṅgha*; the point is extremely important in estimating the position of the laity in early Buddhism. At the same time, it is not justifiable to assert without qualification, as Dr Radhakrishnan has done: 'The Saṅgha contains both lay-members and monks. While the lay-member assents to the doctrine, the monk is the missionary.'[3] The Saṅgha, in the sense of the *sammutisaṅgha*, consists exclusively of bhikkhus and bhikkhuṇis; it does not include *upāsakas* and *upāsikās*. A term '*parisa*', meaning 'company', 'assembly', 'association', is used correctly to cover all these four types of disciples, but the terms '*parisa*' and 'saṅgha' are not interchangeable. The *Kaṅkhāvitaraṇī* categorically explains that an assembly of at least four bhikkhus is called a Saṅgha.[4] In practice, both lay-members and monks—the latter more correctly called 'bhikkhus'—assent to the doctrine, and though the preaching of the Dhamma is an auxiliary activity for the bhikkhu he is not a 'missionary' in the modern sense of the term since he does not engage in 'converting' from one religion to another.

Various definitions have been offered for the word 'bhikkhu'.

[1] Those who have attained to the four supramundane paths (*magga*) and fruitions (*phala*). See also p. 55, note 2.

[2] See p. 55, note 2.

[3] *Indian Philosophy*, Radhakrishnan, London, 1923, Vol. I, p. 437.

[4] Kkvt. p. 2 f.

The Sanskrit 'bhikṣu' derives from *bhikṣ*, beggar, and long before the Buddha's day a *bhikṣu* represented one of many types of ascetics, as did the *paribbājaka*, *ājīvaka* and others;[1] now the terms 'bhikkhu' and '*bhikṣu*' are exclusively Buddhist and the bhikkhus and *bhikṣus* are not 'beggars'. Though they may make spontaneous requests to their parents or close relatives, and may also state a need to professed supporters who have previously requested them to ask for anything they want, the rules of a bhikkhu do not permit him to ask anything from any other person though he may accept gifts of the four 'requisites' of robes, alms, shelter and medicine if they are offered to him.

Nor is it correct to refer to the bhikkhu as a 'monk' since he is not bound by any vows; he may, in fact, leave the order at any time he pleases. Most important in view of frequent mistranslations, he is not a 'priest'. Buddhism recognizing no Deity, there is no being on whose behalf the bhikkhu could act as intermediary with man, either for the performance of ritual and ceremonies, for the asking of favours, or for any other reason. Moreover, no such intervention as the asking for pardon for misdeeds is possible since, automatically, one suffers or enjoys the results of one's actions. Possibly the nearest translation of the word 'bhikkhu' is 'mendicant', though this term may be employed only in the sense of living on alms.

The Buddha was once asked by Mahāli the Liccavi if it was for the cultivation of *samādhi* that the bhikkhus led the religious life under him. He replied that it was not, but that there were 'other things, higher and more excellent'[2] for which they did so. The form in which he proceeded to describe them, though considerably simpler than that adopted in many other places,[3] brings forward clearly the continuity between the moralities side of his teaching and the conditions necessary to attain to the *lokuttara* state from the destruction of fetters and is therefore quoted here.[4]

[1] See Ch. 1. [2] D. I. 156.

[3] D. III. 234; M. I. 432; S. v. 61; A. I. 63 f., IV. 459; v. 16 f.; Vbh. 377, 391.

[4] D. I. 156. There are 10 fetters (*dasa saṃyojanas*) by which beings are bound to the continuity of existence (*saṃsāra*): (i) belief in personality (*sakkāyadiṭṭi*), (ii) doubt, uncertainty of judgement (*vicikicchā*), (iii) belief in the efficacy of ceremonial observances (*sīlabbataparāmāsa*), (iv) sensual lust (*kāmarāga*), (v) ill-will (*paṭigha*), (vi) greed for fine material existence (*rūparāga*)

'First from the destruction of the three fetters,[1] the bhikkhu becomes a *sotāpanna*, one who is sure to have done with all suffering and is sure of liberation at the final end.

'Further, the bhikkhu, from the destruction of the three fetters and from the reduction of the foolishness of sensuous craving and ill-will, becomes a *sakadāgāmī*, one who, having come once more to this world, makes an end of suffering.

'Further, the bhikkhu, from the destruction of the five fetters belonging to the world of desire (i.e. *the aforementioned five*), becomes one who arises independently of the ordinary processes of birth (opapātika), in that condition obtaining final release, one who does not return to a succession of rebirths here.

'Further, Mahāli, from the complete destruction of the influxes (*āsavas*),[2] the bhikkhu, having come to understand thoroughly and to experience for himself, freeing of mind and freeing of insight, here amongst things as seen in the present world, having so attained therein continues. This is the thing, higher and more excellent, for the experiencing of which the bhikkhus lead the religious life under me.'[3]

To Mahāli's next question as to whether there is a 'way of progress by which these things may be experienced', the Buddha replies: 'There is a Way. It is the Noble Eightfold Path (*ariyo aṭṭhaṅgiko maggo*).'[4] He enumerates the components (which were explained earlier in the present work).

(vii) greed for immaterial existence (*arūparāga*), (viii) conceit (*māna*), (ix) restlessness and worry (*uddhacca-kukkucca*), (x) ignorance (*avijjā*).

[1] The three mentioned here are (I) (II) and (III).

[2] *āsava:* The term has been translated 'deadly flood', 'intoxicants', 'bias', 'depravity', 'evil', etc. Skt. *āsrava* which derives from *ā* plus *sru*, meaning 'that which flows', 'discharge from a sore'. According to the Majjhima Commentary (*Papañcasūdanī*, Part I. p. 61: *Ciraparivāsikaṭṭhena madirādayo āsavā viyā ti pi āsavā.*) the meaning extends to 'intoxicants', and, it is used in a psychological sense, hence 'influxes' is reasonable. Since, however, these terms do not convey entirely the idea of a constant flow, it is better to retain, without translation, the Pali or Skt. term which suggests the basic misconceptions of the nature of life to which all the suffering of mankind is due. The *āsavas* are: sense-desire (*kāmāsava*), desire for the process of life (*bhavāsava*) and lack of higher knowledge or ignorance (*avijjāsava*). A fourth is sometimes included, namely *āsava* of views (*diṭṭhāsava*), but this is generally considered to be covered by *avijjāsava*. Lack of 'higher knowledge' is here to be taken as lack of understanding of the truth, as contrasted with a lack of empirical knowledge.

[3] D. I. 156.

[4] *Ibid.* I. 156 f. See also p. 69 ff.

Concerning the beings who have arrived at the supramundane plane, that is to say, *sotāpannas* and beings of still higher development, those who have reached the Goal may be *Sammāsambuddhas*, *Pacceka* Buddhas, or Arahants. A *Sammāsambuddha* is a Fully-Enlightened One who comprehends the Truth by his own intuition, without the help of any others, and who can preach and make others understand the Truth. A *Pacceka* Buddha also comprehends the Truth by his own intuition only, but he is unable to preach to others. An Arahant realizes the Truth after first hearing it from another; he is able to preach and so make others understand the Dhamma. The Buddhas, *Sammāsambuddha* and *Pacceka,* are not members of the Saṅgha; the Arahants and the persons on the three lower stages of the Path comprise the *ariyasaṅgha*.

Bhikkhus of the *sammutisaṅgha* lead the religious life intending to attain to the *ariyasaṅgha,* first 'entering the stream', or becoming *sotāpannas,* then rising to the higher stages. They teach others, both by example and precept, without remuneration. Purity, voluntary poverty, selflessness and service are amongst their characteristics. There are no hard-and-fast rules regarding admission of candidates to the Order. Race, colour, caste and social class are immaterial in this respect, the only rank recognised within the Order being that of length of membership. Entry is debarred to deformed persons, those suffering from such diseases as leprosy or tuberculosis, and to debtors, professional soldiers, or such persons having mundane allegiances. There is no age limit; a boy who is 'old enough to scare away a crow' may join the Order. Entrants below the age of twenty are known as *sāmaṇeras* and later may become bhikkhus. In the meantime they observe the Ten Precepts and prepare for the higher ordination known as '*upasampadā*'. If they possess the necessary qualifications, when they complete their twentieth year they are admitted to the Order of Bhikkhus.

Any senior qualified bhikkhu who has counted more than five years in the Order is empowered to ordain a candidate as *Sāmaṇera*; no self-ordination is permissible. To be initiated into the higher Order there should be at least five Theras at the ceremony.

A newly-ordained bhikkhu is obliged to remain under a

competent teacher for a period of not less than five years, studying and practising the Dhamma, until the teacher considers it advisable for him to live by himself. According to his temperament a bhikkhu may choose either the Studious course (*ganthadhura*) or the Meditative course (*vipassanādhura*). Those who adopt the former study and practice of the Dhamma may travel from place to place preaching the doctrine to others throughout the year except in the rainy season. Those who prefer the latter retire to a place of solitude and engage in meditation.

Having renounced everything wordly the bhikkhu claims no property, does not regret his past, and does not worry about the future; he lives essentially in the present, free from the responsibilities and the trammels of the world. He clings to no abode and in all vicissitudes maintains a balanced mind. The energy at his command is directed to the activities that tend to universal happiness.

Clearly the bhikkhu's self-appointed mission is no easy one for he has no centralized authority in the shape of a governing body on which to base any claim or to which he can look for any support. Though the tradition of the Saṅgha, maintained over a period of some 2,500 years, must count for much in many countries, in the main it is by the example of his own life that he must achieve the good for others that he sets out to do.

CHAPTER 4

SANCTIONS OF MORAL CONDUCT: THE PRECEPTS

(a) *The Five Precepts* (*Pañca Sīla*)

Having taken the Three Refuges, the Buddhist laymen takes it upon himself to observe the Precepts. In the first instance these number five, but in particular cases and on particular occasions they are extended to eight or even ten. The Five Precepts are stated as follows:

(1) *Pāṇātipātā veramaṇī sikkhāpadaṃ samādiyāmi* (I undertake the precept to abstain from the taking of life.)
(2) *Adinnādānā veramaṇī sikkhāpadaṃ samādiyāmi* (I undertake the precept not to take that which is not given.)
(3) *Kāmesu micchācārā veramaṇī sikkhāpadaṃ samādiyāmi* (I undertake the precept to abstain from misconduct in sensual actions.)
(4) *Musāvādā veramaṇī sikkhāpadaṃ samādiyāmi* (I undertake the precept to abstain from false speech.)
(5) *Surā-meraya-majja-pamādaṭṭhānā veramaṇī sikkhāpadaṃ samādiyāmi* (I undertake the precept to abstain from liquor that causes intoxication and indolence.)

The First Precept

Here the Buddhist undertakes to abstain from destroying, causing to be destroyed, or sanctioning the destruction of a living being. 'Living being' implies anything that has life, from insects up to and including man. In taking this precept a Buddhist recognizes his relationship with all living things, a relationship which is so close that the harming of any living creature is inevitably the harming of himself. The Buddha taught the advisability of comparing one's own life with that of other beings: 'Everyone fears violence, everyone likes life; comparing oneself with others one would never slay or cause to slay.'[1] In the conventional sense, however, '*Pāṇa*', or in the Sanskrit '*Prāṇa*', is a 'sentient being'; but in the highest and ultimate sense it is only psychic life or vital force. Preventing the existence of a sentient being is taking away life or killing.

The precept applies to all creatures irrespective of size. It does not exclude the killing of animals for the Vedic sacrifices (*yajña*) or, as do the commandments of some religions, that of lower animals. A Buddhist does not sacrifice living beings for worship or food, but sacrifices instead his own selfish motives; in India the Buddha stopped cow killing and all blood sacrifices. On one occasion he was asked by a well-known Brahman, Kūṭadanta, what was the procedure for an elaborate sacrifice, suitable for the expression of the gratitude he felt for gifts and possessions variously acquired.[2] The Buddha, remarking on the cruelty and suffering involved in the usual type of sacrifice, suggested better means whereby gratitude might be expressed. There were possible, he said, open largesse, perpetual alms such as would guarantee the upkeep of a number of bhikkhus and bhikkhuṇīs, the building of dwelling-places for them, but, he continued, a sacrifice bearing greater fruit and advantage is that of one who, with devoted mind, takes upon himself the precepts: abstinence from taking life, from taking that which is not given, etc., enumerating the Five Precepts mentioned above.[3]

The extent of moral guilt in killing depends on the physical and mental development of the being that is killed and the circumstances under which the deed is committed. The karmic results of killing a man and killing a child vary in proportion to the physical and mental development of the two; patricide, matricide, the slaughter of innocent people and of people of considerable mental development are therefore particularly productive of evil results to the killer. The distinction is drawn between being culpable to a lesser degree (*appasāvajja*), and to a greater degree (*mahāsāvajja*). The particular injunction runs: 'Do not kill a living being. You should not kill or condone killing by others. Having abandoned the use of violence you should not use force either against the strong or the feeble.'[4]

[1] Dh. 130; Uv. v. 19; cf. *Ācārāṅga Sūtra, op. cit.*, I. 2. 3. 92, 93; *Sūyagaḍa, op. cit.*, I. 11. 9, 10.
[2] See D. I. 128 f.
[3] *Ibid.* I. 143–6.
[4] Sn. 394.

There are five conditions which constitute the immoral act of killing: (i) the fact and presence of a living being, human or animal, (ii) the knowledge that the being is a living being, (iii) the intent or resolution to kill, (iv) the act of killing by appropriate means, (v) the resulting death.[1] In the absence of any one of these conditions, the act would not constitute 'killing' even though death should follow; the event would be considered an accident and would not entail any evil effect for the performer of the act.

There are six means of killing: (i) killing with one's own hands (*sāhatthika*), (ii) causing another to kill by giving an order (*āṇattika*), (iii) killing by shooting, pelting stones, sticks, etc. (*nissaggiya*), (iv) killing by digging trenches, etc., and entrapping a being (*thāvara*), (v) killing by the powers of *iddhi*, or occult means (*iddhimaya*), (vi) killing by mantras, or occult sciences (*vijjāmaya*).[2] Whatever device may be used, the individual who kills or destroys the psychic life of a sentient being commits the evil deed of *pāṇātipāta-kamma-patha*. This kamma may be caused through the door of speech since the act of killing could be performed on receiving an order from another person.

Amongst some of the kammic result, as recorded in Buddhist literature, which a man brings upon himself by committing injury to a life may be mentioned suffering in an unpleasant state for a long period, and rebirth in some lower form of being. If born again as a man he may be infirm, ugly, unpopular, cowardly, divested of companions, subject to disease, dejected and mournful, separated from the company of loved ones, and unable to attain to ripe age. So much is recorded in the Suttas. The *Telakaṭāhagāthā* states: 'He who destroys the life of any being may, in his next birth, meet death unexpectedly while in the prime of life, even though he is possessed of all the amenities of life, wealth and beauty, like an Adonis.'[3]

Non-injury (*ahiṃsā*) has also its positive counterpart. It

[1] Dhs. A. 129; Sdhp. v. 58; Kkut. 50; UJ. 62; cf. *Sūyagaḍa, op. cit.*, I. I. 2. 24–9.
[2] Dhs. A. 129; Kkvt. 30.
[3] Tkg. v. 78: *Sabbopabhogadhanadhaññavisesalābhī*
rūpena bho sa makaraddhajasannibho pi
yo yobbane pi maraṇaṃ labhate akāmaṃ
kāmaṃparattha parapāṇaharo naro hi.
'*Makaraddhaja*' mentioned in the second line of the stanza is the Sanskrit

demands not only abstention from injury but also the practice of loving-kindness, *mettā*, to all.

One who wishes to create this force within himself, that is to say, who wishes to meditate on *mettā*, should first sever the impediments inimical to his peaceful surroundings. Then, he should choose a suitable time and a secluded place where he can, without interruption, devote himself to his meditation practice. He should then perceive the danger of anger arising and, at the same time, should realize the advantage of possessing patience, because anger has to be abandoned and patience has to be fostered in the development of this meditation. The dangers of anger should be understood in every possible way. The most effective method would be to understand it in accordance with the teaching of the Buddha.

After that, the aspirant should embark upon the development of *mettā* for the purpose of ridding the mind of hate which is a danger and for the acquisition of patience which is known as an advantage. However, *mettā* should, at first, only be directed towards certain types of persons and not to others. It is absolutely unwise, as well as dangerous, at the commencement of the practice of *mettā*, to direct one's thoughts towards the following six kinds of persons: (i) an antipathetic, (ii) a very dearly-loved, (iii) a neutral, (iv) a hostile or (v) a deceased person, or (vi) a member of the opposite sex.

Why should *mettā* not, in the preliminary stages, be developed towards these six kinds of persons? To direct thoughts of *mettā* towards an antipathetic person, a very dearly-loved one, or a neutral one is mentally fatiguing, and in the case of a very dear person there may be emotional involvement. Anger springs up if a hostile person is recollected. If mettā is directed towards a deceased person, neither absorption (*appanā*) nor access (*upacāra*) concentration is reached. Should mettā be developed towards the opposite sex, lust may arise.

There is a story of a young monk who had started the practice of developing *mettā* but, on making no headway, went to a *mahāthera* and said: 'Venerable Sir, I am quite familiar with the attainment of absorption (*jhāna*) through *mettā*, yet now I cannot attain it. What is the matter?'

equivalent of the Greek Adonis, in the sense that he possesses youth, beauty, grace, and all the good things of life.

The *mahāthera* replied: 'Seek the sign, friend, the object of your meditation.'

When the young monk did so, he discovered that his teacher, to whom he had been directing his thoughts of *mettā*, had died. He then proceeded to develop it towards another and attained full absorption (*appanā*). This, therefore, is the reason why *mettā* should not be developed towards one who is deceased.

For a successful meditation, one should be in a peaceful situation as free from distraction as possible. To begin meditation, the practitioner should be in a posture convenient to him. The proper postures include lying, walking, and sitting. If it is convenient, the ideal position is sitting cross-legged, with spine erect, head straight, eyes half-closed and hands in the lap.

The first step: for the beginner in this practice of meditation on *mettā*, it should be developed first of all towards *oneself*, mentally repeating the following or any other formula similar in sense either in Pāli or in one's own tongue:

'*Ahaṃ avero homi* (may I be free from enmity);
abbyāpajjho homi (may I be free from ill-will);
anīgho homi (may I be free from distress);
sukhī attānaṃ pariharāmi' (may I keep myself happy),

But does this not conflict with what is said in the texts? For there is no mention of any development of *mettā* towards oneself to be found in the *Vibhaṅga*, which says: 'How does a monk dwell pervading one quarter with his heart filled with loving-kindness?'[1] In the *Paṭisambhidā* it is said: 'In what five ways is mind-deliverance of loving-kindness practised with unspecified pervasion? "May all beings be free from enmity, affliction and anxiety and live happily. May all breathing things; all who are born; all individuals of whatever kind be free from enmity, affliction and anxiety, may they live happily."'[2]

In the *Metta Sutta* we find the following:

'May all beings be happy and secure;
May their hearts be wholesome.

[1] Vbh. 272. [2] PS. II. 130.

Whatever living beings there be—
Feeble or strong, tall, stout or medium,
Short, small or large, without exception—
Seen or unseen,
Those dwelling far or near,
Those who are born or who are to be born,
May all beings be happy '[1]

The reason why this does not conflict with the texts is because the latter refer to absorption (*appanā*)[2] alone and not to the initial development of *mettā* in oneself which is only by way of example; for even if one developed it for a hundred or a thousand years in this way mentally repeating, 'May I be free from enmity' and so on, absorption would never arise. Taking oneself as the example, one then extends the wish to other beings welfare and there arises in one happiness.

So first, one should, by way of example, pervade oneself with *mettā*.

The second step: in order to proceed easily, one should recollect gifts received, kind words, etc. (*dānapiyavacanādīni*), that inspire loving-kindness and endearment, such as virtue, learning and so on (*sīlasutādīni*), which give rise to respect and reverence towards a religious teacher, preceptor or his equivalent, developing *mettā* towards him by thinking, 'May this good person be free from ill-will . . .' With thoughts directed to such a person one may attain absorption.

The third step: if, however, one who meditates wishes to proceed further, in order to break down subtler, spiritual barriers (*sīmāsambheda*), one should follow-up the development of *mettā* towards a dearly-loved friend.

The fourth step: one should then develop it towards a neutral person just as one would to a very dearly-loved friend.

The fifth step: finally, one should develop it towards a hostile person, considering him as neutral. As one does this, so one's mind becomes malleable in each case before passing on to the next. On the other hand, if one is the type of individual who perceives none as his enemy, even though one may suffer harm at their hands, this question will not arise.

[1] Sn. v. 145.
[2] Fixing of thought on the object, especially of the attainment of absorption.

Only one who considers he actually has any enemy should develop *mettā* towards a hostile person as a neutral.

Overcoming Resentment

The first method: should resentment arise in one when the mind is directed towards a hostile person because of the memory of past wrong done by him, one should endeavour to overcome this feeling by entering repeatedly into the state of absorption brought about by the development of *mettā* and directed towards any of the aforementioned persons. Thus having emerged each time, one should direct one's feelings of goodwill towards the hostile person in question.

The second method: if, in spite of one's efforts, the feeling of resentment continues to exist, one should strive and strive repeatedly to leave resentment far behind. One should admonish oneself reviewing the *Dhamma* in this way: 'Why should I get angry? Has not the Buddha said this?: "Monks, even if bandits brutally severed limb from limb with a two-handled saw, he who entertained hate in his heart on that account would not be one who carried out my teaching." '[1]

Further, one should admonish oneself by reviewing the teachings of the Buddha as contained in the following verses of the *Dhammapada*:

'In those who harbour such thoughts: "He abused me, he struck me, he overcame me, he robbed me"—hatred never ceases.' (v. 3)

'In those who do not harbour such thoughts hatred will cease.' (v. 4)

'Hatred never ceases by hatred in this world; through non-enmity it comes to an end. This is an ancient law.' (v. 5)

'Some do not think that all of us here one day will die; if they did, their dissension would cease at once.' (v. 6)

'One should give up anger, renounce pride.' (v. 221)

[1] M. I. 129.

'Let a man overcome anger by loving-kindness; let him overcome evil by good; let him overcome the miser by liberality; let him overcome the liar by truth.' (v. 223)

'One should speak the truth, not give way to anger.' (v. 224)

'There is none in the world who is not blamed.' (v. 227)

'One should guard against misdeeds caused by speech. Let him practise restraint of speech. Let him practise virtue with his mind.' (v. 232)

'The wise who control their body, speech and mind are indeed well-controlled.' (v. 234)

'Monks, there are these five ways of removing annoyance, by which annoyance can be entirely removed by a monk when it arises in him. What five? (i) Loving-kindness can be maintained towards a person with whom you are annoyed: this is how annoyance with him can be removed. (ii) Compassion can be maintained . . . (iii) Onlooking equanimity can . . . (iv) The forgetting and ignoring of a person with whom you are annoyed can be practised: this is how . . . (v) Ownership of deeds in a person with whom you are annoyed can be concentrated upon thus: "This good person is owner of his deeds, heir of his deeds, his deeds are the womb from which he is born, his deeds are his kin for whom he is responsible, his deeds are his refuge, he is heir to his deeds, be they good or bad": this too is how annoyance with him can be removed.'[1]

The third method: if, after striving according to the above method, one's resentment subsides, it is good; if not, one should remove irritation by recollecting some controlled, pure and pleasing qualities in that person which, when recalled, help one's anger to subside.

Admonition to Oneself

The fourth method: if, however, in spite of one's efforts, irritation continues to arise, one should think thus:

[1] A. III. 185.

'Suppose an enemy has hurt you
In what is now his domain,
Why try yourself as well to hurt
Your mind? That is not his domain.

'This anger that you entertain
Is gnawing at the very roots
Of all the virtues that you guard—
Where is there such a fool as you!

'Another does ignoble deeds,
So you are angry—how is this?
Do you then want to copy, too,
The sort of acts that he commits?

'Suppose another, to annoy,
Provokes you with some odious act,
Why suffer anger to spring up,
And do as he would have you do?

'If you get angry, then may be
You make *him* suffer, may be not;
Though with the hurt that anger brings
You certainly are punished now.

'If anger-blinded enemies
Set out to tread the path of woe,
Do you, by getting angry too,
Intend to follow heel to toe?

'If hurt is done you by a foe
Because of anger on your part,
Then put your anger down, for why
Should you be harassed needlessly?

'Since states last but a moment's time,
Those aggregates, by which was done
The odious act, have ceased, so now
What is it you are angry with?

'Whom shall he hurt, who seeks to hurt
Another, in the other's absence?
Your presence is the cause of hurt;
Why are you angry, then, with him?'[1]

The Reviewing of Ownership of Deeds

The fifth method: if, however, resentment fails to subside when one admonishes oneself thus, one should then call to mind the fact that oneself and others are owners of their deeds (*kamma*).

Thereupon one should reflect as follows: 'What is the point of becoming angry with another? Will not this *kamma* that has anger as its source lead to my own harm? Since I am the owner of my deeds, heir of my deeds, having deeds as my origin, deeds as my kin, deeds as my refuge; I will become the heir of whatever deeds I commit.[2] It leads not to enlightenment or even to a favourable rebirth in the world, but is rather the kind of action that may lead to my downfall and to manifold suffering in states of woe.

'By allowing anger to arise I am like one who wants to hit another and picks up a burning ember or excrement and by so doing either burn or soil myself.' Having reviewed one's own deeds in this way, one should proceed to review others' also. 'What is the point of his becoming angry with me? Will it not lead to his own harm? For he is the owner of his deeds, heir of his deeds; he will become the heir of whatever deeds he commits. They are not the kind that can bring him to enlightenment or even to a high social position; rather they will lead to his downfall or to manifold sufferings in a miserable state.'

By becoming angry one is like a man throwing dust against the wind—he only soils himself.

The sixth method: if after reviewing ownership of deeds, anger still persists, then one should recollect the special qualities of the Master's former conduct; for when the Master was but a bodhisatta, prior to attaining full enlightenment and whilst engaged in fulfilling the Perfections, he allowed no hate to corrupt his mind even when his enemies on various occasions attempted to kill him. Many are the examples of self-control

[1] Vism. 308; Trn. adapted from the *Path of Purification* by Bhikkhu Ñāṇamoli, Colombo, 1956, p. 326.

[2] See A. III. 186.

to be found in the 'Birth Stories'. It is, therefore, unworthy of one to allow thoughts of resentment to arise if one is attempting to emulate the Blessed One who reached omniscience and whose special quality of patience has no equal in this world.

Reviewing the *Suttas*

The seventh method: but if, as one reviews the special former qualities of the Master, resentment still remains, as one has long been a slave of the defilements, then one should read the *suttas* which deal with the endless round of birth and death.

In the *Saṃyutta Nikāya* we read: 'Bhikkhus, it is not easy to find a being who has not formerly been your mother, or your father, your brother, your sister or your son or daughter.'[1]

Reviewing the Advantages of *Mettā*

The eighth method: should one still be unable to quench the feeling of anger in this way, one should then review the advantages of loving-kindness as follows: 'Has it not been said by the Blessed One: Bhikkhus, when the mind-deliverance of loving-kindness is cultivated, developed, much practised, made the vehicle, made the foundation, established, consolidated and properly undertaken, eleven blessings can be expected.' 'What are the eleven?'

1. One sleeps in comfort.
2. One awakens in comfort.
3. One doesn't have bad dreams.
4. One is dear to human beings.
5. One is dear to non-human beings.
6. *Devas* guard one.
7. Fire, poison and weapons do not affect one.
8. One's mind is easily concentrated.
9. One's mien is serene.
10. One dies unconfused.
11. If one penetrates no higher, one will be reborn in the world of Brahma.

If one fails to arrest the thought of anger, therefore, one will be deprived of these advantages.

[1] S. II. 189.

The Resolution into Elements

The ninth method: but if one is *still* unable to prevent the arising of anger, one should try 'resolution into elements'. How is this accomplished? One should ask oneself when angry with someone: 'What is it I am angry with? Is it the hairs of the head, the earth element therein, etc., or the water element, or the fire element, or the air element that I am angry with? Or among the five aggregates or the twelve bases or the eighteen elements with respect to which this one is called by such-and-such a name—which material aggregate, then, am I angry with? Or the feeling aggregate, the formation aggregate, the consciousness aggregate, the perception aggregate that I am angry with? Is it the eye base that I am angry with or the visible-object base, the ear base or the audible-object base, the nose base or the olfactive-object base, the tongue base, or the gustative-object that I am angry with?

'Or is it the eye-element I am angry with or the visible-object element, or the eye-consciousness element, the ear, audible or ear-consciousness elements, the nose, olfactive or nose-consciousness elements, the tongue, gustative or tongue-consciousness elements, the body, tactile or body-consciousness elements that I am angry with?

'Or the mind, mental-object or mind-consciousness elements that I am angry with?

'For when one tries the resolution into elements, one's anger finds no foothold, like a mustard-seed on the point of an awl or a painting on the air.'

The Giving of a Gift

The tenth method: if, however, one cannot effect the resolution into elements, one should try giving a gift. This can either be given by oneself to the other person or accepted by one from the other. For example, taking the case of a bhikkhu, if his requisites are incomplete, then the gift may be made by oneself and any annoyance with that person will entirely subside.

The Breaking Down of the Barriers

The sign: when one's resentment towards the hostile person has been allayed, then one can turn one's mind with loving-kindness towards that person too, just as one can towards the one who is dear, the very dear friend and the neutral person. One should then endeavour to break down the barriers that separate one from then by practising loving-kindness continuously, accomplishing mental impartiality towards the four persons, that is to say: oneself, the dear person, the neutral person and the hostile person.

The special characteristics of this practice is as follows: suppose this person is sitting in a place with a dear, a neutral and a hostile person, oneself being the fourth. Then suppose a party of bandits come to one who is meditating and say: 'Venerable Sir, let us have any one of you!' On being asked why they answer: 'So that we may kill him and use the blood of his throat as an offering.' If on hearing this the meditator thinks: 'Let them take this one or that one', he had not broken down the barriers. Should he think: 'Let them take me but not any of these three', again he has not broken down the barriers. Why? Because he seeks the welfare of the others only. However, when he does not see a single one among the four of them who should be given to the bandits whilst he directs his mind impartially towards himself and the other three, only then can it be said that he has broken down the barriers.

Thus the sign and access are obtained by this person simultaneously with the breaking down of the barriers. When this has been effected, he reaches absorption without difficulty by cultivating, developing and repeatedly practising the same sign.

At this point, one has attained to the first *jhāna* which, amongst other things, is accompanied by loving-kindness. When that has been obtained, one should continue to cultivate, develop and repeatedly practise the same sign and successively reach the second and third *jhānas*. It is by means of these *jhānas* that one 'dwells intent upon one direction with one's heart endued with loving-kindness, likewise the second direction, the third and fourth directions; also above, below and around; everywhere and equally one dwells, pervading the entire world with one's heart endued with loving-kindness, abundant, exalted, measureless, free from enmity and free from affliction.'[1]

[1] D. I. 250; Vbh. 272.

The Second Precept

The second precept of good conduct, the *adinnādānā veramaṇī,* advises a Buddhist to abstain from taking things that are not given. According to the *Brahmajāla Sutta,* the Samaṇa Gotama 'waits for the gift' (*dinnādayī*).[1] Bhikkhus and bhikkhuṇīs who live on charity should accept their requisites (*paccaya*) only when they are offered. Lay devotees should lead an honest life according to the right livelihood (*sammā-ājīva*). Any sort of thieving, even at the risk of one's life, was denounced by the Buddha.

Two modes of thieving are recognized, the direct and the indirect. The first consists in appropriating anything belonging to another person without first securing his consent.

The second comprises frauds and deceptions whereby a man may cheat another out of something that rightly belongs to him. Of these Buddhaghosa says: 'One or other of these means may be carried out according to circumstances, in stealing by false means and weights, by force, by concealment, by design or by forgery. This is an outlined account of theft.'[2] In short, any scheme, intrigue or device, whether adopted in the sale of houses, horses, cattle or any other commodity, constitutes a violation of the precepts of *adinnādānā veramaṇī,* of the injunction to abstain from taking anything without the consent of the owner, for in such cases the buyer is not aware that the purchase is worth less than he is paying for it. The second precept is therefore an injunction against any form of dishonest dealing.[3] 'One should avoid that which is not given, whatever or wherever it is. The disciple, perceiving this, does not steal or condone stealing. Everything that is not given he should avoid.'[4]

The second precept may be considered also as the reverse of *dāna,* or liberal giving, the first of the ten perfections (*dasa pāramitā*).[5] These are enumerated in *Buddhavaṃsa* and *Cariyāpiṭaka.* They are covered largely in the *Bhikkhuvagga* of the *Dhammapada;* the *Udānavarga* treats of them in a *Sīlavarga* where the following two notable verses occur: 'Firmly established in the moralities, the bhikṣu cultivates his mind and his wisdom; energetic and prudent he will attain to

[1] D. I. 4.
[2] Dhs. A. 130.
[3] For details see Kkvt. 26–30.
[4] Sn. v. 395.
[5] See Ch. 2, p. 72.

permanent destruction of suffering.[1] Those who are pure and moral, and who live by practising vigilance, made free by right penetration, Māra does not know their road.'[2] The first of these verses does not occur in the *Dhammapada* but resembles *Saṃyutta Nikāya* I. 13;[3] the second compares with *Dhammapada* 57.[4] On the other hand, *Dhammapada* mentions the *sīlas* relating to all the five precepts explicitly in verses 246, 247: 'He who in this world destroys life and speaks falsehood, takes what is not given or goes to someone else's wife, and he who takes intoxicating drinks, this person destroys his origin in this world.'[5] However, to complete the observance of *dāna* a strict observance of the precepts *adinnādānā veramaṇī* is necessary, for the practice of *dāna* and *adinnādāna* cultivates the state of mind which gives rise to freedom from cleaving to mortal and changeable things, and it is on the purification from lust and longing that the release from the cycles of *saṃsāra* depends.

Adinna meaning 'that which is not given', and *ādāna* 'taking', the immoral volition to take others' belongings is known as the immoral act of stealing (*adinnādāna-akusala-kamma*). Five factors constitute the immoral act of stealing, namely: (i) others' property, (ii) awareness of the fact that it is others' property that is being taken, (iii) the immoral volition of stealing, (iv) the employment of a device to steal, and (v) the act of removing the property.[6] Whatever device is employed, so long as others' belongings are taken without the consent of the owner, it is the path of retributive kamma (*adinnādāna-kamma-patha*) that is committted. This *kamma* may also be caused through the 'door' of speech, since the act of stealing may be performed on receipt of instructions from another person.

Amongst the Kammic results that accrue to the thief are the following: great suffering in an unhappy state for a long period, or, if by virtue of other merits the thief should be reborn as a man he would lack possessions in this new state. He would be unable to acquire wealth, or if he did so he would be unable to keep it, and would be subject to danger from kings, murderers,

[1] Uv. VI. v. 8.
[2] *Ibid.* VI. v. 19.
[3] S. I. 13.
[4] Dh. v. 57.
[5] *Ibid.* vv. 146, 147.
[6] Dhs. A. 130; Sdhp. v. 61; see UJ. 60 f.

floods, and fire. He would be unable to enjoy sensual pleasures and would be discontented and despised by the people. According to the *Telakaṭāhagāthā*; 'If a man in order to benefit himself is guilty of stealing the property of others, in his next birth he becomes a contemptible beggar clad in dirty rags; with a broken begging-vessel in hand, he ever begs his daily bread at the doors of his enemies while suffering a hundred insults.'[1]

The Third Precept

The third precept of good conduct, *kāmesu micchācārā veramaṇī*, is traditionally interpreted as though '*kāmesu*' were in the singular form and is therefore taken to advise Buddhists to abstain merely from unlawful sexual intercourse. Since this limitation is generally accepted, we defer consideration of the wider significance and take, for the present, that which may be inferred if '*kāma*' had been expressed in the singular.

By '*kāma*' is meant 'lustful attachment to male or female', and by '*micchācāra*' 'wrong conduct'. The immoral act of unchastity (*kāma-micchācāra-akusala-kamma*), is the volition or sense-desire of a male for a female or a female for a male. The Buddha said: 'A wise man should avoid unchastity as if it were a pit of burning cinders. One who is not able to live in a state of celibacy should, at least, not break the purity of another man's wife.'[2]

That the sexual is the strongest instinct of living beings is widely recognized, and man is more sensitive to sexual stimulation than are other living creatures since in the animal world the incentive is periodic and seasonal while in man it is continual. That mental development should result in increase of control of sexual desire would appear to be the logical course of events, but it would also seem logical to suppose that the desire should lessen as the general view of life and its possibilities extends and appreciates in value. In the case of the person of chastity (*brahmacariya*) this is certainly true, whatever his religious views may be or whatever name he calls the religious life; but in the stages intermediary between the least and the most developed of human types the sexual is still the strongest instinct, desire for food and aspiration to

[1] Tkg. v. 79; Sdhp. v. 78. [2] Sn. v. 396.

religious thought ranking second and third. One may take the view that mental development is always challenged by the physical world, that what is popularly called 'nature' makes for quantity and not quality, irrespective of the waste and possible suffering entailed; but if one is not inclined to assume that the physical world exists entirely independently of the mind of man, then one looks to the mind of man to find the ultimate cause of the sex or any other instinct. Here one may consider two factors; the fear of recognizing the impermanence (*anicca*) of things, and the assertion of power. Regarding the first, the urge to make the world seem permanent is reflected in the universal desire to see one's children and grandchildren growing up around one, whether or not these are expected to ingratiate some super-being on behalf of one's welfare in a future state. Briefly stated, the family instinct tends to dispel loneliness for the immediate present and to foster companionship, as well as to furnish a vague suggestion that one will never be entirely alone. Somehow, somewhere, it is felt, there might exist something familiar, to which one can, in a sense, return. Family life represents the aspiration of the bulk of mankind and is by no means to be condemned out of hand. On the contrary one may agree that it constitutes a means whereby some of man's best qualities may be developed, for it obliges him to take an interest in a community whether limited to that of family or extended to that of city or state. Since, however, the present precept refers to misconduct and misuse of a sexual relationship rather than to its conduct in general, we defer consideration of the latter until the following chapter when we may examine the position of the laity, as a whole; we may, nevertheless, include certain remarks since they are pertinent to the whole matter of sex.

Though the highest conduct of life has so often been taken to be that of religious celibacy, still the bulk of the world's population has always been unwilling or unable to adopt it. In the general interest, therefore, marriage must be recognized as a respectable and honourable state if only for the avoidance of promiscuity. In the very early days of Christianity celibacy was the rule for all Christians, but enforcement of this was not possible for long in view of the thriving contemporary of Mithraism; this religion held a creed almost identical with that of the Christians except that it did not enforce celibacy. The Christian objection to marriage for the laity was withdrawn and marriage was celebrated as a holy rite. Centuries before, Indian thought, the Buddha's included, had held that religious celibacy represented the highest form of conduct of one's life, but though the Buddha gave much advice to the laity there was at no time any attempt to bring the state or ceremony of marriage under religious jurisdiction. Rather the line was taken that the householder should achieve the best possible results in his present sphere so that he would become sufficiently advanced in his understanding to choose, of his own volition, the religious life in a future existence.

The second factor is probably not entirely disconnected with the idea of gods as possessing superhuman powers, and, more particularly, with the idea of a creating god or God. If in his struggles to attain to *brahmacariya* man has to contend with the impulse of the large bulk of his fellow-creatures to reject celibacy, he is also faced with their determination to idealize and emulate a 'creator'. The rejection of celibacy implies a materialization of the creating instinct, but the desire to create makes also for a lust for power which brings envy to competition and peoples and nations to war. The necessity to find room for surplus populations then figures as a secondary rather than as a primary cause of bitterness and strife.

The foregoing places consideration of the sexual conduct of man on the level of thought rather than on the level of sensation, and it is noticeable that in his efforts to raise himself above the sensation-level he has engaged in forms of physical training whereby he acquires control over his physique and therefore a certain mental control also. The classic example is that of the Greeks, whose dislike of sex and love of physical fitness stood in marked contrast to the pursuit of luxurious living often attributed to the Semitic races of the day, while in our own times we have seen rapid advances in the standard of physical health and improvement of mental outlook where populations have taken an interest in outdoor exercises. That these are often exploited for commercial and similar reasons is, of course, a matter for regret, but recognition that the first steps in mental control lie in the control of the physique is obvious and essential.

To destroy abnormal sexuality at the root, it is imperative that an individual turns his mind from such thoughts the instant they present themselves. 'As rain gets into an ill-thatched house, so lust penetrates an undeveloped mind. As rain does not get into a well-thatched house, so lusts do not penetrate a well-developed mind.'[1] The man who solemnly undertakes to observe the third precepts of right conduct should therefore purify the source from which actions flow, namely, his thoughts, remembering: 'The harm that an enemy will do to an enemy or a foe to a foe is not so great as that which a wrongly-directed mind will do to oneself.'[2]

Still, as in the case of the person committing an act of theft at the instigation of another, the latter, giving the instruction or impulse to steal, being no less guilty than the person who actually takes the article in question, so persons inciting others to dissolute behaviour are also guilty. The matter is less easy to counter than might at first be supposed, for a large number of even the major works of world literature have sex for their basic theme, while pictorial advertisements displayed in the streets of cities force the lowest aspects of it on the attention of communities at large. Here the person inciting others to dwell on evil is entirely to be condemned, for by dwelling in thought on, and witnessing pictorial examples of, lustful behaviour, sex becomes a demon that drives man to his utter ruin. To sum up the third precept it may be said that indulgence in unlawful sexual conduct is productive of much evil to the person concerned and to the whole of society.

Those in whom sensual thoughts arise should learn to control them by the practice of mindfulness. In the *Satipaṭṭhāna Sutta* it is said: 'Herein, monks, when sense-desire is present in him, the monk knows, "There is sense-desire in me", or when sense-desire is absent, he knows, "There is no sense-desire in me". He knows how the arising of non-arisen sense-desire comes to be; he knows how the rejection of arisen sense-desire comes to be; and he knows how the non-arising in the future of the rejected sense-desire comes to be'.[3]

Among the evil consequences resulting from unlawful sexual intercourse may be mentioned the following: suffering

[1] Dh. vv. 13, 14; Uv. XXXI. vv. 11, 17; Thag. 133, 134.
[2] *Ibid.* v. 42; XXXI. v. 9. [3] D. II. 300; M. I. 60.

in an unhappy state for a long period; when reborn as a man by virtue of merits acquired in a previous existence the birth would occur in a lower form of mankind. Such a person would have many enemies, would be disliked by the people, would be destitute, unable to procure comfortable lodgings, food and clothes, and would be full of anger and rage.[1]

We now return to the interpretation of the precept as with *kāma* in the Locative plural form *kāmesu*. In such form the precept signifies abstinence from all indulgences in the five sensuous objects, namely, visible object, sound or audible object, olfactory object, sap or gustative object, and body impression or tactile object. *Kāmesu micchācāra* is therefore 'wrong or evil conduct with regard to the five sensual organs'. In many places in Pali literature, the fifth factor of *kāma*, that is, body impression, has been interpreted as 'unlawful sexual intercourse'; it seems that it would be the most blameworthy of the five *kāmas*. In representing *kāmesu micchācāra* as relating only to sexual intercourse the grammatical form of *kāma* has been ignored; to achieve complete observance of the precept, one must therefore desist from the five forms of self-indulgence, both directly and indirectly.

The Fourth Precept

The fourth precept of good conduct, *musāvādā veramaṇī*, concerns abstention from falsehood. This covers the act of telling an untruth, the concealing of the truth in such a manner as to convince another person that an untruth is a truth, the use of exaggerated language, in short, everything that is in any sense a departure from a reliable sober statement of fact. Less obvious, but no less to be stressed, *musāvāda* implies the accepting as truth, in one's own mind, of that which one knows to be untrue, lack of diligence in searching out the truth of a statement, or any lack of precision in thought in so far as one is able with one's present understanding and intelligence to probe to the truth that is uttermost.

Taking the obvious features first, 'Lying is applied to the effort of the body and speech, on the part of one who is deceitful, to destroy the good of others; the volition setting up the bodily

[1] See Sdhp. v. 79; Tkg. v. 80.

and vocal effort to deceive, with intent to cheat others.'[1] From the habit of speaking truthfully is acquired confidence since there is no need then to dissemble or conceal the truth. Moreover, the speaker of truth inspires confidence in others who come to know that they may rely implicitly on his words. 'The speech released by a wise man is full of feeling, expressing his true thought. Clumsy people whose language consists only in opening their mouths are not wise people.'[2] Again, 'Truth is the immortal speech, this is the primeval law. In Truth, well-being and law the saints are established.'[3] Conversely, it is disadvantageous to associate with habitual speakers of untruth and the results of lying can bring considerable harm. There are four constituent factors in this offence: (i) the untruth itself, (ii) the intent to deceive, (iii) the effort so involved, and (iv) the act of communicating the untruth.[4] This act becomes the path of retributive kamma (*kamma-patha*) when the false words spoken are taken by others to be the truth. If they are not believed by others, only a bad karmic effect is produced; *kamma-patha* gives rise to both rebirth and to a resultant during the present existence. The immoral act may also be committed as an act of writing, or such communication by hand, and is then said to be performed 'through the door of the body' (*kāyadvārena*).[5]

The habit of speaking the truth must be dependent on the habit of thinking accurately since, in an attempt to give an accurate account of an event one must be clear in one's mind as to exactly what took place. In such an instance the *musāvādā* may represent misapprehension and not a deliberate lie such as that told by a person who is caught in a wrong act and who denies it or tries to explain it away for fear of punishment. Here the sequence of thought of the narrator as he casts about for formulation of a likely-sounding story does have an effect on his later mode of thinking as a whole. With a sustained effort to think precisely, and so to speak precisely, the constant devotee of truth acquires gradually a faculty of detecting the

[1] Dhs. A. 130

[2] Vin. I. 349; Ud. 61; cf. Uv. XV. v. 9.

[3] S. I. 189; Sn. v. 458; Thag. 1229; cf. Uv. VIII. v. 14.

[4] Dhs. A. 131; Sdhp. v. 65; See UJ. 61.

[5] See Kkvt. 16; cf. *Upāsakadaśāṅga*, ed. Kanhaiyalal, Rajkot, 1961, I. 46: writing false statements (*kūṭalekhakaraṇa*).

presence of falsehood whenever he encounters it, to whatever extent it may be disguised.

The penalty that falls on the habitual liar is that he loses all sense of truth, and much the same may be said concerning the casual or superficial thinker. In considering the first of the Three Refuges, The Buddha, attention was drawn to the stress laid in Buddhist teaching on the cultivation of discernment, but if truth and untruth are to be automatically confused there will be no possibility of discernment and the person accustomed to falsehood will be far from an understanding of the teaching of the King of Truth (*Dharmarājā*), the Buddha. On the other hand, the follower of *Dharmarājā*, cleaving to truth in all his words and ways, will qualify himself to arrive at a right understanding; he will proceed steadily in the cultivation of discernment which will make him ever less subject to doubt (*vicikicchā*), one of the Five Hindrances to mental development and vision, and also one of the fetters (*saṃyojana*) binding man to the rounds of rebirth (*saṃsāra*).

In assigning importance of the highest order to the precept relating to *musāvāda*, one may quote in support the *Dhammapada* verse: 'Speak the truth. Do not be angry. When you are asked, give—if only a little. From these three conditions one may go into the vicinity of the *devas*.'[1] If one is accustomed to speaking and thinking with precision, one has sufficient clarity of vision not to feel anger and not to pass over an occasion on which another person is in need of a gift. If, then, one wishes to be 'near the devas', or, in other words, to rise above the human state then the cultivation of thinking and speaking truly is the means *par excellence*. It is, in fact, the foundation of Buddhism.

The Fifth Precept

The fifth precept concerns the Buddhist's abstention from taking distilled and fermented intoxicating liquors. 'He should not take intoxicating drinks. The householder who likes this teaching does not urge others to drink and does not condone drinking, knowing that it ends in madness. Through drunkenness foolish

[1] Dh. v. 224; Uv. XX. v. 16; cf. *Dasaveyāliya*, in Su. Ch. IV. p. 950, Ch. VII. vv. 11, 54.

people commit evils and cause them to be committed by other foolish people. Avoid that which is a realm of evils, maddening, deluding, and the delight of the foolish.'[1]

Though it is recognized at the present day that certain drugs, including alcohol, are efficacious in the treatment of illness or disease, they are not necessary to a person in a normal condition. The basic objection to alcoholic drinks and such drugs lies in the fact that they distort the mental vision if only temporarily; in such case it is not possible to preserve the vigilance and alertness which Buddhists should continuously practise. Possibly the best illustration of this distortion, even though very slight, may be taken from the experience of drivers of motor vehicles who are, as a rule, averse to taking any alcoholic drink when driving or about to drive. If alcoholic drinks and drugs are taken frequently and in large quantities, the harm done to the addict is, of course, very grave, and whatever pleasure he may think to derive from the indulgence temporarily, there can be no source of satisfaction, either to him or to his companions, in experiencing a waning control of his mind or in the subsequent recollection that he has behaved foolishly.

In view of certain current misapprehensions, it should be firmly stated that the use of hallucinogenic drugs for the purpose of attaining allegedly 'higher' meditative states is highly dangerous and is a contravention of the Fifth Precept. In this connection the words of a former Supreme Patriarch of Thailand, Prince Vajirañāṇavarorasa, may be quoted with reference to cannabis:

'INDIAN HEMP. Another kind of narcotic drug is called hemp or Indian hemp (*Cannabis Sativa*). In small doses it may be used for medicinal purposes producing sleep and dullness of the senses. It is also habit-forming and has an intoxicating effect. The addicts prefer to smoke. It reacts mainly on the nervous system, producing both the visionary and auditory hallucination. Thus what a person addicted to it sees or hears is often distorted and exaggerated. Very often a rope is to him a snake and the sound of a drum becomes thunder or the roar of a cannon. This in turn gives rise to a morbid fear and an

[1] Sn. vv. 398, 399.

uncontrollable excitement leading eventually to delirium and insanity.'[1]

The matter of drinking is only briefly alluded to in the Buddhist texts, the causes being of far greater import. Considered in general these consist in an attempt to produce either a sort of exhilaration or a pacification. The former would connect with a temporary and false happiness, the latter with the lulling of a sense of grief. Rather than embark on wholesale denunciation of sufferers in either of these states, one would consider it more helpful to them to show how the states could be understood correctly and so remedied. Such understanding of mental states is an essential part of the Buddhist teachings.

(*b*) *The Eight Precepts* (*Aṭṭhaṅga Sīla*)

The foregoing Refuges and Five Precepts are declared by laymen who wish to account themselves followers of the Buddha, and to them the Refuges and Precepts should be considered as morally binding at all times. Three additional Precepts, bringing the total to eight, form the *aṭṭha sīla*, or *Uposatha Sīla*, since they are observed on *Uposatha* days.[2] The three additional precepts are: (vi) *Vikālabhojanā veramaṇī sikkhāpadaṃ samādiyāmi* (I undertake the precept to abstain from taking untimely meals).[3] (vii) *Nacca-gīta-vādita-visūkadassana-mālāgandha-vilepana-dhāraṇa-maṇḍana-vibhūsanaṭṭhānā veramaṇī sikkhāpadaṃ samādiyāmi* (I undertake the precept to abstain from dancing, singing, music, watching grotesque mime, from using garlands, perfumes, cosmetics and personal adornments.) (viii) *Uccāsayana-mahāsayanā veramaṇī sikkhāpadaṃ samādiyāmi* (I undertake the precept to abstain from

[1] *Pañcasīlapañcadhamma*, published in commemoration of the Third Cycle of the Birthday Anniversary of H.M. King Bhumibol Adulyadej by the Mahāmakuta Educational Council, the Buddhist University, Thailand, December 2506 (1963).

[2] *Uposatha:* Vedic *upavasatha*, the eve of the Soma sacrifice during which day it is prepared. With the advent of Buddhism the word had come to mean the four stages of lunar month's waxing and waning, namely, 1st, 8th, 15th and 23rd. The Buddhists adopted this day as their weekly sacred day (equivalent to Sabbath).

[3] See Vin. I. 83, IV. 274; D. I. 5; A. I. 212, II. 209; Sn. v. 400; cf. *Dasaveyāliya, op. cit.*, Ch. IV., p. 950, Ch. VIII, p. 28.

the use of high seats). Concerning the first of these additions, the sixth precept, on days on which *aṭṭha sīla* is observed the layman takes his main meal at midday and does not eat again during that day. The seventh precept is self-explanatory. The eighth has an ulterior meaning in that the occupying of high beds or high chairs may connect with the assumption of high rank or of personal importance; it need not mean that the bed or chair must be less than a certain height above the floor or ground. For a layman observing *aṭṭha sīla* at intervals, however, the suggestion of avoiding luxury is no doubt paramount.

Regarding the length of time during which the Eight Precepts should be observed, though the keeping may be periodical and therefore constitute 'periodical virtue' (*kālapariyanta sīla*), Buddhaghosa says: 'In the fifth dyad periodical virtue is that undertaken after deciding on a time limit. Lifelong *Sīla* (*āpāṇakoṭika sīla*) is that practised in the same way but undertaken for as long as life lasts. *Aṭṭha sīla* is therefore of two kinds, periodical and lifelong.'[1]

A significant advance in the *Uposatha Sīla* consists in the practice of celibacy. While the daily observance of the Five Precepts preserves the status of family life and only prevents the layman from indulging in unlawful sensual acts, the layman observing the Eight Precepts must practise complete celibacy. A layman strictly observing the *Uposatha Sīla* is confined to meditation and other religious performances in Vihāras, woods, or separate apartments; for the period of observance he is dressed in the simplest of garments. But essentially, while observing *aṭṭha sīla* he must not live attached to his family since the observation constitutes a form of temporary renunciation.

(c) *The Ten Precepts* (*Dasa Sīla*)

The Ten Precepts, *dasa sīla,* were laid down by the Buddha for *sāmaṇeras* and for the more pious of the laity who could remain unattached to their families. They could observe it for a certain period or lifelong.

In the *dasa sīla,* the seventh precepts of the *Uposatha Sīla* is divided into two parts, so that we get for the seventh of the

[1] Vism. 12.

ten: 'I undertake the precept to abstain from dancing, music, singing, and watching grotesque mime'. The remainder, 'I undertake the precept to abstain from the use of garlands, perfumes and personal adornments', forms the eighth of the Ten Precepts. It is thought that the Buddha wished to stress the importance of a longer abstinence, possibly life-long, from all sensual pleasures.

The ninth precept concerns the use of high seats, as in the *aṭṭha sīla*, while the tenth, which exists only in the *dasa sīla*, states: *Jāta-rūpa-rajata-paṭiggahanā veramaṇī sikkhāpadaṃ samādiyāmi* (I undertake the precept to abstain from accepting gold and silver).

CHAPTER 5

THE UNDERLYING IDEALS OF THE MORALITIES

(a) *Relating the Precepts to the Refuges*

Having considered the nature of the Three Refuges and the Precepts separately, we now examine their import when taken together. Two aspects of the conjunction are presented: first the nature of the relationship of the Precepts to the Refuges, second the effect of their being taken together on the whole view of life. Here we come to a study of the Buddha-Dhamma rather than a study of the Buddha and the Dhamma as though with an underlying suggestion that they are separate entities.

Concerning the first aspect, if we try to consider the Buddha alone, we find ourselves postulating something of a transcendental state without the necessary knowledge and equipment for so doing. The result will be merely a 'religion', and the Precepts will represent merely an arbitrary code. But the Buddhist Precepts had their natural root in the Buddha, and we may think of the Buddha both as a man who spent his youth and early manhood living in the world and also as one who experienced the passing from this stage to the attaining of Enlightenment. So will it be seen that the Precepts were never ends in themselves, confined to the mundane life, but were the essential preliminaries, as also the permanent accompaniments, to the attaining to the Highest State.

The Buddha made the following statements regarding himself: 'I am he who has overcome all things, who has found out all things; in all things I am free of taint. I have renounced all things; I am freed of the destruction of craving. From becoming possessed of the Higher Knowledge by myself, to whom should I point as teacher?'[1] The passage occurs frequently in the Buddhist scriptures but is in full context in the *Tathāgatavarga* of the *Udānavarga* in which is included the following stanza: 'I shall go to Banaras; I shall beat the drum of the Deathless State; I shall make turn the Wheel of the Law

[1] Dh. v. 353; Sn. v. 211; M. I. 171; S. II. 284; Vin. I. 8; Uv. XXI. v. 1, etc.

which in this world has not yet been turned.'[1] Having set in motion the Wheel of the Law, the Buddha said later: 'Entered upon this course you will make an end of suffering. The road was declared by me when I had understood the removal of the darts.'[2] The terms *salla*, or *śalya*, for arrow, dart, or thorn, and *śokaśalya* for the arrows or thorns of grief, are common in Indian literature; *Lalitavistara* describes the Buddha as *mahāśalyahartā*, 'the great remover of darts'. The 'darts' consisted in the following: Lust (*rāga*), hatred (*dosa*), delusion (*moha*), pride (*māna*), false views (*diṭṭhi*), grief (*soka*), and indecision (*kathaṃkathā*).[3] They are the equivalents to the Fetters binding one to the rounds of rebirth.[4] Yet with such unparalleled attainments the Buddha is appraised by the average man only with regard to the Moralities.[5]

The second aspect, that of the Refuges and Precepts taken together, with the consequent overall view of life evolved brings up the whole question as to how the Buddha-Dhamma was to be formulated and presented. It might be assumed that the laity would receive elementary instruction and the bhikkus more advanced instruction, but that was not always the case. There is no hard-and-fast line of demarcation between the practise of the Moralities and the understanding of the *Paṭiccasamuppāda*, nor is there any barrier between the intellectual capacity of the bhikkhus and that of the laymen. The point at issue was always the freeing of mind and freeing of insight, and though it was obviously more likely that the bhikkhu would develop these more quickly than would the layman, still there was no holding back of the teaching for those who could absorb it, whatever their status.

We consider the days before the Saṅgha was formed, the days of the *dvevācika*. In the case of Vipassi Buddha, the first of the seven Buddhas mentioned in Chapter I of the present work, a following had formed around him from the time that he took to the homeless life; in order to retire to the solitude during which he became enlightened he was obliged to abandon his followers; but to form a nucleus of properly instructed people to help him after his Enlightenment he went to two

[1] Uv. XXI. v. 6: cf. Vin. I. 8; Mtn. 327; Lal. 406.
[2] Dh. v. 275; Ndi. 59.
[3] See Ndi. 59; cf. *Samavāya*, in Su. Vol. I. 318.
[4] See p. 82, note 4.
[5] See p. 67, note 1.

of his former friends in his native city of Bandhumatī, men whom he knew to be well-informed generally and to be of a high moral standard. Gotama Buddha after his Enlightenment went in search of five of his former companions, all of whom would have had considerable experience in philosophical study. Other than these five he had no following at the time. He went to Banaras, addressed gatherings as did other teachers, and met with considerable success. The story of Yasa and his parents has already been recounted,[1] and while the Saṇgha now counted seven members, three lay-disciples, Yasa's father, mother and wife accrued also. The class of followers known as *upāsakas* and *upāsikās* must therefore have come into being very shortly after formation of the Saṅgha, whether *Sammuti* or the *Ariya* Saṅgha. However, apart from Yasa and his family, Gotama Buddha's teachings soon aroused sufficient interest to cause an outcry in Magadha: 'The Samaṇa Gotama has followed a method by which families are left without sons, women are widowed, and the line of succession of a clan is cut off.'[2] At the same time the prospective recluses were saying: 'The household life is cramping; it is a path choked with dust; to leave it is to come out into the open air. Settled in a house it is not easy to lead the Higher Life in its complete purity, polished like a conch-shell. Surely I should shave my head and beard, put on the yellow robe, and, leaving my home, go out into the homeless life.[3]

(*b*) *Position of the Laity in Early Buddhism*

It is sometimes argued from the above passage, which occurs many times in the Buddhist scriptures, that the Buddha addressed his teaching entirely to recluses, prospective if not recluses already in fact. This is by no means the entire picture of the case, and in forming an opinion thereon it should be borne in mind that recluses were quite common in India in the Buddha's day. Precedent existed as far back as the *Vaikhānasas*[4] and it would have been no particular distinction for any teacher that his students became recluses, at least for

[1] See p. 80, note 5.

[2] Vin. I. 43: *aputtakāya paṭipanno samaṇo Gotamo vedhavyāya paṭipanno samaṇo Gotamo kulūpacchedāya paṭipanno samaṇo Gotamo.*

[3] D. I. 63.

[4] See Ch. 1, p. 30.

the period of study of his doctrine. It was, in fact, the least the student could do. The samaṇas, as a class, were permanently recluses though they did not necessarily follow a particular method of teaching. The distinction for a teacher would lie in the appreciable number of people becoming recluses on account of his particular teaching, and this, according to the Vinaya text quoted above, occurred in Magadha with reference to the Buddha. But the most that could be argued from the circumstance is that the Buddha was more successful than other teachers; he did not lure men from their homes for unworthy reasons of self-aggrandizement or self-advertisement. As far as the daily necessities of life were concerned, householders were accustomed to recluses and to supplying them with food and clothing irrespective of their religious opinions; Buddhist recluses could rely on the householders for alms as much as could any other recluses.

With an increased following and the consequent necessity of an ordered progress for the bhikkhu, contacts with the laity increased as a matter of course. During the rainy season,[1] well-disposed householders attended specifically to the bhikkhus' wants, often taking them their food so that they did not need to make their daily round for it. This custom is still maintained even in countries where the three months' rainy season does not occur. At the end of the rains the householders made the bhikkhus gifts of robes. As would be expected, householders came to like and respect the bhikkhus, listened to their discourses on *Uposatha* days, and frequently declared themselves *upāsakas* or *upāsikās*. However, no more and no less than in any other religion did there exist anything spectacular for the laity to do. Though Buddhist teaching did not include any ceremony, but, to the contrary, pointed out that belief in the efficacy of rites and ceremonies (*sīlabbataparāmāsa*) constituted a tie to the round of rebirths, at the same time no layman would ever have been permitted to participate in the Vedic or Brahmanic ceremonies, other than to the extent of helping provide an audience. Even such an apparently simple act as 'holding up the sacrificial ladle'[2] was fraught with connotation

[1] This is called 'sojourn of rainy season' (*vassāvāsa*) similar to keeping Lent. See Vin. III. 10; Mtn. 16, 8.

[2] D. I. 120: Soṇadaṇḍa brahman, having enumerated the qualities of a

and implied considerable previous study, while the chanting and reciting of hymns were, in the earlier Indian religions, the prerogative of the priests. Again, even in much later religions, the formal reading from a sacred text is rarely entrusted to laymen, though certain arranged responses are uttered by them at prescribed intervals. The contribution of the Buddhist laity would then, as in the case of other religions and 'ways of life' which are not supported by a national church or state grant, consist in studying the teaching, beginning with the keeping of the Precepts, and helping to support the bhikkus or similar personages; but, as will be noticed in the latter part of the present chapter where reference is made to the manner in which the layman is advised to allocate his money, no specific part of it is ever suggested for allocation to the Saṅgha.

Besides the *upāsakas* and *upāsikās*, the Nikāyas refer to '*parisās*'[1] as being also listeners to the Buddha's discourses. The range of *parisās* included the *samaṇa-parisā* and *parisās* of the *deva* worlds, while for the laity of the present world three classes were distinguished: the *Khattiya-parisā*, the *Brāhmaṇa-parisā*, and the *Gahapati-parisā*.[2] Alternatively to *parisā* in these three cases the terms '*mahāsālas*' or '*paṇḍitas*, are employed. In view of the grouping of '*gahapati*' together with '*khattiya*' and '*brāhmaṇa*' it seems that the term is here intended for 'householders' of the upper classes, otherwise professional or business men and craftsmen. The only other one of the four classes considered as forerunners of the caste system, namely, the *suddas*, or servant class, is not mentioned in this connection, but it cannot be inferred that such a class was excluded from the Buddha's teaching. We have, in fact, the notable discourse in *Sāmaññaphala Sutta* which states at the outset: 'A householder or householder's son, or one of some other clan, comes to hear the dhamma. Having heard it he gets confidence in the Tathāgata.'[3] Of the three *parisās*, the *Khattiya* produced the smallest number of followers of the Buddha, the *Gahapatis* the largest, but in the towns suggested specifically to the

true brahman as those of high birth, high scholarship, commanding physical appearance and high morality, concludes: 'He is a wise man and a sage, the first or the second to hold up the sacrificial ladle.'

[1] *parisā:* lit. company, association, assembly.

[2] *khattiyas:* the warrior class; *brāhmaṇas:* the brahman or priestly class; *gahapatis:* the householders.

[3] D. I. 62 f.

Buddha as suitable places for his *Parinibbāna*, namely, *Campā*, *Rājagaha*, *Sāvatthi*, *Sāketa*, *Kosambi*, *Banaras*, there were very appreciable numbers of all three *mahāsālās*.[1]

Of the numerous *vaggas* in the *Nikāyas* bearing the titles *Brāhmaṇavagga* and *Gahapativagga*, the term '*brāhmaṇa*' does not generally refer to members of the Brahman caste; 'Brahman' is taken, in the titles, to signify the ideal type. The *Gahapativaggas*, on the other hand, invariably concern householders, professional men and craftsmen. The extent of the instruction given to the *gahapatis* varied according to the capacity for understanding of the person or persons addressed; for example, in the first two *gahapativaggas* of *Saṃyutta Nikāya* the householder was told to observe the Five Sīlas, develop confidence in the Three Jewels, Buddha, Dhamma and Saṅgha, and understand the law of causation including the Four Noble Truths. *Saṃyutta Nikāya* gives the duties of a householder as (i) the maintaining of one's parents, (ii) paying reverence to elders of the family, (iii) using gentle words, (iv) avoiding malicious talk, (v) giving up of miserliness, (vi) practising generosity, (vii) speaking the truth, and (viii) avoiding anger. *Gahapativagga* of *Aṅguttara Nikāya* gives the special virtues of the householder as: firm confidence in the Three Jewels, charity and generosity, interest in religious discourses, lack of pride in spiritual advancement, and destruction of the five fetters of belief in personality, doubt, belief in the efficacy of rules and ritual, sensuous craving, and ill-will. Householders were also expected to possess the virtues of confidence (*saddhā*), morality (*sīla*), modesty (*hiri*), shame (*ottappa*), much learning (*bahussuta*), charity (*cāga*), and knowledge (*paññā*).

These, however, involve a certain amount of understanding, or at least of Buddhist philosophical learning, and for the more strictly ethical teaching one turns to the *Dīgha Nikāya*. Here it is most concisely put in the *Mahāparinibbāna Suttanta* where the Buddha, on his final tour, was asked by the *upāsakas* of *Pāṭaligāma* to visit their local rest-house.[2] The Buddha did so and in his discourse to them addressed them as '*Gahapatis*'. He gave five bad consequences to the offender against the Moralities: (i) The falling into poverty by reason of indolence, (ii) The acquiring of an evil reputation, (iii) The lack of con-

[1] D. II. 146. [2] *Ibid.* II. 85.

fidence with which such a person approaches a company whether of the warrior caste, of brahmans, householders or samaṇas, (iv) The fear at death, (v) The rebirth in a state of suffering. The five good consequences of keeping the Moralities were given in corresponding terms.

Lakkhaṇa Sutta of *Dīgha Nikāya*,[1] describing the high standard of conduct maintained by the Buddha in his previous existences, still keeps to the strictly ethical side of that conduct, referring to the performance of good deeds, restraint in body, speech and thought, charitable actions, observances of the *sīlas* and *Uposatha* days, care for parents, *samaṇas* and brahmans, exertion for the good of others, and so on. *Sigālovāda Sutta*,[2] prescribing the duties for the householder explicitly, gives: abstinence from killing, lying, stealing and sexual offences, avoiding offences committed through impulse, hatred, delusion or fear, abstinence from drinking and merry-making, from attendance at fairs, associating with bad companions, the avoiding of idleness, the avoiding of enemies posing as friends, the caring for parents, teachers, sons, wife, friends and advisers, servants and workers, *samaṇas* and brahmans.

The goal held before the householder consisted in rebirth in one of the *deva*-worlds, but this conception was pre-Buddhistic and was endorsed by all opinions holding the doctrine of karma. The *Nikāyas* have many instances of good householders being reborn as *devas*. In an address delivered to Venerable Ānanda on the final tour, the Buddha stated that some of the most distinguished of his *upāsaka* followers had been reborn as *anāgāmi*, *sakadāgāmi* and *sotāpanna*, while others who had taken the Three Refuges and observed the Moralities had been reborn among the *devas* of the *Kāmāvacara*. But an advanced *upāsaka* would not wish for rebirth in any of the *lokas* or *āvacaras*, however exalted, since they were all conditioned by birth and death.

The question as to whether a *gahapati* could or could not become an arahant in this life and so avoid rebirth entirely was highly debatable and continued to be the subject of controversy. The view that the householder cannot attain to arahantahood is, however, not supported by the early scriptures. Hence, it may be a postulated view which crept into

[1] D. III. 142–79. [2] *Ibid.* III. 180–93.

the Buddhist scholarship. Arahantaship is a transcendental state beyond the states of bhikkhu, bhikkhunī, *upāsaka* or *upāsikā*. According to the scriptures many householders have attained to Nibbāna. Ananda K. Coomaraswamy rightly says: 'It is true that the layman Arahant is not altogether unknown to Early Buddhism (twenty-one are mentioned in the *Aṅguttara Nikāya*, iii. 451, and Suddhodana, Gotama's father is also specially mentioned), but the fulfilment of worldly duties, however selflessly, was never preached as a way of salvation.'[1] The *Milindapañha* states that the householder who becomes an arahant 'must enter the Order, else die'.[2] This view is also not sanctioned by the early canonical works. It may be 'a contemporary Indian belief' incorporated into his work by its author. It is obvious that a householder after becoming an arahant does not remain attached to his home or family.

The oldest of the Buddhist texts, such as *Dhammapada* and the first half of the *Dīgha Nikāya*, all stress the *āsavas*, representing their destruction as coinciding with realization of the Four Noble Truths; *Dhammapada* does not mention the Fetters (*saṃyojana*), except in the general sense of bonds. Recollecting the Buddha's statement quoted above that his distinguished *upāsakas* and *upāsikās* were reborn as *sotāpannas*, *sakadāgāmīs* and *anāgāmīs*, it remains to be shown they could expect, as *upāsakas* and *upāsikas*, to detroy the *āsavas* in this life and so become arahants. Taking the term with its full implications we have the traditional Indian view that knowledge (*vidyā*) was 'higher' (*parāvidyā*) or 'lower' (*aparāvidyā*), according to whether it concerned 'Brahman' as Absolute Reality, or *Nāma-rūpa*, the things of common experience. *Parāvidyā* does not supply details of particular things but is an insight into the principle of being, and to those possessing the higher knowledge, the lower knowledge is no knowledge at all but merely a form of ignorance. Hence the alternative translation of *avijjā* (Skt. *avidyā*) as 'ignorance' or 'lack of the Higher Knowledge'. But since the entire destruction of lack of the Higher Knowledge coincides with the realization of the

[1] *Buddha and the Gospel of Buddhism* by Ananda K. Coomaraswamy, Harper & Row, New York, 1964, p. 212. Jains also accepted the liberation (*siddhi* or *mokkha*) of householder. See *Paṇṇavaṇā*, in Su., *op. cit.*, Vol. II. 272.

[2] Miln. 264 ff.

Four Noble Truths, and since the Buddha stated this to be the ultimate reason why the bhikkhus led the religious life under him, it would appear that the householder could expect less chance to attain to arahant rank in the present life.

On the other hand, one is not entirely justified in maintaining that only those leading the homeless life could attain to the ideal here in the present existence. In the account given in *Sāmaññaphala Sutta* of the Buddha's discourse to King Ajātasattu, when the King had risen and gone away the Buddha remarked that but for the murder of his father 'the Eye of Truth would have arisen in him even as he sat there'.[1] Again, the *Dhammapada* says: 'Even though a person wears ornaments, if he conducts himself calmly, is constantly tranquil, controlled, leads a life of chastity, and has laid aside sticks in his dealings with other living beings, he is a brahman, he is a *samaṇa*, he is a bhikkhu.'[2] And again: 'A man is not a bhikkhu merely because he seeks alms from others. He is not a bhikkhu merely for having taken all the Rules of the Dhamma. He who, having gone beyond merit and evil, leads a life of chastity, walks in this world as though it were an appearance, that one is truly a bhikkhu.'[3] The comprehensive view is perhaps most succinctly expressed in two *gāthās* peculiar to the *Dhammapada*: 'There is no track in space; externally one is not recluse. Mankind delights in manifoldness; Tathāgatas are without variety of expansion.'[4] 'There is no track in space; externally one is not recluse. Conditioned things are not eternal; there is no instability in the Buddhas.'[5]

If from these and similar quotations one wishes to infer that the terms 'bhikkhu', 'brahman', '*samaṇa*', 'householder', or 'worldling' held in truth no differentiation other than that of states of mental development, one may support one's conclusion with a statement made by the Buddha at the end of the lengthy discourse on the nature of the 'self'. He said: 'But these are only designations, figures of speech, expressions, concepts, belonging to the world, and the Tathāgata makes use of them without being bound to, or holding onto, any of them.'[6] They do, however, 'belong to the world', and it was according to the standing and understanding of people of the

[1] D. I. 86. [2] Dh. v. 142. [3] *Ibid.* Dh. vv. 266, 267; Uv. XXXII. vv. 18, 19. [4] *Ibid.* v. 254. [5] *Ibid.* v. 255. [6] D. I. 202.

world that he must declare his teaching in words. If the term 'bhikkhu' had no mundane significance, why advocate the religious life? And if the religious life were to be advocated, must it not carry an advantage which would not accrue to those remaining in the world? The advantage lay in a formality of reserving the attainment of arahantship in the present life specially for those who had gone out into the homeless life. If those who did not so go out thought they could attain to arahantaship, there was nothing to prevent them making the effort.

With regard to observances arising at a date after the *Parinibbāna* of the Buddha, and of considerable interest at the present day, are those of visits or pilgrimages to Buddhist sacred places. Shrines, or *cetiyas*, were common in India long before the Buddha's day and generally consisted in a tree, stone, or small area of ground often believed to be inhabited by a good or evil spirit.[1] Vinaya mentions two *cetiyas* at which the Buddha stayed,[2] while *Pāṭika Suttanta* and *Mahāparinibbāna Suttanta* contain references to *cetiyas* round *Vesāli*.[3] The latter *suttanta* names also the *cetiyas* of *Sārandada* and *Cāpāla* at Vesāli,[4] *Ānanda-cetiya* in Bhoganagara, and *Makuṭabandhana-cetiya* of the Mallas at Kusinārā.[5] To the Buddha the Vesāli *cetiyas* would be attractive, no doubt, since they would lie away from the town and would constitute the type of 'lonely' place suitable for meditation after the food collected as alms on the morning round had been eaten.[6]

The erection of mounds (*stupas*), on the relics of persons distinguished for their social rank or outstanding spiritual attainment was also a custom of ancient India. According to *Mahāparinibbāna Suttanta* the Buddha is represented as having said that *stupas* should be erected over the relics of a Tathāgata, a Pacceka Buddha, a Tathāgatasāvaka and a Rājā Cakkavatti.[7]

[1] See p. 55, note 1, and associated text.

[2] Supatiṭṭha-cetiya and Aggālava-cetiya at Ālavi near Rājagaha, Vin. I. 37; II. 172.

[3] Udena-cetiya to the east of Vesāli, Gotamaka to the south, Sattamba to the west, and Bahuputta-cetiya to the north. D. III. 9; also II. 10.

[4] *Ibid.* II. 107. The beauty of Vesāli and its six cetiyas was commented on by the Buddha when, with Venerable Ānanda, he had gone to spend the day at the Cāpāla-cetiya.

[5] *Ibid.* II. 123 and II. 163 respectively.

[6] *Ibid.* I. 71.

[7] *Ibid.* II. 142.

According to the same suttanta, a *stupa* should be erected at the place where four highways meet, the direction following an account of the manner in which the Buddha's earthly remains should be cremated.[1]

Immediately preceding the instruction regarding the visiting of the earthly remains of the Buddha is the detailing of the four places of pilgrimage; these were: the birth-place of the Buddha, the site of his Enlightenment, the site of the preaching of the First Discourse, and the site of the *Parinibbāna*. Persons who died in the course of such a pilgrimage would be reborn in a happy world.[2] However, the honouring of the remains of the Tathāgata was to be left to *khattiya*, brahman and *gahapati paṇḍitas*; the bhikkhus were to reserve their energies for their own spiritual development.[3] It is stated: 'The bhikkhu or bhikkhuṇī, *upāsaka* or *upāsikā*, who lives in conformity with the Dhamma, who has entered on and who walks in the proper course conforming to the Dhamma, he is the one who pays the highest and most excellent honour and reverence to the Tathāgata.'[4]

The pilgrimages to the sacred places of Buddhism are today by no means confined to the laity. They are not undertaken in the conventional sense of 'worship' but represent acts of extreme reverence.

(c) *The Buddha's approach to his teaching of the Moralities*

Whatever the position assigned to the laity, whether in the Buddha's day or whether visualised to cover the centuries, the statement of the Four Noble Truths must, in the last instance, determine the role which the layman should assume and play in the Buddhist life. In the characteristics of *anicca, dukkha* and *anattā* lie the philosophy of Buddhism, and those the layman must come to consider early on as he strives to live according to the Precepts. So we are brought again to the dictum: 'Morality is washed all round with wisdom, and wisdom is washed all round with morality. Wherever there is morality there is wisdom, and wherever there is wisdom there is morality. From the observing of the moralities comes wisdom and from the observing of wisdom comes morality. Morality

[1] D. II. 142. [2] *Ibid.* II. 140, 141. [3] *Ibid.* 141. [4] *Ibid.* II. 138.

and wisdom together reveal the height of the world. It is just as if one should wash one hand with the other or one foot with the other; exactly so is morality washed round with wisdom and wisdom with morality.'[1] Again, the *Dhammapada* statement: 'Avoiding the doing of all evil, the accomplishing of good, purifying one's own mind: that is the teaching of the Buddhas'[2] gives the logical procedure. Further, the *Dhammapada*: 'Cut down the forest, not only one tree; from the forest is born fear'[3] points to the need of the understanding of the nature and extent of the 'forest' and therefore to the understanding of the philosophical implications of the teaching.

In the Buddha's day philosophical discussion was rife, and on occasion he took up the position of setting aside philosophy for the moment to consider the whole question of method or path as starting from the general moralities. In such cases he proceeded to confirmation of the superiority of the Buddhist philosophical views by pointing to their effects on his own conduct and on that of his Saṅgha. A notable instance of this occurs in his conversation with Kassapa, the naked ascetic, and since this covers other important matters pertinent to the present consideration the conversation is quoted at length.[4]

'At one time the Exalted One was staying in the Kaṇṇakatthala deer park at Ujuññā. Kassapa, a naked ascetic, came up to him and, after exchange of friendly and courteous greetings, stood to one side and said: "I have heard, Sir: 'The Samaṇa Gotama disapproves of all penance and religious austerities; all who practise them and lead a miserable life thereby he censures entirely.' Those who say thus, do they report you correctly, or do they accuse you falsely? Do they declare in conformity with your teaching, or does some co-religionist misinterpret you for contemptible reasons? Indeed we have no pleasure in representing you falsely, Sir."

' "Those who spoke so, Kassapa, have not reported me correctly. They have accused me falsely from lack of mindfulness. With the purity of the Celestial Eye, beyond the human faculty of sight, I see these things: of those leading a miserable

[1] D. I. 124.
[2] Dh. v. 183.
[3] *Ibid.* v. 283; Uv. XVIII. v. 3.
[4] D. I. 159–63.

life of self-mortification in this world, at the destruction of the body at death some arising in states of wretchedness and suffering, and others arising in a happy and celestial world. Since I have come to know, as they really are in Absolute Truth, the coming and passing away of these ascetics, the consciousness disconnecting the present life and the re-uprising, how shall I disapprove of, or censure, all asceticism? How shall I reproach and condemn all who lead a miserable life practising it?

' "There are, Kassapa, certain samaṇas and brahmans, clever, skilful in disputation, experienced in controversy, hair-splitters, so to speak, who go about as if breaking into pieces by their 'wisdom' the speculations of their adversaries. Between them and myself there are some matters on which we agree and some on which we do not agree.

' "I went to them and said: 'Friends, concerning those things in which we do not agree, let us leave them alone. For those in which we do agree, let the wise put questions and ask reasons—discuss the matter either with teachers or their followers in this way: Of those things that are bad or accounted as bad, reprehensible or accepted as such, undesirable of association, unsuited to the Noble Ones, evil or accepted as such, who exists with these things completely destroyed? The Samaṇa Gotama or other teachers with many followers?'

' "It may be found, Kassapa, that the wise, from cross-questioning, from asking for reasons, conversing together, would say: 'These things that are bad, or accepted as bad, reprehensible or accepted as such, undesirable of association, unsuitable to the Noble Ones, evil or accepted as such, these the Samaṇa Gotama conducts himself as having destroyed without remainder. For the other teachers of many, that is not so'.

' "And again: 'Concerning those things which are good, without blame, desirable of association, in keeping with the Noble Ones, pure or accounted pure, who exists having completely taken upon himself these conditions? The Samaṇa Gotama or other teachers with large followings?' " '[1]

The Buddha pointed out that in such discussions it would transpire that he alone of all teachers had taken the conditions

[1] D. I. 162 f.

upon himself completely, and that his followers were more addicted to good and refrained more from what was considered evil than the followers of other teachers. He proceeded to instruct Kassapa in the Noble Eightfold Path.

The passage makes clear the following points. In the first place the rigid austerity attributed to the Buddha's teaching by later generations was by no means fully endorsed by his contemporaries. In the second, the Buddha made clear that mere philosophic discussion was unlikely to lead to any appreciable results. Third, a discussion which would lead to useful results would be better begun with points of agreement of the debaters than with their differences. Fourth, that these hopeful beginnings would deal with things accepted commonly by all shades of reputable opinion as definitely 'good' or definitely 'evil'; in other words, the starting points should be moral values. Fifth, that the highest moral tone would be that of the persons with the soundest philosophical outlook.

If then the Buddha's teaching may be referred for re-appraisal back to the general morality, to the things that are good or bad or generally accepted as such, what were the general virtues recommended, what effect had they on the individual, and how might they be utilised for the benefit of a community?

(*d*) *Advice to the individual Layman*

Of the discourses addressed specifically to Householders that of the *Mahāparinibbāna Suttanta* was delivered to a group and that of *Sigālovāda* to an individual. The former has already been described earlier in the present chapter; the latter, which goes into much greater detail, is given under specific headings. The circumstanses of delivery were as follows.

Sigāla, son of a householder who had recently died, had previously shown no interest in religion. At his father's death however, he consented to observe the practice of paying devotion to the various quarters of the earth and sky[1] imme-

[1] 'In the *Śatapatha Brāhmaṇa* (Sacred Books of the East, XII, 283; XLIII, 277, 314) five, and also seven *disās* as well as four are mentioned in rites. In the *Grihya Sūtras* (S.B.E. XXIX, 320, cf. 232; XXX, 171, 194, 213, 278. These *Sūtras* contain the rules of Vedic domestic ceremonies. *Grihya* means 'houseness') the four quarters are to be worshipped in connection with certain rites. And so much self-anointing or contact with water is enjoined that the

diately after his morning bathe. In such state he was once found by the Buddha who asked him what he was doing, then proceeded to explain the real significance of those quarters and of Sigāla's actions in adoring them. The six quarters, east, south, west, north, the nadir and the zenith, should be taken as representing parents, teachers, wife and children, friends and companions, servants and workpeople, and religious teachers and brahmans respectively. As a preface to this explanation, the Buddha speaks of the necessity of abandoning the evil actions arising from four motives and the six practices leading to loss of property or wealth. He points out that the householder's son is a disciple of the Noble Ones in so far as he has abandoned the four impurities of conduct, does not act on the four conditions or causes of evil doing, and does not pursue the six practices bringing about loss of means.[1] The four impurities of conduct consist in the violation of the precepts not to take life, not to take that which is not given, not to commit sensual offences, and not to indulge in falsehood. The four motives on which one should not act are: impulse (uncontrolled) or partially (*chanda*), hatred (*dosa*), fear (*bhaya*) and delusion (*moha*).[2]

However, the *suttanta* gives only the result of the pursuit of the evil motives, remarking that persons acting on them are brought to ruin just as the moon wanes with the passing month, but more detailed treatment is given in various of the suttas of *Aṅguttara Nikāya*. Here, as advocating self-restraint in contrast to uncontrolled impulse, we have the story of two aged Brahmans who, fearing the approach of death, went to the Buddha for comfort.[3] They explained that they had performed no noble deeds or meritorious acts. The Buddha pointed out that the world is swept on by old age, sickness and death, and that the only remedy lay in practice of self-restraint in body, speech and thought. Such restraint would form a shelter, defence and resting-place and support for one who goes beyond.[4]

lay celebrant may well have had both hair and garments wet as Sigāla had'. *Dialogue of the Buddha*, Part III by T. W. and C. A. F. Rhys Davids, Pali Text Society, London, 1965, p. 170, and also see pp. 168–72. For further information of the quarter-worshippers (*disāpokkhiyas*) see the *Bhagavatī*, in Su., *op. cit.*, Vol. I. *śataka*, 11, *uddeśaka*, 9.

[1] D. III. 181. [2] *Ibid.* III. 182. [3] A. I. 155.

[4] Cf. p. 27, note 6; *Thāṇa*, in Su., Vol. I. 204.

For the second evil motive, that of hatred or enmity, the *Dhammapada* points out that these achieve nothing of advantage whatever; more, that a person who even dabbles with them is playing with death since they are part and parcel of the realm of death.[1] The *Uragavarga* gives us: 'Whatever a man may do in anger, whether he thinks it bad or good, once the anger has disappeared he feels a burn as if he has touched fire.'[2] And again: 'One should conquer anger by non-anger, conquer evil with good, avarice with generosity, lying with truth.[3] From where should come anger to one who cannot be provoked to anger, who is controlled, leads a right life, who is set free through right knowledge? For that one anger does not exist.[4]

Concerning delusion, this quality may be considered strictly as '*moha*', one of the three evil roots (*hetus*) of action, the other two being greed (*lobha*) and hatred (*dosa*). *Dosa* is mentioned specifically amongst the present four motives from which no action should be committed; but *moha* is often considered to be a synonym of *avijjā*, ignorance, and in that connection has a much more extensive significance than 'delusion'. The wider meaning seems necessary here in order to cover *lobha* which is not synonymous with *chanda*, but since consideration of *avijjā* would take us beyond the advice to the householder's son in *Sigālovāda Suttanta* we point out here merely the two qualities typical of the ignorant man's lack of investigation (*ananuvicca*) and lack of understanding or lack of having penetrated (*apariyogāhetvā*) in contrast to those of the wise man who accomplishes both investigation and penetration. 'Having investigated, having penetrated (the wise man), speaks blame of one who should be blamed, and praise of one who should be praised.'[5] Such a person therefore gives a considered and reliable judgment.

The fourth motive from which no action should spring is that of fear. This may be of four varieties: fear of self-reproach (*attavādānubhaya*), fear of the reproach of others (*paravādānubhaya*), fear of punishment (*daṇḍabhaya*), and fear of bad results in the life to come (*duggatibhaya*).[6] Such fears act as a

[1] Cf. p. 28, note 2. [2] Uv. XX.. v 4.

[3] Dh. v. 223; J. II. 4; Uv. XX. v. 19; cf. *Dasaveyāliya*, *op. cit.*, Ch. VII. vv. 38, 39.

[4] S. I. 162; Thag. 441; Uv. XX. 20. [5] A. I. 89. [6] A. II. 121 ff.

deterrent, but if they are disregarded and, in spite of their bases, an evil action is committed, the doer of that action is considered to have acted from fear rather than in spite of fear.

The fears are analogous to moral shame and dread (*hiri-ottappa*), which are two mental concomitants present in types of good consciousness, while awareness of fright (*bhayatūpaṭṭhāna*) comprises knowledge of the fact that the conditions and continuity of existence appear to oneself as fear, or fright. Whoever recognizes the impermanence of existence sees the karma-formations (*saṅkhāra*) as fear since they drive on to death. To one who considers the *saṅkhāra* as a misery, the continuity of existence appears as fear in that it is oppressive. Whoever considers the *saṅkhāra* as impersonal, these, as well as the continuity of existence, appear as fear, like an empty village or a mirage. Such is one of the eight kinds of knowledge which are free from defilements, are following the right process, and are considered as Insight.

In the more popular sense, *hiri* and *ottappa* are considered as the 'bright' states which protect the world, for without them there would exist no differentiation as between mother and mother's sister, uncle's wife, teacher's wife, or wife of an honourable man, but the world would come to a condition of promiscuity such as exists among animals.[2] *Hiri* is also numbered amongst the four good qualities praised by virtuous men and leading to the realm of the *devas*.[3]

The six courses mentioned in *Sigālovāda Suttanta* as being conducive to loss of property and wealth are: indulgence in intoxicants, sauntering in the streets at unseemly hours, frequenting entertainments, gambling, associating with evil companions, and idleness. The first of these leads not only to loss of wealth but fosters quarrels, increases liability to disease, the acquiring of an evil reputation, indecent exposure, and impaired intelligence. The frequenting of the streets at unseemly hours results in a man's leaving his wife and family alone, and his property unprotected. Addiction to entertainment leaves him directing his thoughts constantly to locating such entertainment, while gambling, in addition to the loss of wealth, leads to grieving for that wealth and hatred towards the winner. No reliance is placed on the gambler's word in a court of law;

[1] A. I. 51. [2] *Ibid.* IV. 236; Uv. X. v. 1.

he is despised by his friends and associates, and no one will consider him as a possible husband since he is obviously unfit to look after a wife. Association with evil companions may involve association with any gambler, any libertine, any drunkard, swindler, cheat or man of violence. The lazy person does not work, excusing himself on the ground that it is too cold, too hot, too late, too early, that he is very hungry or has eaten too much. In the meantime, what he should do remains undone, and any wealth he already possesses dwindles away.

However laziness may be considered in more extensive form than is done in *Sigālovāda Suttanta* for, under the synonyms of Torpor and Languor (*thīna-middha*), it represents one of the Five Hindrances to mental development and vision and constitutes an immoral factor of consciousness. In this connection 'laziness' would not be considered merely as doing nothing at all, but as failing to put forth one's maximum efforts for good on whatever occasion. Contrasting laziness with its opposite, vigilance, we get the *Dhammapada* chapter *Appamāda Vagga*, with the characteristic verses: 'Vigilance is the way leading to the deathless state; negligence is the road to death. Those who are vigilant do not die; those who are negligent are as if dead already.'[1] 'By means of energy, vigilance, control, self-mastery, the wise man builds an island which the flood does not overwhelm.'[2]

The foregoing teaching relates explicitly to the individual and before passing to consideration of his relationship to his associates we may consider the effect in general of the good man on his surroundings. *Aṅguttara* uses the simile of the scent whose savour spreads both in the direction of the wind and against it.[3] Here the Buddha says that recluses and brahmans, *devas* and non-humans, all praise the man who takes the Three Refuges, keeps the Five Precepts, who is virtuous, of lovely nature, who settles in the houschold life with heart free from stinginess, who is open-handed and delights in giving, who is one of whom one would ask a favour, and is one who delights in sharing gifts with others. The effects of such virtues is also likened to the defence enlisted by a king for his country[4] and the effect of a good supply of rain on crops.[5]

[1] Dh. v. 21; Uv. IV. v. 1. [2] *Ibid.* v. 23; *ibid.* IV. v. 3. [3] A. I. 225 f. [4] J. I. 280. [5] J. IV. 244, 245.

CHAPTER 6

THE LAYMAN'S DUTIES TO HIS ASSOCIATES

Children and Parents

The duties of children to their parents were stressed in India from a very early date. *Rukkhadhamma Jātaka* expressed the value of the solidarity of a family, using the simile of the trees of a forest; these are able to withstand the force of the wind whereas a solitary tree, however large, is not.[1] The Buddha confirmed and emphasized the family relationship, exhorting all persons who decided to remain in the worldly life to maintain the family ties together with the honour and dignity of the family as a social unit. The Asoka *Edicts* concern themselves very much with the duties of children to parents; we have, for example: 'Meritorious is obedience to mother and father';[2] 'Right conduct to mother and father is obedience';[3] 'Obey mother and father';[4] 'Listen to mother and father'.[5] These are, however, modifications of the Upaniṣadic dictum: 'Be one to whom mother is a god. Be one to whom father is a god.'[6]

Aṅguttara Nikāya records that great approval is accorded to families where the parents are held in high respect. Such families, said the Buddha, counted as belonging to the Brahma rank (*sabrahmakāni*) and with the early great teachers (*sapubbacariyakāni*); they were 'worthy of offerings' (*āhuṇeyyā*),[7] an expression indicating great distinction since it was used also by the Buddha in reference to the members of the Saṅgha. He pointed out that parents do much for their children, bringing

[1] J. I. 329:

Sādhu sambahulā ñāti api rukkhā araññajā,
vāto vahati ekaṭṭhaṃ brahantam pi vanaspatiṃ.

[2] Rock Edict, Girnar, III. line 4: *sādhu mātari ca pitari ca susūsā.*

[3] *Ibid.* XI. line 2: *samyapatipatī mātari pitari sādhu sususā.*

[4] *Ibid.* XIII. line 3: *māta pitri suṣushā.*

[5] Pillar Edict, Delhi Topra, VII. line 29: *mātāpitisu sususāyā* (for the above references see *Corpus Inscriptionum Indicarum*, Vol. I. ed. by E. Hultzsch, London, 1925).

[6] *Taittirīyopaniṣad*, I. ii. 2: *mātṛ devo bhava pitṛ devo bhava.*

[7] A. I. 132; It. 109 f.

them up (*āpādakā*), taking care of them (*posakā*), introducing them to the world (*lokassa dassetāro*).[1] The duty of supporting one's parents is included in the three good things proclaimed by the wise, the other two being the practice of charity (*dāna*) and the going forth into the homeless life (*pabbajjā*).[2] The debt to one's parents is, in general, impossible to repay; it can be discharged only in a case where the child arouses in his parents confidence in the Dhamma, settles and establishes them in morality, replaces their meanness by generosity, or, dispelling their foolishness, settles and establishes them in wisdom.[2]

Sigālovāda Suttanta gives five ways in which a child should minister to his parents. He should maintain: (i) I will support my parents since they at one time supported me, (ii) I shall take upon myself the duties incumbent on them, (iii) I shall establish a succession, (iv) I shall follow a method of inheritance, and (v) I shall make gifts in due course to the dead. In return, the parents should show their love for their children by (i) restraining them from vice, (ii) exhorting them to virtue, (iii) training them for a profession, (iv) arranging a suitable marriage for them, and (v) in due course handing over to them the inheritance.[3]

An occasion is recorded when certain sons fulfilled none of the duties prescribed; rather they followed the course taken by the children of Shakespeare's Lear. The story is told in *Saṃyutta Nikāya*[4] where an elderly and once-wealthy Brahman, coarsely dressed and very weary, visited the Buddha at Sāvatthi. He stated that he had four sons who, with their wives, had put him out of their houses. The Buddha advised him to recite the following verses when the populace had assembled in their local Hall:

> 'Those in whose birth I took delight,
> For whose existence I had longed,
> They now together with their wives,
> Reject me as one would a hog.

[1] A. I. 62, 132; It. 110.
[2] *Ibid.* I. 151.
[3] D. III. 180. See A. I. 61 f.; UJ. 270; cf. *Ṭhāṇa* in Su., Vol. I. 260.
[4] S. I. 175–7.

'Wicked, contemptible are these
Who spoke familiarly like sons,
Yet far from filial care of me
Now leave me, aged and alone.

'Just as a worn-out horse is forced
Away from food and driven from his shelter,
So do these children drive away their father
To beg for alms at other people's doors.

'Better a stick, I say, would be
Than disloyal sons estranging me;
At least it keeps away an ox
Or drives away a pariah dog.

'Yet—once bewildered, in the dark,
Now I have gained a solid hold.
Supported firmly by the hold,
Though once I stumbled, now I stand.'

The aged Brahman followed the Buddha's advice and his sons amended their behaviour.[1]

For reward for keeping the rules of conduct, there is given the case of Sakka, ruler of the *devas*. Sakka, when a man, declared he would observe the following seven conditions: (i) That he would maintain his parents, (ii) Revere the head of the family, (iii) Use gentle language, (iv) Speak no slander, (v) With a mind free from stain conduct himself in his home with generosity, delighting in renunciation, be willing to listen to petitions, and delight in sharing gifts, (vi) Speak the truth, and (vii) Not give way to anger; if anger should arise in him he would repress it quickly. As a result of so living and conducting himself, the Tāvatiṃsa *devas* conferred on him the name 'Good man' (*sappurisa*) and in due course he became the Ruler of the *devas*.[2]

Husband and Wife

Of the more advanced type of advice given to householders much was of necessity directed to the relationship between

[1] S.I. 175–7. [2] S. I. 228.

husband and wife since they were to be considered by their children as *devas*. The story of Nakula's parents is a case in point.[1] Here the father lay ill, and the mother, reminding him that death with a worried mind was followed by bad results, reassured him on these points: that she could support the children and maintain the household by spinning cotton and carding wool; that since she and the father had led a good life together for sixteen years she would not re-marry; that she would welcome the Exalted One and members of the Saṅgha even more warmly than before; that as long as there existed any *upāsikās* she would keep the Moralities in full, would acquire calmness of mind, become established in the dhamma and discipline (*dhammavinaya*), put an end to doubt, abolish indecision, be self-confident, not relying on others, and live in the Teacher's teaching. The reassurance was sufficient to heal her husband. He rose from his bed and not long after, with the aid of a stick, visited the Buddha. The Buddha remarked on his great gain in having such a wife as Nakula's mother, compassionate and solicitous for her husband's welfare, for a counsellor and teacher, and said that as long as he had any women lay-disciples at all she should be one of them.

For interpretation of *Sigālovāda*'s adoration to the direction of the West, the *suttanta* gives five ways in which a wife should be ministered to by her husband: (i) by being courteous to her, (ii) by not despising her, (iii) by being faithful to her, (iv) by handing over authority to her, and (v) by providing her with necessary adornments. In return, the wife should minister to her husband: (i) by ordering the household well, (ii) by hospitality to their relatives, (iii) by fidelity, (iv) by taking care of his wealth, and (v) by her industry.[2] *Aṅguttara Nikāya* takes into account the case of the wife who fulfils her task perfectly, and here the Buddha enumerates the four qualities by which woman wins power in this world and has this world in her grasp.[3] There are as follows:

She is capable in her work; whatever her husband's home industries, whether in wool or cotton, she is skilful, gifted with an enquiring mind into the work, and able to carry it out. She is able to manage her servants, knowing the duties of each

[1] A. III. 295–8. [2] D. III. 190. [3] A. IV. 269.

and seeing these are carried out; further, she knows something of sickness and is able to allot the food suitably. She studies the approval of her husband and keeps safe whatever money, corn, silver or gold he brings home. With these qualities, said the Buddha, 'she wins power and this world is within her grasp'.[1]

This, however, does not establish her ultimate limitation. She may win power in the world beyond, have the world beyond in her grasp. By what means? By establishment in confidence, virtue, charity and wisdom. For confidence she knows the arising of a Tathāgata and such and such is so.[2] She is accomplished in virtue by the keeping of the Five Precepts. She is accomplished in charity, living at home with thought free from avarice, delighting in alms-giving. She is wise in the penetration into the rise and fall of things and in the complete destruction of suffering. With these four qualities she wins power and has the world beyond in her grasp.[3] Yet though these last four qualities contain realization of the destruction of suffering, her reward is only formally acknowledged as rebirth in the *deva* worlds.

Instructions to girls about to marry are recorded in *Aṅguttara Nikāya* as having been given by the Buddha at the invitation of a man whose daughters were shortly going to their husbands. The Buddha advised them to rise early, work willingly, order their affairs smoothly, and to cultivate gentle voices. They should honour and respect all persons honoured and respected by their husbands, whether parents or recluses, and on the arrival of these should offer them a seat and water. Other instructions were similar to those given to wives, namely, skill in the various handicrafts, care of servants and sick people, and care of the wealth brought home by the husbands.[4]

A further point raised by the Buddha concerned appreciation of the trials of women who, in addition to the disabilities of their sex, were called upon to leave their own families and to live with their husbands'.[5] From that time on, the wife

[1] A. IV. 270: *mātugāmo idhalokavijayāya paṭipanno hoti, ayaṃ sa loko āraddho hoti.*

[2] See p. 57, note 2.

[3] A. IV. 271: *mātugāmo paralokavijayāya paṭipanno hoti, parassa loko āraddho hoti.* [4] *Ibid.* III. 26–8. [5] S. IV. 239.

was cut off from her former associates and was entirely dependent for her happiness on the new conditions and surroundings. While the Buddha speaks of ill-assorted couples, and of couples in which both the husband and wife are bad or good,[1] a particular address dealing with what would appear to be a form of frustration is also extant. The persons concerned were Anāthapiṇḍika, owner of the famous park, and his daughter-in-law, Sujātā.[2] The Buddha, going one morning to the house of Anāthapiṇḍika, heard a great noise therein; likening it to that due to fishermen who had just made a haul of fish he enquired the reason for it. Anāthapiṇḍika replied that the commotion was due to Sujātā who was rich and had been brought from a wealthy family; she took no notice of her parents-in-law or of her husband, nor did she respect the Buddha himself. The Buddha called to her and she came and sat down by his side. He said that there were seven kinds of wives, one like an executioner inflicting punishment, one like a thief, one like a mistress, one like a mother, one like a sister, one like a companion, and one like a slave. The Buddha asking her which of the seven she herself was, Sujātā replied that she did not understand, he had put the matter too briefly; but would he teach her the Dhamma so that she might understand? The Buddha expounded. The executioner wife was pitiless and corrupt, a prostitute. The thief robbed her husband of his gains. The lazy gossip and shrew with loud voice was a mistress. The mother-wife cared for her husband and his possessions as she would for an only son. The sister-wife behaved like a younger sister to an elder. The companion-wife behaved as the term would indicate, as a companion. The slave-wife endured all things, remaining calm and pure in heart, and obedient. The last four kinds of wife would, at death, wander in a heavenly world. Sujātā said that she would be the seventh kind. Exactly what she had in mind is left to the interpretation of the reader, but the fact that she found herself in a responsible position in a Buddhist household could hardly have been independent of an inner awareness of the nature of life and therefore of a subconscious desire for knowledge of the Dhamma. The Buddha did not refuse her request to be taught.

[1] A. II. 57–9.
[2] *Ibid.* IV. 91–4.

Friends

If the matter of selection of the family into which one is born in the present existence is closely connected with the karmic effects of previous lives, the selection of one's friends is clearly more directly associated with the circumstances and acts of the current life. Physiologically the world is perpetuated by the family relationship, but the Buddha has also given the quality of making friends as one which is instrumental in 'making the world go round'. 'The person who is kindly, who makes friends, makes welcome, is free from avarice, is understanding, is a conciliator, such a one obtains good repute. Generosity, kindly speech, doing good to whatever person, fairness in all things, everywhere, as is fit and proper, these are indeed the means on which the world turns, just as a chariot moves on quickly depending on the pin of a wheel axle.'[1]

Concerning the selection of one's friends, and one might also say the including of oneself in their selections, the following observations are made. One makes friends with a person who gives what is hard to give, does what is hard to do, and is forebearing when it is hard to be so.[2] A person who is inferior to oneself in morality, concentration and one-pointedness of mind, and wisdom, should not be followed, served or honoured except for reasons of compassion. A person who is one's equal in them should be followed since one's conversation with him would be on these subjects and so conducive to mutual profit and comfort. A person who is one's superior in them should be followed, served and honoured with reverence since one would increase one's own virtue and understanding thereby.[3] One should not be angry with an ungrateful person but merely avoid him,[4] while a wise enemy is better than a foolish friend.[5] One should not loiter amongst enemies; a night or two nights with such brings suffering.[6] One may recognize a potential enemy in that he will not smile at sight of one, will not show a welcome, but will deliberately turn his eyes away.[7]

In the case of good companions where a mutual friendship is already established, certain duties are incurred. Loyalty to

[1] D. III. 192. [2] A. I. 286. [3] *Ibid.* III. 124 f. [4] J. III. 27.
[5] *Ibid.* I. 247. [6] *Ibid.* I. 413. [7] *Ibid.* II. 131.

one's friends brings service and support, freedom from enemies, a welcome home after one's travels, and success in one's undertakings.[1] One should live up to one's promises[2] and should regard with friendliness any object or person that has done one a service. For example, one should not break a branch of a tree that has sheltered one; if one has accepted hospitality for a night and taken food and drink from a person, one should never entertain unfriendly thoughts of him or contemplate any unkind act towards him.[3] If one hears gossip concerning a friend one should examine the matter carefully before accepting it as true; a chance word of a stranger should never separate friends.[4]

Returning to the simile of the quarters, *Sigālovāda Suttanta*, giving as the northern that of the ministrations of friends, asserts the following.[5] A genuine friend is one who is a help and support, is the same in happiness and sorrow, who advises for one's welfare, and who is sympathetic. As a help and support he guards one when one is negligent, protects one's property when one is neglectful of it, is a refuge in anxiety, and, on occasion, undertakes twice the amount of service needed. As one who is the same in happiness and sorrow, he does not withhold confidences, does not forsake one in distress, and even sacrifices his life for one's welfare. Advising one for one's welfare, he prevents one from doing evil, establishes one in good, tells one what one has not heard, and points out to one the road to happiness. As one who is sympathetic, a genuine friend does not rejoice in one's mishaps but rejoices in one's successes; he restrains a person speaking disapprovingly of one and commends a person speaking in praise of one. A wise person should recognize such a friend and be thoroughly devoted to him. As opposed to the above, an enemy posing as a friend may be recognized by his greed, his superfluity of words as compared with his acts, his flattery and spendthrift habits. Such a person appropriates one's possessions, expects much from little, does his duty through fear, and gets all he can for himself out of anything. Again, he makes vain protestations regarding the past and future, but when an opportunity for service arises he does nothing about it. A flatterer consents

[1] J. VI. 22. [2] *Ibid.* III. 253. [3] Pv. 23; UJ. 299.
[4] J. III. 192. [5] D. III. 187; UJ. 268 ff.

to do wrong and avoids doing right; speaking in praise of one to one's face, he speaks ill of one in one's absence. A spendthrift is a willing companion in indulging in intoxicants, sauntering the streets at unseemly hours, frequenting entertainments, and gambling. Such friends are to be avoided as one would avoid a dangerous road.[1] It is therefore incumbent on one to conduct oneself towards one's true friends with generosity and courteous speech, acting in their interests, treating them as one treats oneself, and living up to one's word. In return, friends protect one from negligence, including negligence of one's belongings, are a refuge in anxiety, do not forsake one in one's distress, and show honour to one's family. So does one minister to one's friends and associates as the northern quarter.[2]

However the selection of friends is not always a matter for entirely free choice, for besides the people one would try to cultivate as friends are those to whom one gravitates through similarity of character and those who are thrust upon one. 'He who strikes finds another who strikes; the enemy finds emnity; the injurious find the injurious and the angry find the angry.'[3] 'Breakers of bones, takers of life, thieves of oxen, of horses, riches, and even revilers of kingdoms, between them there is always unity. Between you, how should there not be, you who know the Dharma?'[4] The sentiment is expressed succinctly in the western proverb: 'Birds of a feather flock together.'

Only one's own improvement will disembarrass one of the undesirables towards whom one may gravitate, while for those who have undesirables thrust upon them the advice and assertions given above should be followed. There are, however, potential associates whom it is difficult to avoid, namely, the matters presented by the radio and television set. These are thrust upon one to an extent which one human being could not thrust himself upon another, for the stream of them is continuous and, under some circumstances, often wears down a person's resistance. In making one's selection of programme one may bear in mind the following: 'Whatever a friend does, whatever he practises, by association with him one becomes of such quality.'[5]

[1] D. III. 185 f.; *ibid.* 267.
[2] *Ibid.* III. 190; *ibid.* 267.
[3] S. I. 85; Uv. XIV. v. 3.
[4] M. III. 154; Uv. XIV. v. 6.
[5] It. 67 f.

It is frequently pointed out in the Buddhist texts that one's estimates should not be the result of superficial or hasty observation; the dictum holds also with regard to friends. 'Not by the texture of his skin is a man known. Not in a passing glance should one put trust. The unrestrained wander about the world disguised as the well-restrained.'[1] A person's morality should be assessed with consideration over a long period; similarity with regard to his purity, strength in distress, and wisdom in conversation. A person's actions may prove, over a spell of time, to be inconsistent in character. Intimacy with a person may lead one to see that he behaves in one way with some persons and in quite another with others. Again, a person afflicted with misfortune, loss of wealth, of relatives, of property, may come to reflect thus: One is born, lives in the world, acquires a personality, in so far as that in the being born, living in the world and acquiring a personality, eight things of the world keep the world turning and the world keeps turning on eight things. These are: getting and losing, disrepute and fame, blame and praise, happiness and suffering. In his affliction a man may be overwhelmed with distress and utterly bewildered; on the other hand, a person so afflicted may not grieve or become confused. Further, by conversation with a man one comes to know his uncertainty or resolution. One sees whether or not he utters profound words, calming, beyond the realm of logic and reasoning. Concerning his conversation on the Dhamma one comes to know whether he is able to offer explanations, analyses, clarification of matters: consequently one is able to gauge his wisdom.[2]

One may summarize the foregoing in the words of the scriptures: 'If a man finds a companion well-versed, always comporting himself well in the world, overcoming all obstacles, he should walk with him with mind receptive and reflective. If a man does not find a companion with experience, always conducting himself well in the world, like a king leaving his lost kingdom let him walk alone and commit no evil. And if, in walking, you do not meet a companion who might be your equal and be suitable for you, continue resolutely your solitary walk. A fool is not company. The solitary walk is more worth-

[1] S. I. 79. [2] A. III. 187 ff.

while; a fool is no companion. Walk alone and do not do evil, having few desires, like an elephant in the forest.'[1]

Teacher and Pupil

Since ignorance (*avijjā*) is considered the greatest impurity,[2] and since considerable sympathy and understanding are necessary on the part of one person helping another to rid himself of this impurity, the relationship between teacher and pupil is one which is very highly valued in Buddhism. Considering the teacher as the southerly direction, *Sigālovāda Suttanta* gives five ways in which a pupil should conduct himself towards the teacher and five in which the teacher should conduct himself towards the pupil.

The five devolving on the pupil are stated in Pali terms which may be construed both literally and figuratively. In the literal sense, (i) the pupil should rise from his seat in salutation, (ii) wait on the teacher, (iii) desire to hear him, (iv) render him personal service, and (v) honour him by reception. Figuratively these may be taken as displaying energy, understanding the teacher, paying attention, showing obedience, and preparing the work thoroughly.[3]

The teacher should show his compassion on, or love for, the pupils by teaching and training them well and happily, seeing that they grasp all the arts and crafts equally and thoroughly, teaching them in the respectful manner he adopts towards friends, and by making them secure in every way including the knowledge of their duties to persons represented by the other directions.[3]

Aṅguttara Nikāya recognizes five ways of growth: growth in confidence based on knowledge and personal experience (*saddhā*), in morality (*sīla*), in learning (*suta*), in the practice of giving up things or generosity (*cāga*), and in wisdom (*paññā*).[4]

The foregoing shows a considerable advance on the attitude adopted by the Brahman guru. According to McKenzie, 'It is characteristic of the Indian guru that he imparts the highest

[1] Vin. I. 350; M. III. 154; Dh. vv. 328–30; Uv. XIV. vv. 13–16. Cf. *Dasaveliya op. cit., cūliā* 2nd v. 10.

[2] A. IV. 195; Dh. v. 243: *avijjā paramaṃ malaṃ.*

[3] D. III. 189; UJ. 274.

[4] A. III. 80.

instruction very reluctantly and as a profound secret, only to those whom he considers fit to receive it.'[1] Again, 'A father may therefore tell that doctrine of Brahman to his eldest son, or to a worthy pupil. But no one should tell it to anybody else, even if he gave him the whole sea-girt earth, full of treasure, for this doctrine is worth more than that; yea, it is worth more.'[2] According to Muller, the teaching by the father was superseded by that of teaching by *ācariyas*, or professional teachers, and already in *Chāndogya Upaniṣad* we have the story of Svetaketu who, having studied for twelve years under a teacher, guru or *ācariya*, returned to his father 'conceited, considering himself well-read'. His father enquired if he had ever asked for that instruction by which 'we hear what cannot be heard, by which we perceive what cannot be perceived, by which we know what cannot be known'. After some preliminary remarks by his father, Svetaketu said: 'Surely those venerable men (my teachers) do not know that. For if they had known it, why should they not have told me? Do you, Sir, therefore tell me that?' 'Be it so', said the father.[3] There is, however, nowhere any suggestion of a free discussion of doctrine amongst friends conducted for their mutual advantage.[4]

Servants and Workpeople

According to *Sigālovāda Suttanta*, a gentleman (*ayirakena*)[5] should conduct himself towards his servants and employees in these ways: (i) by arranging their work according to their strength and capabilities, (ii) by providing them with food and salaries, (iii) by looking after them when they are sick, (iv) by sharing occasional good things with them, and (v) by giving them leave at times. In return, (i) the employees so treated should rise before the master rises, (ii) go to rest after he has done so, (iii) take what is given them, (iv) work well, and (v) establish a good reputation for him.[6] Many of the Rock Edicts

[1] *Hindu Ethics*, John Mackenzie, Oxford, 1922, p. 83.
[2] *Chāndogya Upaniṣad*, III. II. 5. See *The Upanishads*. SBE. I. Max Muller's trn., Oxford, 1900, p. 44.
[3] *Ibid*. VI. I. 5–7. See Muller's trn., pp. 92, 93.
[4] See p. 140, note 2, and associated text.
[5] *ayiraka, ayira, ayya:* nobleman, gentleman, man of letters, man of culture.
[6] D. III. 190 f.; UJ. 275 f.

bear out this advice: 'Now in this practice lies great fruit, namely in the practise of dhamma, in which is included right conduct towards employees.'[1] Or again: 'Right conduct towards servants and employees.'[2]

The sentiment of the above was in marked contrast to that previously maintained. According to passages in *Ṛgveda*, misdeeds were classified as those committed 'against the gods, our friend, and our house's chieftain',[3] and again as actions against 'the man who loves . . . a brother, friend or comrade, the neighbour ever with us or a stranger'.[4] Towards the aboriginal inhabitants of India, who were always contrasted with the 'noble Aryans', no special duties were recognized.[5]

Duties connected with means of Livelihood

It is clear from the preceding account that a high standard of duty is expected regarding one's family, friends and associates generally; if one remains in the household life one must fulfil those duties. No less demand is made in the conduct and management of one's professional or business affairs, and, moreover, it is recognized that a moral person should expect and achieve success in his ventures. The Buddha gave five reasons why a moral person should desire to be possessed of means. Firstly, by his work, diligence and clear-sightedness he could make happy himself, his parents, wife and children, servants and workpeople. Secondly he could make happy his friends and companions. Thirdly, he would be able to keep his property from the depredations of fire, water, rulers, robbers, enemies and heirs. Fourthly, he would be able to make suitable offerings to his kin, guests, deceased (*petas*), kings and *devas*. Fifthly, he would be able to institute, over a period, offerings to recluses and others who abstain from pride and negligence, who are established in patience and gentleness, and who are engaged in every way in perfecting themselves. At the same time, whether his wealth increases or whether it does not, he

[1] Rock Edict, Girnar, IX. line 4: *ayaṃ tu mahāphale maṃgale ya dhamma-maṃgale tata dāsabhatakamhi samyapatipati.*

[2] Rock Edict, Kalsi XI. line 4: *dāṣabhaṭakaṣi samyāpaṭipati.* For both the references 52 and 53 see *Corpus Inscriptionum Indicarum,* Vol. I. ed. by E. Hultzsch, London, 1925.

[3] *Ṛgveda,* I. 185. 8. [4] *Ibid.* V. 85. 7. [5] *Ibid.* I. 51. 8.

should not be disturbed in his mind if he knows that his reasons for trying to amass it were good.[1] In the meantime the householder successfully amassing wealth by lawful and honourable means, by his own energy and effort, enjoys ownership, well-being, independence in the sense that he does not run into debt, and blamelessness.[2] His parents, wife and children, servants and workpeople, honour him, as do also the recluses and priests to whom he is accustomed to give alms and make charitable gifts. All of these wish him long life and protection, and by reason of his virtue it may be expected that he will not go into decline.[3]

There are, however, certain trades and pursuits which the householder should not follow since these are not in accord with the Precepts; these are enumerated as: trade in weapons, trade in human beings, in flesh, intoxicants, and trade in poison.[4] Apart from these, a shopkeeper is recommended to be alert, capable and dependable. His clear-sightedness consists in judging the possibility of sale and amount to be obtained thereby, and his capability in technique as a salesman. That he becomes a dependable person will be evident from the willingness of people to invest their money in his ventures.[5] It is possible to start business in a small way: according to a simile employed in the *Cullaseṭṭhi Jātaka:* 'By means of accumulation of small money, the wise man establishes himself even as by skilful application small particles are fanned to a fire.'[6]

Having attained to some success, it is necessary to make it enduring. Four reasons are given for failure to do so, namely, failing to seek what has been lost, not repairing what is decayed, eating and drinking to excess, and putting immoral and unreliable men or women in responsible positions.[7]

Again, having acquired and consolidated one's wealth, one

[1] A. III. 45 f. The gift to '*petas*' mentioned here consists in donations made with the object of perpetuating the memory of deceased persons. This act of goodwill and gratitude is called the 'transference of merit' (*pattidāna*) which is the sixth one of tenfold meritorious deeds (*dasakusala*). See UJ. 12 ff., 305; Sdhp. vv. 497, 500.

[2] *Ibid.* II. 69 f. [3] *Ibid.* III. 75–8. [4] A. III. 208. [5] *Ibid.* I. 116 f.

[6] J. I. 122:

Appakena pi medhāvī pābhatena vicakkhaṇo
samuṭṭhāpeti attānaṃ aṇuṃ aggiṃ 'va sandhamaṃ.

[7] A. II. 249.

should distribute it suitably. No benefit accrues to the miser who merely hoards it, or to the person who uses it entirely for selfish ends. Of the miser it is said: 'At no time whatever does he get himself clothing, food, garlands or perfumes, nor does he give any to his relatives. He guards them, crying: "Mine! Mine!" Then rulers, thieves, his heirs, having taken his wealth, go away in disgust. Yet still he cries: "Mine! Mine!" as before. The wise man, having acquired wealth, helps his relatives and gains their respect; after death he rejoices in a heavenly region.'[1]

The Buddha was once visited by Pasenadi, King of Kosala at the unusual hour of noon.[2] The king explained that there had just died a wealthy man who had left no instructions regarding the disposal of his property; therefore Pasenadi had ordered that the goods should be brought to the royal residence. Vast quantities had arrived, gold and silver. Yet the deceased had always dressed in very poor garments and had been in the habit of eating only sour husk-gruel. He had gone about in a wretched little chariot with only a leaf-awning. Since this man had not utilized his wealth properly, either on his own account or on that of his parents, wife, children, work-people, friends, samaṇas or brahmans, it would be confiscated by ruler or robbers, destroyed by fire or water, or appropriated by heirs for whom he had had no regard. The Buddha confirmed that this would have been the natural order of events, and that in the opposite circumstances, when the wealthy man would have allocated his wealth properly, he would have been happier himself, would have made others happy, and his charitable deeds and almsgiving would have been productive of a happy future state. His riches would not then have been wasted.

Both the squandering and hoarding of wealth are therefore deplored. The ideal disposition lies in a division into four parts: one part should be used by the householder for his own ease and convenience, two parts for his business or occupation, and the fourth should be saved in case of adversity.[3] It is noticeable that no mention is made here of charitable contributions, and it is considered that the omission was intended

[1] J. III. 302. [2] S. I. 89 ff.
[3] D. III. 188; cf. *Uvāsagadasāo* in Su., Vol. I. 1127.

since the amount of these is always left to the discretion and inclination of the giver.

Advice to one agricultural worker is less detailed, but it is stated that his fields should be well-ploughed and well-prepared, that sowing and watering should take place at the proper time, and that the worker should be quick at his work.[1] But whatever the nature of one's occupation, one must be diligent. Any man leading the life of a householder who is prudent and possesses the qualities of truth, self-control, firmness, liberality, will escape enduring affliction in his next existence.[2]

From the foregoing it is clear that no blame attached to the householder as such; he was merely advised that, as a householder, he must try to make a success of his chosen work. To achieve this he must exercise all the moral and physical effort of which he was capable, and if at times he was unsuccessful he must take for consolation the thought that he had acted rightly as far as such action could be judged under the circumstances. On such occasions he should not give way to distress but should turn immediately to consider: 'How shall I use my strength in the present situation?'[3] He was told to use his wealth, not only for others but to some extent on his own behalf. He was even told to live in a suitable locality.[4] But, in the end, of course, the wealth must be left behind. Therefore the wise man, discerning this, should enjoy and share his benefits. Blameless he would attain to rebirth in a happy place.[5]

There were, of course, many people who thought often of the final parting with their belongings and so looked for something of more durable nature than wealth to which they could devote their energies. King Pasenadi once asked the Buddha if there were anything of profit attainable in the things of the present world which would also be of value in the world beyond.[6] The Buddha replied simply: 'Vigilance (*appamāda*).'

On one occasion when the Buddha was staying at the Koliyans' market town of Kakkarapatta, he was approached by one Dīghajānu[7] who remarking that he and other house-

[1] A. I. 239 f. [2] Sn. vv. 187, 188.
[3] A. III. 56: *kammaṃ daḷhaṃ kin ti karomi dāni.*
[4] Sn. v. 260; A. II. 32. [5] S. I. 31. [6] *Ibid.*, I. 87. [7] A. IV. 281–5.

holders were absorbed in the affairs of the present world, suggested that the Buddha should preach the Dhamma to people like them. They wished to know the things that would be of advantage to them in the future world. The Buddha gave the four things leading to happiness in the present world as attainment of energy (*uṭṭānasampadā*), attainment of watchfulness (*ārakkhasampadā*), association with people of high moral standing (*kalyāṇamittatā*), and the leading of a balanced life (*samajīvikatā*). Whatever one's occupation, whether that of farming, trading, cattle-herding, archery, civil servant, or craftsman, one should be skilful and industrious, be possessed of an enquiring mind, able to do and to arrange the work; these qualities constitute attainment of energy. The second, attainment of watchfulness, should be interpreted as care of one's possessions, so that they would not be stolen or taken from one or come to any harm. By associating with friends of high moral standing one should emulate the virtues of confidence (*saddhā*), morality (*sīla*), charity (*cāga*) and wisdom (*paññā*) displayed by the best of one's associates. Regarding the leading of a balanced life, whether one is experiencing an easy or difficult time, one should neither be unduly elated nor depressed; further, one should order one's affairs according to one's income.

The four things leading to welfare and happiness in the world beyond were given by the Buddha as confidence based on understanding and experience, morality, generosity or charity, and wisdom; these are also the four that the layman should seek in his associates. Here 'confidence' is the certainty of the qualities of the Buddha, such as his enlightenment.[1] Achievement in the Moralities lies in the keeping of the Precepts, while achievement in generosity and charity lies in the freeing of thought from avarice and the practising of giving up things. Achievement in wisdom lies 'in the rise of that wisdom leading to welfare, to the penetration of the noble way leading to total destruction of suffering'.[2] The Buddha concluded his address with the following gāthas:

[1] See also D. I. 62. Cf. p. 57, note 2.

[2] D. III. 237, 268; M. I. 356. II. 95, 128; S. V. 197, 199, 392 and *passim: udayatthagāminiyā paññāya samannāgato ariyāya nibbedhikāya sammādukkhakkhayagāminiyā.*

'From rising and taking action, arranging his matters with care,
He who is vigilant orders his living, guards and protects his wares.
With confident understanding, moral and willing to hear,
Free from the taint of the niggard, he clears a continuous road
Leading to things that are excellent, things of the world beyond.
By one who is named the 'Truth' there are declared eight things
To bring the understanding layman present joy
And joy in future worlds. For increased merit
Let him be generous, happy to make a gift.'[1]

To Ugga, the King's chief minister, the Buddha gave seven states that are not subject to fire, theft and other such damage:

'The riches of confidence, riches of morals, of shame and fear of wrong-doing,
The riches of listening, of charity, wisdom are seven.
Of whom is possessed these riches, or woman or man,
That one is invincible either to devas or men.
Because confidence, morals, are brightness, the vision of Truth,
Give yourselves up, wise one, to remembering
That which the Buddha has taught.'[2]

Such were the ethics prescribed for the householder and that states to which the practice of them led.

[1] A. IV. 285.
[2] A. IV. 6 f.:
Saddhādhanaṃ sīladhanaṃ hiri-ottappiyaṃ dhanaṃ
sutadhanañ ca cāgo ca paññā 'me sattamaṃ dhanaṃ.

Yassa ete dhanā atthi itthiyā purisassa vā,
sa ve mahaddhano loke ajeyyo devamānuse.

Tasmā saddhañ ca sīlañ ca pasādaṃ dhammadassanaṃ
anuyuñjetha medhāvī saraṃ Buddhānasāsanaṃ.
See also A. IV. 4 f.

CHAPTER 7

THE LAYMAN'S RELATION TO THE STATE

It might have been expected that, with the attention given to the conduct of the laity and the frequency of his advice in social matters, the Buddha would at some time have sketched the political construction of an ideal state: yet no thought of any reform in the existing political set-up is apparent. The warrior class (*Khattiyas*), priestly class (*Brāhmaṇas*), householders, Gahapatis, Seṭṭhis, Suddas, all occupied a definite status and there is no suggestion in the Buddha's Discourses that this distribution would become modified, except in cases of reference to a general promiscuity resulting from the collapse of morality.[1] Nor does it seem that the Buddha felt the need for any such change since his teaching was designed for, and addressed to, 'a householder, or householder's son, or son of some other clan.'[2] It seems that he attributed the success of a system to the morals of the people working it rather than to any virtue inherent in the system itself. This, surely, is sound enough, if it is taken that a community develops a system according to its own understanding of life and improves on it as that understanding improves, always assuming that no other system is forced on it from the outside against its will. Since, however, the disposition of the present consideration was set forth in comparison with the study of ethics as inaugurated by the Greek thinker Aristotle, and since his predecessor at the Academy, Plato, who flourished only a short while after the Buddha, did in fact produce the Republic, a full-scale work envisaging a political system, further in view of the Socratic and Platonic thought as forming so largely the foundation of Western thought of the present day, one may with advantage compare the conditions in India and Greece which made the outlining of a political system seem necessary to Greek thought but not to Indian Buddhist.

[1] A state foreshadowed if no fear of shame or wrong-doing (*hiri-ottappa*) existed. See A. I. 51.

[2] D. I. 62 f.

It has been said that Socratic enquiry 'implied a standard of truth and good, undiscovered but endlessly discoverable, and to be approached inductively'.[1] Plato, however, was explicit in the identification of virtue with knowledge as an 'art of measurement'[2] and in the vision of an absolute object of desire.[3] He would not break with experience, and in his *Dialogues* often contrasts what ought to be with what is, which is to say the principles of truth and right with the practices of man. His basic aim is always virtue and the furtherance of virtue. But good has more than one aspect, and the beautiful or noble when realized in action constitute the just, while closely allied to the consideration of justice is that of the political state. The trial of Socrates had represented merely a show of justice in which clever rhetoric played a large part, and Socrates, maintaining that his real 'trial' would take place before the judge of the world, showed no fear of death since he knew he had done no wrong. Inspired with the wisdom and courage of Socrates, Plato showed that the more clearly he appreciated the qualities of Socrates the more clearly he saw this philosophic idealism to be separated from the everyday world. In Plato's case the world was that of the restored Athenian democracy, and here was no place allotted for philosophers. In the Republic all governing power rests with the philosophers since the remainder of the community is unable by its ignorance to prosecute virtue.[4] Yet the philosopher, in so governing, is making a sacrifice.[5] He has a

[1] *Encyclopaedia Britannica*, 13th ed. 1926, p. 815, article on 'Plato' by Lewis Campbell.

[2] *Protagoras*. B. Jowett's translation, extensively rev. by Martin Ostwald, New York, Liberal Arts Press, 1956. For definition of the 'art of measurement' see Plato's *Gorgias;* translated with an introd. by W. C. Helmbold, New York, Liberal Arts Press, 1952, and *Philebus*, Plato's examination of pleasure; a translation of the Philebus, with introduction and commentary by R. Hackforth. Cambridge, the University Press, 1945. The extent to which virtue can be taught, and the distinction between transcendental and commonly acquired knowledge, are debated in various aspects in many of the *Dialogues*, the types of knowledge being comparable to the *parāvidyā* and *aparāvidyā* of early Indian thought.

[3] *Lysis*. In Phaedrus, Lysis and Protagoras, translated by J. Wright, London, Macmillan, 1888.

[4] *Politicus* 293A. *In* Lewis Campbell's *The Sophistes and Politicus of Plato,* Oxford at the Clarendon Press, 1867; *The Republic, with an English translation* 428D, by Paul Shorey, London, W. Heinemann, 1937.

[5] *Ibid.* 519.

special education of an advanced type which enables him to perform his duties as a ruler, and these must supersede all private ties and interests. That in the process the individuality of the subjects would be lost to sight was of no particular consequence since the aim lay in the education of the people to virtue.[1] Excellent educational systems, which, incidentally, included in their curricula music and gymnastics, were devised to that end. Even the existence of the state was of value only in so far as it constituted the sole means of preserving virtue and controlling that preservation. It was considered that a state which represented merely a collection of people was not worthy of consideration.

But the state must be defended from without and therefore a second, if much lower, section of the community must be formed. This consisted of naval and military personnel. The third section was composed of farmers, peasants, and people following trades and professions, so that obviously something of a caste system must shortly evolve.

The Republic was not merely a politico-economical treatise since, though it contained many inconsistencies of which Plato may or may not have been aware, he was clearly more confident concerning moral than political matters. At the same time, he believed that the state he designed was attainable by man and that it represented man's highest development. The work contains ten sections, the first of which raised the main question of justice; the next three outlined the perfect state, including the education of the 'Guardians' and defining of justice in the State as well as in the individual. Sections 5, 6 and 7, thought by some to be additions to, and by others to be the kernel of, the whole production, provide for a community and for the education of the philosopher-rulers. Section 8 and 9 show the decline, through four stages, of the State and the individual, terminating in the complete injustice which is a tyranny. The final section, number 10, reviews some of the previous matter and ends with a vision of judgement.

Though the Buddha left no 'Republic', the attitude expressed in the *Nikāyas* is clear enough to be compared with Plato's.

[1] *Gorgias* 464. *In* W. R. Lamb's *Plato with an English translation*, London, W. Heinemann, 1932; *The Republic with an English translation* 500, by Paul Shorey, London, W. Heinemann, 1937.

We may first consider a point common to Socrates, Plato and the Buddha, this to the effect that one's first duty lies towards oneself and only in the second to the community.[1] This combines with the idea that there is no place for the philosopher in the everyday world; moreover one must increase one's own virtue in order to be able to do anything for others, for one cannot teach that which one does not know. The *Dhammapada* has: 'Let each one establish himself in that which is proper; then he should advise others, and not become impure.'[2] And again: 'Let no one neglect his own good for the sake of another's however great. Let it be that, having understood the ideal, he engages himself in it.'[3]

Returning to the comparison, if for 'philosophers' we may take the *samaṇas* who wished to live apart from the world, preferring always the life of the mind, it was never envisaged by the Buddha that these should attempt to 'govern' the rest of the community. They were there for guidance and advice if they were asked for it, but from the Buddha's teaching of Suffering no perfect State could be possible here in the present world. The caste system, potential in the Republic, was already established in India to the extent that the brahmans represented the thinkers and educated portion of the population, the Kshatriyas the warrior class, the gahapatis the householders and occupational men, and the sudras the servants and work-people. These did not attempt to follow each others' callings, but with the advent of the recluses any member of the four classes could leave his calling and aspire to the most select rank. Within the Saṅgha, 'rank' was determined solely by length of membership. The Buddha took the line that, with the cultivation of the Moralities, any person of any social rank could improve, be successful in the mundane sense, and, if he took the Refuges and kept the Precepts, could be certain of an improved status in future lives. Finally, with the understanding

[1] *Symposium*, 216A. *In* W. R. M. Lamb's *Plato with an English translation: Lysis, Symposium, Gorgias*, London, W. Heinemann, 1932.

[2] Dh. v. 158.

Attānam eva paṭhamaṃ patirūpe nivesaye
ath'aññam anusāseyya na kilisseyya paṇḍito.

[3] *Ibid.* v. 166.

Attadatthaṃ paratthena bahunā pi na hāpaye
atthadattham abhiññāya sadatthapasuto siyā.

that he would acquire in conjunction with the keeping of the Moralities, he could rise entirely above the world.

Regarding the formulation of a definite scheme of government which would last indefinitely, producing always satisfactory results solely by reason of its own excellence, it seems unlikely that any person of vision, or even any thinking person, would ever have embarked on the task. In the last two thousand years, Western Europe has worked out many types of governments, but, in the main, they present a series of checks and modifications tending towards one side or the other of the principle for which the Greeks of the fifth century BC fought the Persians at Marathon and Salamis, namely, freedom of individual thought *versus* regimentation of thought. To some extent it might be considered that Plato was advocating the latter, but there is no question that the Buddha entirely advocated the former. In forming an estimate, however, it is necessary to bear in mind the conditions under which the schemes worked or were to work. Life in Greece was always hard; riches as understood by contemporary Indians would have been to them fabulous. With the Greeks, austerity was largely a matter of necessity and housing a major problem. In the sense that a wealthy Indian might leave the household life to devote himself to meditation, the average Greek had much less to leave. Where the Indian was constantly exhorted to lead a moral life, to the Greeks sex was already contemptible. If one is inclined in the present consideration to devote a certain space to such a comparison, some justification may lie in the fact that the alleged Christianity on which the Western world has supported itself for so long has a large Greek philosophical component, and it is this, not the Hebraic or Zoroastrian components that have furnished its outlook on, and general conduct of, life. The ideal to the Westerner has always been physical fitness, simplicity of living, reasoning, 'doing beautifully whatever needs to be done' (*aretē*);[1] these are entirely Greek concepts. They contrast with the love of luxury and ease so often considered typical of the Semitic races. If therefore, with faith in the mythical and mystical

[1] *aretē:* sometimes translated 'virtue'. To the Greeks it combined all the moral and social qualities which go to the making of the perfect man and citizen.

side of Christianity having given way in face of the faculty of Greek reasoning, one comes to see the basic qualities of the Westerners as those which the Buddha gave as 'extolled by the wise',[1] one understands the present Western interest in the Buddha's teachings.

By reason, then, of the importance assigned to the moral standards and outlook of man in the Buddha's teachings, one must look for a description of the qualities of the people who will operate a scheme rather than for any intrinsic virtue in the scheme itself. If the scheme is one of an autocracy such as prevailed in the Buddha's day, then one must look for political teaching of the nature that will render that autocracy benevolent; this will consist in injunctions to the kings and their proclaimed duties to their peoples. Of such we have several examples.

The leader of a community should realize that by his integrity and foresight will be constructed the course which his people will naturally follow. The case is compared to that of a bull crossing fields by a devious route with the kine straggling in disorderly fashion behind him. When the ruler keeps to righteous ways his people will be righteous also and peace will reign in the realm.[2] A fool in an exalted station causes great trouble.[3] When kings are evilly disposed, so are their ministers, brahmans and householders. Seasons become disordered, the rains and winds occur at the wrong times, and the crops are deficient. The people are weak and sickly. If, however, the king is a good man, the people are like him and the kingdom is a happy one.[4] To enlist a following, a gift, a kindly word, a good turn, or equality of treatment, according to the nature of the person desired as a follower, may be counted as advisable means.[5]

Two *suttas* describe at length the conditions of a kingdom. In *Cakkavatti-Sīhanāda Suttanta*[6] we have the story of Daḷhanemi, a universal monarch. After a very long reign he commanded a certain man to let him know if the Celestial Wheel[7] should at any time move back or lag. In due course the Wheel did so and the king was informed. Inferring from this that he had

[1] See p. 54, note 1, and associated text. [2] J. III. 111.
[3] *Ibid.* I. 445. [4] A. II. 74 ff. [5] *Ibid.* IV. 216, 218. [6] D. III. 58 f.
[7] According to a very old Indian tradition, the Celestial Wheel was the first of seven treasures belonging to a great ruler at whose birth it had been foretold that he would become either a universal monarch or, if he went out into the homeless life, 'an arahat, fully enlightened, who removes the veil

not much longer to live, he handed over his domain to his son and went out into the homeless life to devote his remaining years to contemplation of celestial joys. Seven days later the Wheel disappeared. The son went lamenting to his father who explained: 'The Celestial Jewel of the Wheel is not an inheritance passing from father to son. See, my dear! By means of the service in the noble duty of the universal monarch, a place exists in that duty in which you are functioning. At Uposatha, once in every fifteen days, if the leader, having bathed and having observed the Eight Precepts, goes to the upper storey of his palace, there will become manifest before him the Jewel of the Celestial Wheel with a thousand spokes, rim and hub, complete for working.'[1] The son asked:

'What, then, Sir, is this noble duty of the Universal Monarch?'

The King replied:

'That duty consists in one's support in honouring the Dhamma, paying reverential homage to it, being one who reveres it, is a symbol and banner of it, one to whom the Dhamma is the overlord, a righteous screen and protection in arranging for the family units, army, nobles (*Khattiyas*), subordinates, Brahmans, householders, country people and people of the market-towns, *samaṇas*, and brahmans, animals and birds. Do not, my dear, in your kingdom set going or continue wrong action. Whoever in the kingdom should be without means, to him should be handed some. Whoever in the kingdom, *samaṇas* and brahmans who, having from vigilance abstained from sensual attachments and become established in patience and gentleness, such a one training himself, calming himself, bringing himself to approach final rebirth, if coming to you from time to time should inquire: "What, Sir, is good and what is not good? What is to be censured and what not censured? What should be made use of and what should not? What over a long period will be valueless and painful to one, and what over a long period will be beneficial and of happiness to me?" then, having heard, you should make them avoid and get rid of evil, and take up that which is good. This, surely, my dear, is the noble duty of the Universal Monarch.'[2]

from the eyes of the world'. (*Sace kho pana agārasmā anagāriyaṃ pabbajati arahaṃ hoti Sammāsambuddho loke vivattacchaddo.* D. I. 89.

[1] *Ibid.* III. 60.

[2] D. III. 61.

The son followed his father's advice and to him was manifested the Celestial Wheel. Desiring to become a world-monarch, he confirmed the wish by taking in his left hand a pitcher, and with his right sprinkling water from it over the Wheel. With the Wheel always before him, he travelled with his armies, horses and chariots, elephants and men, all over the world. The rulers of the regions through which he passed welcomed him and asked him to teach them; he did so by declaring the Five Precepts, not to kill any living thing, not to take that which is not given, not to commit sexual offences, not to lie, and not to drink intoxicants. He concluded his teaching with the injunction to enjoy their possessions as they had always done, and then passed on leaving them willing vassals.

The same events occurred in respect of many succeeding rulers until at length there arose one who, on the disappearance of the Wheel, did not consult his hermit father. Instead he ruled according to his own ideas. The results being unsuccessful, nobles, officials, councillors, ministers, courtiers and reciters of verses went to him complaining. They suggested that he should consult with the many persons in the kingdom who knew the noble duty of a great ruler, and that he should govern on those lines. In accordance with their recommendation he provided the necessary protection for the well-to-do but did not attend to the poorer people. Poverty became widespread and a case of theft occurred. The thief, being brought before the king, gave as his reason for the theft his entire lack of means of subsistence, whereupon the king made him a gift. A second case occurred with similar result. Many persons taking to thieving, the king decided to put a stop to the whole matter by making an example of one culprit. The man was drummed round the town and executed at one of the main gateways. Thieves now began to conduct their operations with violence and murder became common. The physical appearance of people deteriorated and the span of life reduced from a former eighty thousand years to forty thousand. Lying became common, and with the spread of this and other evils the life span became reduced to twenty thousand years. The *Suttanta* then records the case of a thief who was denounced by a certain man; this denunciation was considered as yet another evil in that it involved the speaking of evil of another person. The life span became reduced to ten thousand years. Physical appearance deteriorated to the extent that many persons were ugly; these, coveting the more beautiful, misconducted themselves towards other men's wives. A further succession of evils arose: immorality, abusive speech, trivial talk, covetousness and ill-will, false opinions, lust and poisonous greed. Consequent on these the respect previously shown to mother, father, *samaṇas* and brahmans, and the elders of the clan, decreased continuously. By this time the span of life had become reduced to a hundred years.

Before proceeding to the description of further deplorable states provided in the *Sutta*, one may consider some of the points so far advanced. The idea that man has descended to his present state from some higher life appears to have been widespread amongst the early peoples, and attached to it is the notion that he enjoyed a much longer span of life than he now knows. Modern research has put the length of time since man first evolved a civilization as some eight thousand years ago, but recent employment of the isotope 'carbon-fourteen' in excavation work in Asia Minor had indicated figures in the region of twenty thousand years. Viewing the question from another standpoint, the 'King-Lists', schematic lists of kings drawn up by Sumerian scribes about 2000 BC as a framework for a history of Sumer, give reigns of many centuries each, the ten antediluvian kings accounting for 432,000 years between them. Recalling that excavations at Ur and Kish have yielded elaborate palaces and much grave-furniture containing material of which the nearest source of supply must have been the west coast of India and, in the case of lapis-lazuli, the Pamirs, one can hardly fail to attribute this and similar facts to a close association with the people of the ancient Indus cities and to at least some similarity of ideas. It is known that by 3500 BC Sumer had attained to a standard of architecture employment of the arch, dome, colonnade construction and so on, which was not attained in the western world for many centuries, while a notable feature of important Sumerian buildings consisted in an elaborate flight of steps leading to the pillared entrance. This is the subject of a simile well-known in the Buddhist *suttas*. Again, the port at the mouth of the Narbuda River, Broach, known to Ptolemy as Barygaza, is mentioned in the *Jātakas* as a very ancient port from which trading was conducted to and from the Mesopotamian countries.

Yet though the estimate of a very long life was not peculiar to Indian thought, it is by no means suggested that Buddhism flourished in either Sumer or the Indus cities; to the contrary the ultimate fall of these and other civilizations is attributed to failure to develop the higher levels of thought. The extent to which such thought does develop should determine the persistence and improvement of the race; once this ceases to develop the race would decline. In the case of Sumer, beyond an ethical code and the high degree of civilization, nothing was achieved but interminable works on magic. Regarding any suggestion of Buddhist thought, one may turn to the quotation given in the early part of the present work, namely, that of the Buddha's declaration: 'I shall go to Banaras; I shall beat the drum of the Deathless State; I shall make turn the Wheel of the Law which in this world has not yet been turned.' But this does not preclude the possibility of existence of earlier phases of man's occupation of the earth, for, according to the account given in *Mahāpadāna Suttanta,* Vipassi Buddha was the first of the six Buddhas who flourished in previous aeons. Still, whatever interpretation one decides to put on the length of aeons or the possibility of a human life ever extending to eighty thousand years, or even if one abandons the estimates as wholly fictitious or legendary, there are two points involved which the present generation has seen proved in its own experience; they consist in the one mentioned above, namely, the fate of a race whose higher thought has stagnated either due to indifference or weight of dogma; secondly, the source and progression of evils which will reduce a state, and finally the entire world, to anarchy and destruction.

So far the decline may be taken to have originated in an initial poverty, and it is noticeable that the list of evils, as contrasted with those given according to the Precepts or at other places in the Buddhist texts,[1] is now arranged with the first three components as stealing, violence and killing. In the instructions given to householders as set forth in the earlier

[1] According to D. I. 3 f. the order would be: taking of life, stealing, sexual intercourse, lying, slander and gossip, harsh speech, frivolous talk.

part of the present chapter, where the theme is largely success in one's professional or business undertakings, little is said of poverty apart from the aspect of dissipation of wealth, while the observations apply to the individual person. The present homily deals with the danger of increasing individual poverty as regards the State, and we learn here that if rulers do not prevent the spread of poverty in their domains they not only induce disorder therein but create disrespect for all recognized forms of authority, so contributing to the deterioration of the human race. We have, moreover, further stress on the inter-relation of physical conditions, collective as well as individual, with morality. The present generation is, of course, all too familiar with such a state of affairs, and stands in no doubt regarding the dangers of mass poverty.

From a life span of a century the *suttanta* goes on to consider a reduction to ten years.[1] In these circumstances the marriageable age will be five years. The tastes of ghee (*sappi*), fresh butter (*navanīta*), oil (*tela*), honey (*madhu*), molasses (*phānita*) and salt (*loṇa*) will disappear, and the highest kind of food will be the grain *kudrūsaka*.[2] The ten moral ways of action will have disappeared and the ten immoral ways will be very much in evidence.[3] The word 'good' will no longer exist; whence, then, a doer of good? Honour and respect will be paid to the evil doer, just as at present they are paid to a doer of good. The world will become lawless as with goats, sheep and such animals. Enmity will be the rule, until a period of general slaughter occurs. After seven days, some persons will decide to abandon the killing and will take refuge in dens, rocks, holes in trees, living on the produce of the jungle. Emerging after another seven days, people will feel well-disposed towards each other, will rejoice to find someone else is left alive, and will comfort each other. Tracing their heavy losses of kin to their former conduct they will distinguish between good and bad, and will cease to take life. Working up through the range of virtues they will come back to their span of life of eighty thousand years, when they will have regained their beautiful appearance. In that condition the marriageable age will be five hundred years. There will be only three kinds

[1] D. III. 71 f.

[2] A course type of grain resembling rye.

[3] See Vbh. 391. The 'ways' are practically those given in the present *sutta*.

of affliction, desire, fasting and old age.[1] India will be rich and prosperous, with cities and towns so close to each other that a cock could walk from one to another; the population will be enormous. The city of Bārāṇasi will be called Ketumatī, will be crowded with well-fed prosperous people, and will be the chief of the eighty-four thousand towns of the country. Here will arise Saṅkha, a universal monarch who has conquered the world not by the sword but by goodness. The Buddha Metteyya will then arise, and Saṅkha, having raised up the palace built long ago by King Mahāpanāda,[2] will give up his possessions and go forth into the homeless life under the Buddha Metteyya.[3]

In the *Kūṭadanta Sutta* a similar subject is treated of, though in a rather more circumscribed manner. Here we have the story of a king of a distant date, by name Mahāvijita, who, finding himself possessed of great wealth, his treasure-houses and storehouses full, felt that he should perform a great sacrifice to show his gratitude.[4] He consulted with his religious adviser who said: 'Sir, it is remarked that the king's territory is oppressed with murderous attacks, the sacking of villages, market-towns and cities, with ambush and robbery. If now the king would uproot this oppression by imposing a tax, he would not be fulfilling his duty. It may be that the esteemed king feels: "I should put an end to that robbery-trouble by punishment, imprisonment, fine, or by making an example of somebody, or by exile"; but it is not by that means that violence is rightly exterminated. Those who survive cause fresh difficulties. But by adopting this method the robbery-trouble is rightly exterminated. In this case, to those in the king's territory who work on the land, cultivating and farming, let him distribute food and seeds; to those who are traders let him make a grant; to those who are in his service let him consider food and wages. These men, attached to their own work, will not make trouble; they will help in the raising of revenue and the country will be free from oppression. People will be pleased and happy, and, rejoicing in the rearing of their children, will surely dwell with their houses open.'[5]

[1] D. III. 75: *asītivassasahassāyukesu manussesu tayo ābādhā bhavissanti icchā anasanaṃ jarā.*

[2] See Thag. 130.

[3] D. III. 75 ff.

[4] *Ibid.* I. 134–42. See also Ch. 3 of the present work.

[5] *Ibid.* I. 135.

The king, following the advice, found his territory to become secure and peaceful, his people happy and loyal. The religious adviser was now called to prepare a great sacrifice and to instruct the king concerning the procedure. Accordingly, notable personages were invited, representatives of the Khattiyas, Ministers of State, Brahmans and Householders, all of whom brought much wealth which they offered to the king. He declined it since he had already sufficient revenue and possessions, and the gifts were funded to constitute a perpetual charity. The 'sacrifice' consisted entirely of ghee, oil, butter, milk, honey and molasses, and to it the king himself brought his personal gifts of wealth and power, his confidence and understanding, and his intelligence. His religious adviser brought his scholarship, virtue and wisdom.

That an underlying spirit of such nature will bring peace and happiness to a country is evident from the report of Fa-hsien, the first of the Chinese Buddhist pilgrims whose records are still extant. Passing through Central India some eight centuries after the *Parinibbāna* of the Buddha, Fa-hsien writes: 'Of all the countries of Central India, this (i.e. *Magadha*) has the largest cities and towns. Its people are rich and thriving and emulate one another in practising charity of heart and duty to one's neighbour. Regularly every year, on the eighth day of the second moon, they have a procession of images, . . . there may be some twenty cars, all beautifully ornamented and different from one another. On the above-mentioned day all the ecclesiastics and laymen in the district assemble; they have singing and high class music, and make offerings of flowers and incense . . . the elders and gentry of these countries have instituted in their capitals free hospitals, and hither come all poor or helpless patients, orphans, widowers and cripples. They are well taken care of, a doctor attends them, food and medicine being supplied according to their needs. They are all made quite comfortable, and when they are cured they go away.'[1]

It cannot, of course, be assumed that the peace and prosperity of Magadha had continued without interruption over the centuries. King Bimbisāra, mentioned frequently in the *Nikāyas* as being favourably disposed towards the teachings of

[1] *The Travels of Fa-hsien* or *Record of the Buddhistic Kingdoms*, Trn. H. A. Giles, Routledge & Kegan Paul, Second impression 1956, p. 47.

the Buddha, was an ambitious ruler who by conquest and matrimonial alliances added appreciably to his dominions. His son and successor, Ajātasattu, continued the policy and less than a year before the *Parinibbāna* of the Buddha was projecting an attack on the powerful Vajjians. The chief minister of Magadha was sent to the Buddha with the information and with instructions to find out as far as possible the extent of the chances of success. Venerable Ānanda, who was present at the interview, confirmed to the Buddha that the Vajjians had followed advice given to them by the Buddha some time previously regarding their conduct, and from this the minister inferred that Ajātasattu would be definitely the loser. The advice given had been: (i) that the people should attend habitually the formal assemblies, (ii) that they should assemble in a spirit of unity and harmony, pass the time there harmoniously, and do what had to be done harmoniously, (iii) that they should not make new laws or abolish old ones but should continue in the old Vajjian manner, (iv) that they should honour and respect their elders, paying heed to them, (v) that they should not detain by force women or girls of their clans, (vi) that they should honour the Vajjian shrines in their country and continue with their former religious offerings, (vii) that they should protect and provide for the Arahants among them and admit new ones. If the Vajjians would fulfil these conditions, said the Buddha, they might be expected to prosper and not to decline.[1]

It is not known whether the particular attack intended did take place within the near future, but at length Ajātasattu gained control of Kosala and Vaisāli; his son and successor, Udayana, continued the tradition. The programme of expansion seems to have been halted by a succession of weak rulers until the usurper Sisunāga annihilated the only outstanding rival state, Avanti. In this building up of a Magadha empire it was inevitable that Buddhist interests should have been adversely affected, and it seems hardly strange that the earliest Buddhist scriptures, whether they were ever written down or not, should have disappeared as a collection. Of them we have evidence only in the *Dhammapada* and the oldest of the *Sutta* and *Vinaya* texts, but it seems possible that the major groups of

[1] D. II. 72–6.

Buddhists, though these need not necessarily have been representative of different sects, each possessed its compendium if only for purposes of reference for teaching. The *Mahāvastu* would be a case in point. Though it carries as its full title 'The *Vinaya Piṭaka* according to the text of the *Lokottaravādins*[1] belonging to the *Mahāsāṅghikas*',[2] in the form in which we know the compilation at present there is practically no *Vinaya* material, though the contents include narratives, poems, *Jātakas*, early versions of the *Mahāgovinda Sutta*[3] and others of the well-known Pali suttas, the whole of the *Sahassavagga* of the *Dhammapada*, the *Khuddakapāṭha*,[4] and *suttas* of the *Sutta Nipāta*. That a concentrated effort was made at some time to reassemble the early scriptures is clear from the compilation of the *Āgamas* and the *Nikāyas*, for these were drawn from a common source and it would appear that this source represented a stage intermediate between the very early texts and the *Āgamas* and *Nikāyas* as we know them at present. One fact at least is outstanding, namely, that the compilers of the *Nikāyas* were unaware of the origin of the texts they incorporated in the *Khuddaka Nikāya*, to the extent that these '*Khuddaka*' texts were already survivors of a complete and larger collection.

However, the fact that attempts were made to hold collections of texts amongst groups of Buddhists, and also when at times more favourable conditions prevailed to reassemble or reconstruct the whole body of scriptures, bears witness to upsurges of Buddhism in parts of India even to the level of that described in Magadha by Fa-hsien. The efforts of some of the sections of the community to follow the Buddha's instructions to the Vajjians were therefore not made in vain.

Still we have no indication that amongst these earlier works there was ever included a formal treatise of the nature of Plato's Republic. As always, the Buddha stressed the thought behind a thing, and if the happiness and well-being of a state were dependent on the moral quality of its rulers we have to recognize, also according to the advice given to the Vajjians, the duties of the populace that it should attend and co-operate

[1] Transcendentalists. They considered that the Buddha was not a human being but was raised far above the life of the present world.

[2] An early sect of Buddhists which tended to raise the Buddha above the human level and to identify his personality with that of former Buddhas.

[3] D. II. 220–52.

[4] See p. 78, note 2.

in the public gatherings where the discussion of legislation took place. Moral responsibility lay not only with the rulers but also with the masses; there was no question of a dictatorship. In short, each person should share in the responsibility of making decisions, and, in the working out, the community should present a united front. Here, obviously, the moral character of the individual must be a factor of primary importance.

CHAPTER 8

THE ULTIMATE GOAL

(*a*) *Statements of the Aim*

The Ultimate Aim of the Buddha's Teaching is, without question, the attainment of Nibbāna with the realization of the Four Noble Truths. Various aspects of the Goal may be presented in the course of dissertation and various terms employed which are intended to convey a similar meaning, but these are all tributary to the statement that the Goal consists in the realization of the Truths. The standards of moral conduct must therefore always be those which are conducive to this realization; perfection in *sīla, samādhi* and *paññā* must always represent the means of accomplishment. It is never sufficient to say merely that the Goal, by whatever name it may be called, is not of the order of logical deduction (*atakkāvacara*), and so hint that in order to attain to it one has only to wait for some kind of supernatural revelation; for the Fourth Noble Truth is that of the Way to the Cessation of Suffering (*dukkha-nirodha-gāminī paṭipadā*), which, we are told, must be followed continuously and diligently throughout the present life. In support of this statement we will now consider the Goal according to two well-known aspects, first the one indicated by the popular term of 'Nirvāṇa' or 'Nibbāna', second according to the Buddha's description as freeing of mind and freeing of insight (*ceto-vimutti paññā-vimutti*).

(*b*) *Nirvāṇa, Nibbāna*

For etymology we have the Vedic association of *nirvāṇa* as *nir* plus *vā*, to blow, the suggestion being 'to make cool by blowing'; later this came to connect with *vr*, to cover, the sense then associating with the extinguishing of fire. The imagery of flame and fire in the early *Upaniṣads* was frequently used by the Buddha, while the nature of the residue of the fire, if any, has long been a matter of consideration. However, before embarking on the question of residue, we will consider the general statements found in the Buddhist texts concerning 'Nirvāṇa' or 'Nibbāna'.

The Pali *Dhammapada* gives the following information regarding Nibbāna. A generalization occurs in the statement: 'The Buddhas declare Nibbāna to be the highest of all things.'[1] For indications by comparison we have: 'Hunger is the most extreme of afflictions; the conditioned state is the utmost suffering. Having understood this according to absolute truth, Nibbāna is the extreme of happiness.'[2] Or again: 'Health is the greatest of gifts; one's own contentment is the greatest wealth. Confidence (intimacy) is the most excellent of relationships; Nibbāna is the highest happiness.'[3] But more specifically we have: 'For those who maintain vigilance, who study day and night, who strive for Nibbāna, their *āsavas* disappear.'[4] In this case the Sanskrit text contains the variation 'who strive for deathlessness'.[5] Again: 'Those wise ones who meditate constantly and with strong effort touch Nibbāna, the unsurpassed release from attachments.'[6] But the key to the situation lies in the *gāthā*: 'Cut out the love of self as you would an autumn-lily with the hand. Develop the way to Nibbāna, taught by the Happy One.'[7]

The first of these quotations occurs also in *Mahāpadāna Suttanta* as part of a '*Pātimokkha*' spoken by Vipassi Buddha to the assembly of bhikkhus who had just returned to Bandhumatī after seven years of teaching the Dhamma in distant

[1] Dh. v. 184:
Nibbānaṃ paramaṃ vadanti Buddhā.

[2] *Ibid.* v. 203:
Jigacchā paramā rogā saṅkhārā paramā dukhā
etaṃ ñatvā yathābhūtaṃ nibbānaṃ paramaṃ sukhaṃ.

[3] *Ibid.* v. 204:
Ārogyaparamā lābhā saṃtuṭṭhīparamaṃ dhanaṃ
vissāsaparamā ñāti nibbānaṃ paramaṃ sukhaṃ.

[4] *Ibid.* v. 226:
Sadā jāgaramānānam ahorattānusikkhinaṃ
nibbānaṃ adhimuttānaṃ atthaṃ gacchanti āsavā.

[5] Uv. XV. v. 8:
Jāgaryam anuyuktasya ahorātrānusikṣinaḥ
amṛtam anuyuktasya astaṃ gacchanti āśravāḥ.

[6] Dh. v. 23; Uv. IV. v. 3:
Te jhāyino sātatikā niccaṃ daḷhaparakkamā
phusanti dhīrā nibbānaṃ yogakkhemaṃ anuttaraṃ.

[7] See p. 31, note 2.

places.[1] The full context is: 'Patient endurance is the extreme austerity; the Buddhas declare Nibbāna to be the highest. One who injures is not a recluse; the *samaṇa* does not harm others. Avoiding the doing of all evil, the accomplishing of good, purifying one's own mind: that is the teaching of the Buddhas. Not blaming, not injuring, restraint according to the *pātimokkha* rules, moderation in food, walking, sleeping, and sitting, exertion in the concentration of the mind: that is the teaching of the Buddhas.'[2]

In the second of the *Dhammapada* quotations given above we have the contrast between the extreme suffering of the conditioned state and, by inference, the extreme happiness of the unconditioned, the latter brought about by the realization of the nature of suffering. Recalling the Three Characteristics of Existence,[3] in which all sankhāras are impermanent and imbued with suffering, while all things, whether conditioned or unconditioned, are without substratum, the amplification of the present *Dhammapada* verse lies in the words: 'This is the road to purity.' According to the *Sarvāstivāda* philosophy, the *asaṃskṛta* dharmas[4] are space (*ākāśa*), extinction through intellectual power (*pratisaṅkhyā-nirodha*), and extinction due to lack of a cause (*apratisaṅkhyā-nirodha*), which is to say: not by any type of knowledge but by nature. *Sautrāntika*[5] is also in agreement with this view. *Vijñānavāda* adds three other such dharmas: extinction by a motionless state of heavenly meditation (*āniñjya*), extinction by the stoppage of idea and sensation (*saṃjña-vedayita-nirodha*) as achieved by an *arahant*, and *Tathāgata*. Nirvāṇa is considered as an example of extinction through intellectual power. Examination of the reasons why space is classed as an unconditioned *asaṃskṛta* dharma may serve as suggestion for the inclusion in the class of the other dharmas; the reasons are: (i) that space gives no hindrance, (ii) that space penetrates through any hindrance

[1] D. II. 38 f. The incident referred to here occurred after Vipassi Buddha had acquired a large following and had sent out bhikkhus to teach.

[2] *Ibid.* II. 49 f.; Dh. vv. 183–5. [3] See p. 43, note 1, and associated text.

[4] See the *Central Conception of Buddhism* by Th. Stcherbatsky, 3rd ed., Calcutta, 1961, p. 334.

[5] An early school of Buddhist thought which claimed that nothing, either matter or mind, exists at all. See Kvu. 3, 5. The word 'Sautrāntika' derives from *sūtrānta*, scripture, the tenets being based on the sutras in contrast to the *Sarvāstivāda* which is based on the Abhidharma.

freely, (iii) that space manifests no change. With no interference of any kind, one may think of Nirvāṇa as being essentially calm, therefore happy, as contrasted with the constant commotion in a conditioned state.

Two important instances are extant wherein the Buddha employed the terms conditioned and unconditioned (*saṅkhata* and *asaṅkhata*). He put the question: 'What is the *asaṅkhata*?' and himself replied: 'That which is the destruction of lust, hatred and delusion, bhikkhus, is called "*asaṅkhata*".'[1] Again he said: 'Whatever the thing, whether *saṅkhata* or *asaṅkhata*, that which is declared the highest is dispassionateness, absence of desire—which is to say: the subduing of pride, the removal of thirst, the uprooting of desire or attachment, the breaking of the cycle of rebirth, the destruction of craving, dispassionateness, cessation, Nibbāna.'[2]

Deferring for a moment further consideration of happiness, or the 'highest happiness' as mentioned in the third of the *Dhammapada* quotations given above, we turn to the fourth quotation with the attainment to Nirvāṇa as connected with the removal of certain conditions. Venerable Sāriputta once stated: 'That which is the destruction of lust, hatred and delusion is said to be Nibbāna.'[3] He proceeded to declare that the way to accomplishing these destructions lay in following the Noble Eightfold Path. The three qualities to be destroyed are known as the three evil roots (*hetus*), and with them the Buddha combined destruction of the *āsavas* as a means of attaining to the Goal. Asked by a certain bhikkhu what the removal of the three bad *hetus* implied, the Buddha answered: 'The expression "removal of lust, hatred and delusion", because it means the destruction of the *āsavas*, is called the sphere of Nibbāna.' Asked further by the same bhikkhu, 'What is the deathless state (*amata*)?' the Buddha replied: 'That which is the destruction of lust, hatred and delusion is called the "deathless state". The way to it is the Noble Eightfold Path.'[4]

[1] S. IV. 359: *Katamañ ca bhikkhave asaṅkhataṃ yo bhikkhave rāgakkhayo dosakkhayo mohakkhayo idaṃ vuccati bhikkhave asaṅkhataṃ.*

[2] A. II. 34; It. 88: *yathā bhikkhave dhammā saṅkhatā vā asaṅkhatā vā virāgo tesaṃ aggam akkhāyati yad idaṃ madanimmadano pipāsavinayo ālayasamugghāto vaṭṭūpacchedo taṇhakkhayo virāgo nirodho nibbānaṃ.*

[3] S. IV. 251 f.

[4] S. V. 8: *Nibbānadhātuyā kho etaṃ bhikkhu adhivacanaṃ rāgavināyo*

The destruction of the *āsavas* covers that of the three evil *hetus* and it is in respect of the former that the realization of the Four Noble Truths and therefore attainment to Nibbāna is contingent. At the end of the discourse recounted in *Sāmaññaphala Sutta* we have the following, given directly by the Buddha: 'He comes to know what, according to absolute truth, are suffering, the origin of suffering, the cessation of suffering, and the way to the cessation of suffering. He comes to know, according to absolute truth, the *āsavas*, the origin of the *āsavas*, the cessation of the *āsavas*, and the way to their cessation. From knowing and seeing thus, his mind is freed from the *āsava* of sense-desires, from the *āsava* of craving for existence, and from the *āsava* of lack of the Higher Knowledge. In this freedom he knows: Exhausted is birth, the Higher Life has come to perfection, that which should be done has been done, there will be no more to be done for the present state (*nāparaṃ itthattāyā ti*).'[1] By attainment to Nibbāna must therefore be understood the destruction of sense-desires, craving for the process of life, and ignorance, so that 'Nibbāna' will then imply a cessation of the processes which constitute life, and also the acquisition of a Perfect Knowledge and Vision, otherwise, seeing according to absolute truth (*yathā bhūtaṃ*).

Regarding the *āsava* of sense desires, a conversation is recorded between Venerable Sāriputta and Venerable Udāyi[2] according to which the former, when addressing a gathering of bhikkhus, stated that Nibbāna is happiness. Venerable Udāyi asked what is the happiness in Nibbāna which is not that of the senses. Venerable Sāriputta replied to the effect that the happiness of Nibbāna is just that which is not recorded by the five physical senses; the well-being arising from the five senses is merely sensuous happiness. With the improvement of understanding, the forms of happiness become of an order higher than that of the senses. That which was happiness, or ease, at one mental level becomes a dis-ease as one attains to a

dosavināyo mohavināyo āsavānaṃ khayo tena vuccatī ti. Yo kho bhikkhu rāgakkhayo dosakkhayo mohakkhayo idaṃ vuccati amataṃ ayam eva ariyo aṭṭaṅgiko maggo amatagāmimaggo.

[1] D. I. 83 f. and *passim* in the scriptures.

[2] The Udāyi mentioned here is the 'Great' Udāyi, as distinguished from the theras Lāludāyi and Kāludāyi who also figure in the Buddhist texts. See also D. III. 115 and S. V. 83.

higher level. Tracing the refinements of mentality according to the Jhānic states, he at length reached the highest *Jhāna*; with perception and feeling ended, and with the *āsavas* destroyed genuine happiness is attained.[1] It should be noted, however, that in this dissertation Venerable Sāriputta included all the Jhānic states, *Rūpa* and *Arūpa*,[2] whereas in the *Sāmaññaphala* discourse the Buddha did not include the *Arūpa Jhānas*. The principle of elimination is, however, the same in both cases.

Regarding the second *āsava*, that of love of the process of life, we have many statements in the *Nikāyas* to the effect that the ceasing of the process is Nibbāna.[3] From this it has been mistakenly inferred that, since there is no basic substratum to a personality, Nibbāna must be total annihilation. The Buddha's verdict on the soul theories, as also on annihilation, have been set forth in a previous chapter, but we have also his dictum that Nibbāna is impossible of definition, as recorded in the following incident.

A statement was once made by a Brahman and endorsed by the Buddha to the effect that the five senses have each their particular 'pasture', or 'roaming-ground' (*gocara*), do not interfere with each other, but that mind is the repository for all of them. The Brahman putting a series of questions, the Buddha in reply took each of them in turn. He said that the repository of mind is mindfulness, that of mindfulness is release or deliverance, and that of deliverance is Nibbāna. For the repository of Nibbāna he said: 'Taking the question to the limit it is transcendental, not to be directly observed. Living the religious life is the approach to Nibbāna; its end and perfection is Nibbāna.'[4] That the religious life is not to be taken merely as a form of asceticism is clear from the following. Venerable Ānanda once remarked to the Buddha that half of the religious life (*brahmacariya*) is friendship and intimacy with that which is lovely; to this the Buddha replied: 'It is the whole, not the half, of the religious life. Of a bhikkhu who is a friend, an associate, of that which is lovely, morally good, is

[1] S. IV. 279 ff.

[2] See Ch. 1, p. 23 f. and associated text.

[3] S. II. 117: *bhavanirodho nibbānaṃ*.

[4] S. V. 218: *Ajjhaparam brāhmaṇa pañhaṃ nāsakkhi pañhassa pariyantaṃ gahetuṃ nibbānogadaṃ hi brāhmaṇa brahmacariyaṃ vussati nibbānaparāyanaṃ nibbānapariyosānan ti.*

intimate with it, it may be expected that he will develop and progress according to the Noble Eightfold Path.'[1] It may be taken, therefore, that constant association and intimacy with the lovely, the morally good, is a means of progress to Nirvāṇa.

Regarding the third *āsava*, that of ignorance (*avijjā*), it is necessary to recall the type of knowledge of which *avijjā* indicates a lack. This is the lack of the Higher Knowledge and besides the *āsava* aspect, it represents, inevitably, a component of the *Paticcasamuppāda*, instrumental in maintaining the round of rebirths. It is also the last of the Ten Fetters binding to the round of rebirths. 'But the superlative impurity, greater than all others, is ignorance; having struck down that impurity, bhikkhus, be pure.'[2] Ignorance is considered to be the origin of lust and hatred, and, in fact, all evil states of mind are bound up with it, while ignorance in the sense of 'blindness' is an unconscious state, a ṛemainder from death, a remainder consisting of the effect of deeds performed in the previous life or lives. Such ignorance should not be considered as merely lack of knowledge since it includes both knowing and not-knowing. It is the characteristic of the blind mind, leading to a blind activity, which, in turn, has its effect in the 'will to live', the strongest characteristic of living beings. Again, the cutting off of obstructions caused by lust or desire, or even the production of a cessation of consciousness, is by no means Nirvāṇa; both represent merely a return to the *avijjā* which is termed 'blindness'. Only complete Enlightenment destroys this blindness.

We may now consider the alternative reading of 'deathlessness' (*amṛtam*) as employed in the corresponding verse of the Sanskrit.[3] On the principle that at death the consciousness normal to a person during his life becomes reduced to an infra-consciousness which persists to form the basis of a rebuilding in the coming life, then if a state of deathlessness is not to occur either consciousness must never so sink down, or alternatively, some entity must be present or have been realized whereby the former normal consciousness will be

[1] S. V. 2.

[2] Dh. v. 243:
Tato malā malataraṃ avijjā paramaṃ malaṃ
etaṃ malaṃ pahatvāna nimmalā hotha bhikkhave

[3] See p. 166, note 5.

entirely superseded. There will, in fact, be no basis on which another normal consciousness could build up. With the blind consciousness absent there will be no 'will to live', consequently there will be no further 'life', that is, there will be 'no more to be done for the present state'.[1] The view taken by some of the Brahmans, such as the Gotama's early teacher Udraka Rāmaputra,[2] that the 'Neither-Perception-Nor-Non-Perception' (*nevasaññānāsaññāyatana*) stage of *Arūpa Jhāna* is tantamount to Nirvāṇa is understandable if one could relate the cessation of normal consciousness to entire exhaustion of the infra-consciousness but this is not possible; as in the case of death, the normal consciousness is only temporarily suspended, so that the cessation is comparable only to a type of blindness. We have therefore to take it that a deathless state represents complete abrogation of the life which consists in an assembly of processes and processing.

The definition of Nibbāna according to the fifth quotation given from the *Dhammapada* consists in 'the unsurpassed release from attachments'. Here the term '*yoga*' for 'attachment'[3] is synonymous with '*āsava*'. Four *yogas* are recognized,[4] three of them identical with the *āsavas* already considered, while the fourth, attachment to wrong views or speculative theory, is also sometimes taken as a fourth *āsava*. Since however the term 'ignorance' covers false views and speculative theory, the *āsavas* are very often limited to three in number. Taking remarks applying to the *āsavas* to hold also for the *yogas*, in the sense in which '*yoga*' is here employed, we may proceed to the last of the six *Dhammapada* quotations under review.

'Cut out the love of self as one would an autumn water-lily with the hand. Develop the way to Nibbāna, taught by the Happy One.'[5] In the present consideration attention has

[1] *nāparaṃ itthattāyā ti*. See p. 169, note 1. [2] See p. 35, note 1.

[3] The term 'Yoga' also means a method of meditation or mental-control which has been known in India from very early days. This technique is explained in *Upaniṣads* and *Bhagavadgītā*. The system of philosophy established by Patañjalī (c. fifth century AC) in his *Yogasūtra* defines the term as 'cessation of the mental activities' (*cittavṛttinirodha*). The term, however, is derived from *yuj* to employ or join and it means the practice of spiritual discipline or way to union with ultimate reality. The *Dhammapada* also says: Indeed from meditation wisdom arises (*Yogā ve jāyate bhūrī*. v. 282).

[4] *kāma-yoga, bhava-yoga, diṭṭhi-yoga, avijjā-yoga*. See D. III. 230; A. II. 11.

[5] See p. 166, note 7.

already been drawn to the Buddha's repudiation of the idea of a permanent in-dwelling self, to his expositions on the identification of feeling with the self,[1] to the attainment to final release from the 'self',[2] and to the fact that all dhammas are without a self.[3] Regarding the release from the self, it is essential to be clear on the point that the Pali *attā* is by no means identical with the Sanskrit *ātman*; *ātman*, having a much longer history than *attā*, has many connotations which could not apply to *attā*. Prior to the personification of Brahman, the Absolute Reality of the *Upaniṣads*, *ātman* represented a far more profound concept than 'soul', and in some respects signified the non-self rather than the self. Nearer to the soul, self or *attā*, was the *jīva* which was the transmigrating portion of the being. When 'Brahman' was personified, though with the *saprapañca* aspect some distinction could still be drawn between the *ātman* and the *jīva*, with the *niṣprapañca* aspect[4] *ātman* and *jīva* are inextricably confused. But as though to disclaim any relationship between the Tathāgata of Buddhism and the aspects of Absolute Brahman or Brahma we have the statements already quoted: 'Mankind delights in manifoldness; the Tathāgatas are without variety of expansion,'[5] and: 'There is no movement with the Buddhas.'[6] There is no indication in the *Nikāyas* as to whether the Brahmans as a body inclined to the *saprapañca* or *niṣprapañca* ideal; 'Brahman' appears merely as 'Brahma'; therefore the question so frequently put to the Buddha: 'Is the *jīva* the same thing as the body, or is the *jīva* one thing and the body another?[7] represented no idle enquiry but was the result of much disputation and hair-splitting over the philosophical problems presented by the personification of Brahman. Sometimes the Buddha refused to reply, in conformity with the reasons given to Poṭṭhapāda;[8] at other times, as in the case of Maṇḍissa and Jāliya, he adopted the procedure of describing the training of a bhikkhu and then asking if to such a person the question would be

[1] See p. 40, notes 1, 2, 3. [2] See p. 41, note 2

[3] See p. 43, note 1. [4] See p. 20, notes 2, 3.

[5] Dh. v. 254: *papañcābhiratā pajā nippapañcā Tathāgatā.* See p. 121, note 4.

[6] *Ibid.* v. 255: *n'atthi Buddhānam iñjitaṃ.* See p. 121, note 5.

[7] *taṃ jīvaṃ sarīraṃ udāhu aññam jīvaṃ aññaṃ sarīran ti.* D. I. 157. and frequently in the Buddhist texts.

[8] See p. 62, note 6, and associated text.

even intelligent.[1] Any quotations regarding '*ātman*' should therefore be treated with circumspection before applying their content to the *anattā* of Buddhism. The Buddhist '*anattā*' is to be considered always as the absence of a permanent indwelling 'self' or essence of any kind; this is confirmed in the presentation of life as a stream of consciousness.

'*Burning*' (*āditta*)

The employment of the simile of 'burning' (*āditta*)[2] with regard to the life of a living being may be extended to a comparison well beyond the field of poetic imagery; in fact, the details of 'burning' correspond to many details of the basis of progress of an existence and of the passing from one existence to another. In the usual sense of the term, however, 'burning' is so common that few people have paused to consider what happens exactly when a thing is 'burnt'. Primitive man produced a fire by rubbing two sticks together until sparks appeared and the sticks caught alight, thereby supplying directly from himself the energy necessary to start the process going. It was not until the third century CE that it was recognized that the presence of air was essential for 'burning', and fourteen more centuries elapsed before the suggestion was advanced that respiration and burning are similar processes. At the time the idea seemed fantastic, but after another century there was liberated from the atmosphere a gas which was found to be essential to both processes. This gas was called 'oxygen' (Grk. *oxus*, sharp, and *genes*, produced), and the processes were found to be those of oxidation. Three conditions are necessary to 'burning': something to burn, the oxygen in which to burn it, and the application of some form of energy which will raise the temperature of the surroundings sufficiently to start the activity. Similarly for respiration there are needed: something that can breathe, some oxygen for it to breathe, and a supply of energy to start the process going. Failing any one of these specific conditions, we have neither burning nor breathing, neither combustion nor respiration.

[1] D. I. 158: *yo so āvuso bhikkhu evaṃ jānāti evaṃ passati kallaṃ tass' etaṃ, vacanāya taṃ jīvaṃ taṃ sarīran ti vā aññaṃ jīvaṃ aññaṃ sarīran ti vā.*

[2] See Vin. I. 34; S. III. 71, IV. 19 f.; Sn. v. 591 and *passim;* (*ādīpita*) S. I. 31.

If the processes are in active condition, in order to halt them one of the three conditions must be withdrawn. If the fire has been allowed to 'burn itself out', in other words if all the wood—assuming this to be the sticks of primitive man—that would burn at the temperature supplied has now burnt, there remains ash which might or might not be rekindled if a higher temperature were available. The energy supplied to start the reaction has been converted into the heat and light of the attendant flame; these have been dissipated and one must look for them 'somewhere' in the universe. According to older Indian thought they have returned to a universal stock of such forms of energy; but in any case they cannot be recovered in the form in which they were previously expended. If we take the parallel of human life, the removal of one of the three conditions for breathing would result in the cessation of breathing and therefore in the 'death' of the individual concerned. The physical body disintegrates, and, in the words of Hamlet: 'Why may not imagination trace the noble dust of Alexander till he find it stopping a bung-hole?' But we have the dictum: 'This is my body, possessing material qualities, formed of the four great elements, produced by mother and father, an accumulation of rice and fluid, a thing by its nature impermanent, fragile, perishable, and subject to total destruction; and this is my consciousness, bound up with and dependent on it.'[1] What becomes of the consciousness?

At death the mentality is reduced to the level of infra-consciousness which continues, without a break, as the first form of pre-natal consciousness of a new existence. In terms of the burning wood one may say that, given sufficient incentive, the ash is ready to break again into fire; in terms of the human being the infra-consciousness continues as the potential to be energized into a new existence. In the term 'Nirvāṇa' we have the implication of the dying-out of fire, but since 'Nirvāṇa' is, literally, 'making cool by blowing', we have to reckon that the extinguishing is due to deliberate effort to remove the condition making any further reaction possible,

[1] D. I. 76: *ayaṃ kho me kāyo rūpī cātum-mahā-bhūtiko mātā-pettika-sambhavo odana-kummās-upacayo anicc-ucchādana-parimaddana-bhedana-viddhaṃsana-dhammo, idañ ca pana me viññāṇaṃ ettha sitaṃ ettha paṭibaddhan ti*. See also p. 67, note 4.

whether or not the equivalent of the ash remains. That any potential should remain at death is impossible if the person has become enlightened during the present life. It could be taken, however, that sufficient potential remains to carry him through the remainder of his present life in the everyday world, and that in this remainder he is merely carrying on in conformity with his antecedents. In this connection the Buddha used the simile of a mango branch.[1] Such a branch, though severed from its parent plant, continues to maintain its previous appearance and habits and to produce mangoes of the same type as the fruit of the parent tree until it finally dies, then subsiding into complete decay. There remains nothing to be re-energized.

Taking the attaining to Nibbāna to be synonymous with becoming enlightened, we may recognize two kinds of Nibbāna, that with substrata remaining, and that with no substrata remaining. The Buddha once considered the case of a bhikkhu who had destroyed the *āsavas*—has done what ought to be done, has laid down his burdens, attained a good welfare, destroyed the Fetters of existence, and is emancipated by Perfect Knowledge.[2] If he rejoices in his feelings he has a remaining substratum and the Nibbāna is *saupādisesa*; if he does not rejoice in his feelings these will become burnt out and there will be no substrata remaining. This is the *anupādisesa* condition of Nibbāna. The extinction of human passion is therefore called the 'Nibbāna with the condition of being still remaining', or, more literally, the 'Nibbāna with the *upadhi* remnant', where *upadhi* is the material and immaterial condition of being. This would represent a person without passion while yet alive. The total extinction of the conditions of being, as well as that of passion, represents the Nibbāna without any remainder, the complete and perfect freedom.

But though with the final disappearance of the potential to live there will be no more of the present state, that is by no means to say that there has not transpired a situation of an entirely different kind from that previously known. We have the parallel in the case of 'splitting the atom' when, though no new material substance was found within the atom, there did transpire what is now referred to as a micro-world. Here the

[1] D. I. 46. [2] It. 38 f.

problems of the macro-world for the most part ceased to exist; there is no similarity of the factors creating them. The laws of time and space of the everyday world do not here govern in the same way, and in place of substantial bodies we have something more of the nature of fields of force or spheres of influence. It is by no means suggested that Nirvāṇa is a micro-world with the present as a macro-world, but it is definitely suggested that, in the research into one type of situation or the solving of one set of problems, one may arrive at some novel state which is quite unpredictable from the viewpoint of the former state. But regarding living beings, what passes on from one life to another is at least the potential of the past life or lives whatever the visible surroundings may be; what exists at attainment to Nibbāna may be perfected and true vision, but there is no content that we recognize from the present state. Hence it was logical that, though after the Parinibbāna of the Buddha neither man nor *devas* would perceive his body,[1] it would be incorrect to say that after death the Tathāgata exists, does not exist, both exists and does not exist, or neither exists nor does not exist.[2]

The position taken up by the commentators Buddhaghosa and Upatissa consists largely in agreement that 'the Blessed One preached about the Cessation of Suffering by way of the Origin of Suffering'.[3] Upatissa does not embark on a direct description of Nibbāna but Buddhaghosa treats of the subject in *Visuddhimagga*[4] where he recognizes eleven kinds of 'fire': that of lust, hatred, delusion, sickness, decay or old age, death, grief, lamentation, suffering, melancholy and tribulation.[5] On the other hand Buddhaghosa does not comment on the word 'dhamma' but Upatissa says of it: 'Thus is the Dhamma, Nibbāna, and the way of progress to Nibbāna. What is that way of progress? The Four Applications of Mindfulness, the Four Right Efforts, the Four Roads to Power, the Five Guiding Faculties, the Five Forces, the Seven Factors of Enlightenment,

[1] D. I. 46: *kāyassa bhedā uddhaṃ jīvita-pariyādānā na dakkhinti devamanussā*

[2] See p. 41, note 3, and associated text.

[3] *Vimuttimagga and Visuddhimagga, op, cit.*, p. 107.

[4] Vism. 67–70.

[5] *Rāgo ca doso ca moho ca vyādhi*
jarā ca maraṇam pi ca sokam eva
paridevadukkham pi ca domanassaṃ
'pāyasam ekādasa aggim āha.

and the Noble Eightfold Path. This is called the Way of Progress leading to Nibbāna.'[1] This is exactly the enumeration given by the Buddha when addressing bhikkhus shortly before his *Parinibbāna*. He put the question: 'What are the things I have taught you? What are the Truths I have perceived, that you, having thoroughly learnt them, should practise them, cultivate them, take them up seriously, so that the religious life, lasting a long time, may be perpetuated, that it may be for the good of the many, for the happiness of the many, for compassion on the world, for the sake of the welfare and happiness of *devas* and men.'[2] He then gave the list of the 'things' he had taught, as quoted immediately above.

Other statements concerning Nibbāna

Other statements made by the Buddhas concerning Nibbāna include the following: Speaking of his own *Parinibbāna* the Buddha said: 'On the night the Tathāgata attains to the Highest Perfect Wisdom, and on the night in which he attains to the Final Release, to the state without substratum, the natural condition of Nibbāna, on these two occasions the skin of the Tathāgata is of complete purity and perfection.'[3] Again, when Vipassi Buddha had discerned the second and third of the Four Noble Truths and had been freed from the *āsavas*, he considered preaching the Dhamma;[4] then he decided: 'This generation is attached to pleasure and delights in the attachment and because of this it is difficult for it to understand the matters, namely this Causation and the Law of "This arises depending on That". These too are matters difficult to understand, namely, the calming of all mental concomitants, the forsaking of all substrata of rebirth, the destruction of craving, dispassionateness, no prevention, no obstruction, Nibbāna.[5] The latter part of this quotation, 'the calming of all mental con-

[1] *Vimuttimagga and Visuddhimagga, op. cit.*, p. 107.

[2] D. II. 119 f.: *Katame ca te bhikkhave dhammā mayā abhiññāya desitā, ye vo sādhukaṃ uggahetvā āsevitabbā bhāvetabbā bahulīkātabbā yathayidaṃ brahmacariyaṃ addhaniyaṃ assa ciraṭṭhitikaṃ, tad assa bahujana-hitāya bahujanasukhāya lokānukampāya atthāya hitāya sukhāya devamanussānaṃ? Seyyathīdaṃ cattāro satipaṭṭhānā cattāro sammapaddhānā cattāro iddhipādā pañc' indriyāni pañca balāni satta bojjhaṅgā ariyo aṭṭhaṅgiko maggo.*

[3] *Ibid.* II. 134. [4] *Ibid.* II. 35. [5] *Ibid.* II. 36.

comitants' and onwards, is given elsewhere in the *Nikāyas* as a definition of Nibbāna.[1]

According to the *Paṭiccasamuppāda* the cessation of consciousness is contingent on cessation of the *saṅkhāra*, and the cessation of the *saṅkhāra* is contingent on cessation of ignorance (*avijjā*), and *vice versa*. The associations of the *saṅkhāra* have already been considered so that we may now examine the question of craving, or thirst (*taṇhā*).

Craving, Thirst (Taṇhā)

It has been stated that ignorance is the greatest impurity;[2] by reason of this ignorance one mistakes the true nature of life, and because of the sustained and intensified effort to hold on to existence in the form in which one knows it at present one brings on oneself all manner of ills. As a result of ignorance comes the blind will to live, the thirst, not merely for incidental things, but for the whole process of life.

'What is the Noble Truth of the Origin of Suffering? It is the craving, leading to rebirth, that is connected with impassioned delight, rejoicing first in one place then in another, namely: the sensual craving, the craving for the process of life, and the craving for the negation of the process of life.'[3]

Here craving for existence is intended to cover not only existence in the present world but also that in the fine-material (*rūpāvacara*) and non-material (*arūpāvacara*) realms.[4] All such forms are condemned as 'craving', as is also the desire for annihilation. The verdict is given frequently in the Buddhist texts, as for example: 'Beings held in the bonds of craving, with minds infatuated with existence and non-existence, who are harnessed to the yoke of Māra and have fear of the bonds, so difficult to avoid in this world, are pursued by birth and death. But he who abandons craving, is without craving for

[1] *Sabbasaṅkhārasamatho sabbūpadhi-paṭinissaggo taṇhakkhayo virāgo nirodho nibbānaṃ.* S. I. 136; A. II. 118.

[2] See p. 171, note 2.

[3] *Katamañ ca bhikkhave dukkha-samudayaṃ ariya-saccaṃ? Yāyaṃ taṇhā ponobhavikā nandi-rāga-sahagatā tatra tatrābhinandinī, seyyathīdaṃ: kāma-taṇhā bhava-taṇhā vibhava-taṇhā.* Vin. I. 10; D. II. 308, III. 216, 275; M. I. 48, 299, III. 250 and *passim.*

[4] See p. 24f.

existence or non-existence; a bhikkhu without craving, who has destroyed craving, attains to *Parinirvāṇa*.'[1]

The above verses occur in the *Udānavarga* chapter on Craving (*tṛṣṇāvarga*) and are followed by others which, occurring also in the *Dhammapada* and other Pali texts, appear to be part of a discourse delivered by the Buddha. They run: 'Whoever is subject to that contemptible craving, so difficult to overcome in this world, for him sorrows increase like the *bīraṇa* grass after rain. But he who overcomes this contemptible craving, difficult to pass over in this world, from him sorrows fall off like drops of water from a lotus. I tell you this good thing: as many of you as are assembled here, dig up the root of craving as one digs up the *bīraṇa* to find the fragrant root of *usīra*.'[2]

The *Udānavarga* proceeds here to stress non-existence: 'A man who has associated with craving for a long time, again and again follows the road of birth and death; again and again without ceasing he submits to the process of life, in this way or that, coming and going.[3] But abandoning craving he is without craving for existence or non-existence; he is not subject to rebirth, indeed to him craving does not exist.'[4] But peculiar to the Pali texts is the employment of the word '*vāṇa*', craving, to which there is no corresponding Sanskrit, and which is used in connection with *taṇhā* and *nibbāna*. We have, for example, '*vāṇa saṅkhātāya taṇhāya nikkhantattā nibbānaṃ*'—the departure from craving is called nibbāna.

For the remainder of the definition of Nibbāna quoted above[5] we have '*virāgo, nirodho, nibbānaṃ*'. *Virāgo*, signifying dispassionateness, without colour, without passion, is often considered to be synonymous with 'nibbāna'; '*nirodho*', if interpreted as 'extinction' can be misleading, yet taken as *ni* plus *rodho*, no prevention, or no obstruction, we have an aspect of the Goal which is rarely presented and which is in

[1] It. 50; cf. Uv. III. vv. 7, 8.

[2] Dh. vv. 335, 336 and 337; Thag. 402; J. III. 387; Cf. Uv. III. vv. 9, 10, 11.

[3] A. II. 10; Sn. v. 740; It. 15; Uv. III. v. 12.

[4] Uv. III. v. 13:

Tāṃ tu tṛṣṇāṃ prahāya hi vītatṛṣṇo bhavābhave
nāsau punaḥ saṃsarate tṛṣṇā hy asya na vidyate.

(No Pali equivalents.)

[5] See p. 179, note 1.

keeping with the statement 'There is no movement (*instability*) with the Buddhas',[1] and with the classification as an *asaṃskṛta dharma.*[2]

Recognizing that the basic obstruction to realization of Nibbāna lies in craving, therefore in ignorance, and that until these are removed the vision to perceive Nibbāna is obscured, we turn to the consideration of 'freeing of mind, freeing of insight'.

(c) *Freeing of mind, freeing of insight* (*ceto-vimutti paññā vimutti*)

When the Buddha was asked by Mahāli if it was for the purpose of the cultivation of *samādhi* that the bhikkhus led the religious life under him he replied that it was not, that there were other things, higher and more excellent, for the realizing of which they did so.[3] He then described the Stages of the Path, the highest occurring with the destruction of the *āsavas*. Then he continued: 'The bhikkhu, having come to understand thoroughly and to experience for himself, freeing of mind and freeing of insight, here amongst things as seen in the present world, having attained therein continues.'[4] The destruction of the *āsavas* being coincident with the attainment of the Goal, one may take it that this attainment consists in the freeing of mind and the freeing of insight here in the present life. In this passage from *Mahāli Sutta*, quoted immediately above, the Buddha states that the way to reach such understanding lies in following the Noble Eightfold Path, but here the terms *ceto-vimutti paññā-vimutti* are not expressly mentioned. We will therefore examine their associations according to other parts of the Buddhist texts.

The assumption that '*ceto-vimutti*' and '*paññā-vimutti*' are synonymous is incorrect, while the statements that '*ceto-vimutti*' is 'always with *paññā-vimutti*', and '*paññā-vimutti*' is 'always paired with *ceto-vimutti*' are also not accurate.[5] For example, *ceto-vimuttiyā* occurs alone in *Tevijja Sutta*,

[1] See p. 173, note 6. [2] See p. 168, note 1. [3] See p. 83, notes 1–3.

[4] D. I. 156: *Puna ca paraṃ Mahāli bhikkhu āsavānaṃ khayā anāsavaṃ ceto-vimuttiṃ paññā-vimuttiṃ diṭṭhe va dhamme sayaṃ abhiññā sacchikatvā upasampajja viharati.*

[5] See Pali Text Society's Pali-English Dictionary, p. 272 and 390.

Dīgha Nikāya XIII, where an account is given of the states known as the '*Brahmavihāras*' which lead to *ceto-vimutti*. The discourse was delivered when a young Brahman, Vāseṭṭha, enquired of the Buddha the way to 'Union with Brahma'.[1] The Buddha described the Moralities and *Samādhi* in the terms of the *Sāmaññaphala* address,[2] up to and including the abolition of the Five Hindrances and the consequent joy attained, but instead of proceeding to the description of the Jhānic states he continued as follows: 'From his thought imbued with loving-kindness (*mettā*), the bhikkhu suffuses with loving-kindness one quarter of the world and so continues. Then he suffuses a second, a third, a fourth quarter. Above, below, across, everywhere, the entire world, he suffuses with loving-kindness from the mind, extensive, becoming unlimited, without ill-will or trace of hurt, and so remains. Just, Vāseṭṭha, as a powerful trumpeter reaches with little difficulty to the four quarters of the world, so with the freeing of the mind by loving-kindness he who fulfils this example will not remain standing there. This, Vāseṭṭha is the way to union with Brahma.'[3] The Buddha then describes how the bhikkhu imbues his thought with compassion (*karuṇā*), sympathy for the welfare of others (*muditā*), and equanimity (*upekkhā*). In each case he uses the simile of the trumpeter, and, emphasizing that one who follows this example 'will not remain stationary, or standing, there', states that this is the way to union with Brahma. In striving to effect the union, or as the Buddhist teaching enunciates the projected result '*ceto-vimutti*', all four *Brahmavihāras* must be taken into account; too frequently, and probably because the western translations of the text give in full only that for *mettā*—as has been done here—there is a tendency to overlook the practice of *karuṇā*, *muditā* and *upekkhā*. This, of course is not legitimate. It must further be established that there is no identity between the Brahmanic

[1] D. I. 235 ff. [2] See p. 67, notes 1–3, and associated text.

[3] *Ibid.* 250 f.: *So mettā-sahagatena cetasā ekaṃ disaṃ pharitvā viharati, tathā dutiyaṃ, tathā tatiyaṃ, tathā catutthaṃ. Iti uddham adho tiriyaṃ sabbadhi sabbattatāya sabbāvantaṃ lokaṃ mettā-sahagatena cetasā vipulena mahaggatena appāmāṇena avereṇa avyāpajjhena pharitvā viharati. Seyyathā pi Vāseṭṭha balavā saṅkha-dhamo appakasiren'eva catuddisā viññāpeyya, evaṃ bhāvitāya kho Vāseṭṭha mettāya ceto-vimuttiyā yaṃ pamāṇa-kataṃ kammaṃ na taṃ tatrā-vasissati na taṃ tatrāvatiṭṭhati. Ayam pi kho Vāseṭṭha Brahmāṇaṃ sahavyatāya maggo.*

goal and any stage on the Buddhist *magga*; the use of the expression 'Union with Brahma' was made by Vāseṭṭha and accordingly continued with by the Buddha during the conversation.

The *Brahmavihāras* were already familiar to Indian thought before the Buddha's day; so also were the Jhānic states whose position according to the *Sāmaññaphala* discourse is, in *Tevijja Sutta*, taken by the *Brahmavihāras*. But whereas in the *Sāmaññaphala* the *Jhānic* states—and it must be remembered that only the *Rūpa Jhānas* are there described—are followed by the section comprising '*paññā*', with the *Brahmavihāra* in the *Tevijja* we have only the assurance that the person practising them does not 'stand' there. Notably, in both cases the highest point reached is that of *upekkhā*, equanimity; it may therefore be considered that the study and development of *paññā* is the natural sequence also in both cases.

Regarding a mention of '*paññā-vimutti*' without the accompaniment of '*ceto-vimutti*', in *Mahānidāna Suttanta*,[1] the Buddha described the seven stages of sentient beings and two spheres of consciousness as follows: The first stage, in which there is a variety of bodily states and states of intelligence, as in the case of men, certain devas, and certain people born in miserable states; the second stage, in which there are beings with a variety of bodily states but with uniform intelligence, like the devas of the company of Brahmā having attained to rebirth in the Brahma world for the first time; the third stage, in which beings have one kind of body but diversity of intelligence as in the case of the Ābhassara *devas*; the fourth stage, in which are beings with uniform body and uniform intelligence, like the Subhakiṇha *devas*;[2] the fifth stage in which are beings who, from the passing beyond the perception of form, from the setting-down of the perception of the opposing nature of objects, and from non-attention to discriminating between the diversity of objects—thus: 'Space is infinite'—attain to the field of consciousness on which arises the consciousness of the infinity of space; the sixth stage, in which beings attain to the consciousness dwelling on the infinity of

[1] D. II. 55–71.

[2] *Devas* of the *Rūpāvacara* who were reborn there because of their experience of Third *Jhāna*.

consciousness; the seventh in which consciousness dwells on 'nothingness'. The sphere of beings without consciousness is the first and where consciousness is so subtle that it barely exists, if it exists at all, is the second sphere of consciousness. The last four of those stages will be recognized as stages of Consciousness of the Formless, or *Arūpa* Consciousnesses, already mentioned. The Buddha having enumerated these stages, and having pointed out that it would not be fitting that a person who had come to know them, their origin, passing away, satisfaction and disadvantages, and the way of departure therefrom should take any delight in them, continued: 'From the time the bhikkhu has found out, according to the Truth, the origin of these seven stages and two spheres, their passing away, their satisfaction and disadvantages, and the way of departure from them, then he is said to be freed by insight.'[1]

The Buddha followed with an enumeration of eight stages of deliverance, known generally as the Eight Freedoms (*Vimokkhas*), but these do not correspond throughout to the stages described in the previous paragraph. The first three of the *Vimokkhas* are given in a very condensed form of Pali, while the remaining five, which represent the four *arūpajhānas* and the final cessation, are in more academic Pali, in the standard form in which they appear in both the Pali and Sanskrit texts. The *Vimokkhas* are: (i) The seeing of material compositions as being material qualities, (ii) Having oneself perception of formlessness one sees material compositions as exterior (without intrinsic nature), (iii) That 'pleasantless' is one's inclination to a thing, (iv)–(viii) the *arūpajhānas* and the cessation of consciousness.[2] It is not until the Buddha has added to these stages the destruction of the *āsavas* that he employs the terms *ceto-vimutti* and *paññā-vimutti* in conjunction. He concludes: 'Having

[1] D. II. 70: *Yato kho Ānanda bhikkhu imāsañ ca sattannaṃ viññāṇaṭṭhitīnaṃ imesañ ca dvinnaṃ āyatanānaṃ samudayañ ca atthagamañ ca assādañ ca ādīnavañ ca nissaraṇañ ca yathābhūtaṃ viditvā anupādā vimutto hoti, ayaṃ vuccati Ānanda bhikkhu paññā-vimutto.*

[2] *Ibid.* II. 70 f.: *Rūpī rūpāni passati ayaṃ paṭhamo vimokkho, ajjhattaṃ arūpa-saññī bahiddhā rūpāni passati ayaṃ dutiyo vimokkho. Subhan't'eva adhimutto hoti. Ayaṃ tatiyo vimokkho. Sabbaso rūpasaññanaṃ samatikkamā paṭigha-saññānaṃ atthagamā nānatta-saññānaṃ amanisikārā ananto ākāso ti ākāsānañcāyatanaṃ upasampajja viharati ayaṃ catuttho vimokkho. Sabbaso nevasaññānāsaññāyatanaṃ samatikkamma saññā-vedayita-nirodhaṃ upasampajja viharati ayaṃ satthamo vimokkho.*

understood and experienced for himself the freeing of mind and freeing of insight, here amongst things as seen in the present world, and having attained therein continues, then it is said that the bhikkhu has attained freedom by both ways; further or more excellent freedom than this does not exist.'[1]

(*d*) *Origin of the Attainment*

The essential condition for attaining to Nibbāna being therefore a freeing of insight, *paññā-vimutti*, we turn to consider the *paññā* of *paññā-vimutti* in relation to the Noble Eightfold Path. The components of the Path have already been stated: Right View and Right Aspiration constituting *Paññā*, Right Speech, Right Action and Right Livelihood constituting *Sīla*, and Right Effort, Right Mindfulness and Right Concentration or One-pointedness of Mind constituting *Samādhi*. Here we are reminded of the main groups into which the Buddha divided his teaching, namely, *sīla, samādhi* and *paññā*, and also of the simplest form in which he described his teaching: 'Avoiding the doing of all evil, the accomplishing of good, the purifying of one's own mind.'[2] In the latter case the *samādhi* and *paññā* components may be combined under the heading of purification of the mind; in the Noble Eightfold Path the components are interrelated but certain qualities are common to them all. Just as it was possible to point to the existence of ignorance or craving as the essence of the bonds tying one to the rounds of rebirth, so it is also possible to point to certain radical features as providing the means of attainment to the Goal. These features are investigation (*vīmaṃsā*) and vigilance (*appamāda*).

In the instructions given to householders it was clear that the qualities they were advised to cultivate were exactly those which would be needed throughout their journey along the Path, the Road (*magga*). There was never any question of arguing that the householder, whether formally he could or could not attain to Nibbāna in the present life, need not

[1] D. II. 71: *āsavānañ ca khayā anāsavaṃ ceto-vimuttiṃ paññā-vimuttiṃ diṭṭhe va dhamme sayaṃ abhiññā sacchikatvā upasampajja viharati, ayaṃ vuccati Ānanda bhikkhu ubhatobhāga-vimutto, imāya ca Ānanda ubhato-bhāga-vimuttiyā aññā ubhato-bhāga-vimutti uttaritarā vā paṇītatatarā vā n'atthīti.*

[2] Dh. v. 183.

exert himself in current affairs. There was no pseudo-puritanism to the effect that he should welcome poverty or live meanly; on the contrary he was expected to be successful, live in a suitable locality, dress himself suitably, and conduct himself in a hospitable manner towards his associates. He was, in fact, to use all his possessions, material and non-material, to the utmost advantage for good. The difference between the training for the householder and that for the recluse lay not in the faculties employed but in the specific ends to which they were directed; therefore, when in the course of time a householder came to see an unworthiness in his specific objects and to look for something better and higher, he had already acquired the habits of virtue which he would need to use. More, it was in the practising of these virtues that he would have come to a better understanding and to something of a mental vision that would lead to a quest for the higher life. If the objects on which, as a householder, he had concentrated his energies were among the toys of his mental childhood, they had not been unserviceable, for in the lawful pursuit of them he had come to search for others more worthy of his attention.

Regarding *vīmaṃsā*, even the housewife was told to go about her duties in a skilful, able, energetic manner and with a spirit of investigation (*dakkhā analasā tatrupāyāya vīmaṃsāya*). In the conversation with Vyagghapajja the Koḷiyan, the Buddha gave four qualities for alertness: 'By whatever activity he makes a living, whether by cultivation of the soil, by trading, by cattle-rearing, by archery, in government service, by whatever craft, he is skilful, energetic, able, and of an investigating mind, able to carry out his work satisfactorily. This is called the origin of attainment.'[1] In the *Kālāma Sutta* the Kālāmas were told to investigate every doctrine before adopting it.[2] Finally, this spirit of investigation is one of the four ways to *Iddhi*.[3]

The Buddha enumerated three kinds of *iddhis*; that of mystic wonders (*iddhi*), that of prophecy (*ādesanā*), and that of instruction (*anusāsanī*).[4] The first two, by reason of their

[1] A. IV. 281. [2] *Ibid.* I. 189 f.

[3] *Iddhi:* originally used in the sense of potential, a possession of latent power. Later the term came to signify 'wonder', 'an extraordinary happening'.

[4] D. I. 212.

misuse, he said 'distressed, vexed and disgusted' him, but the third was to him the genuine wonder. It was attained by cultivation of the four essential conditions for the striving for concentration and one-pointedness of mind, namely: the impulse to strive, the energy to strive, the consciousness of the procedure, and the investigation of it.[1] According to *Visuddhimagga*, the 'roads to power' (*iddhipāda*) are so called 'for they, as guides, are indicating the road to power connected therewith and because they are forming, by way of preparation, the roads to power constituting the fruition of the Path.'[2] He who has reached the four roads to power has reached the right path leading to the cessation of suffering. Hence the importance of the investigating mind, and so of the need to stress the cultivation of it from the commonplace of life and onwards.

Concerning vigilance, one recalls the occasion on which King Pasenadi asked the Buddha if there were anything profitable in the things of the present world which would be of value in the world beyond. The Buddha replied in one word: 'Vigilance'.[3] The *Dhammapada* chapter on Vigilance (*appamāda*) has already been referred to, and *gāthās* concerning the connection of vigilance with the deathless state have been quoted,[4] but the final reference to vigilance is contained in the Buddha's last instructions. *Mahāparinibbāna Suttanta* gives the following: 'Now, bhikkhus, I call upon you: Conditioned things are things of decay; with vigilance try to accomplish.' These were the last words of the Tathāgata.[5]

If the qualities of the investigating mind and vigilance are to be understood as the basic and irreducible minimum for the following of the Path throughout its entire length, one may ask why, in the cultivation of them, it should have been necessary to introduce such matters as the *deva*-worlds, Jhānic states, and so forth. It must be appreciated, however, that the Buddha addressed a community of people who had themselves evolved these ideas over a period of many centuries, and that the ideas were therefore, as one may say, the very alphabet

[1] D. II. 213; A. II. 256.
[2] Vism. 373 ff.
[3] S. I. 87.
[4] See p. 69, note 3.
[5] D. II. 156: *Handa dāni bhikkhave āmantayāmi vo vayadhammā saṅkhārā appamādena sampādethā ti ayaṃ Tathāgatassa pacchimā vācā.*

of their thinking. Having stated his principle of the Four Noble Truths, he had the choice of denouncing the current concepts in entirety or of employing existing terminology and remodelling and restating the concepts which lay behind it. The first alternative he was not always disposed to adopt, as, for instance, in the matter of asceticism. When the naked ascetic Kassapa asked him if it were correct that he condemned all ascetic practices,[1] the Buddha asked Kassapa, how, since he knew the coming and passing away of the ascetics, the consciousness disconnecting the present life and the reuprising, he should censure all asceticism. Though he had had his own severe experiences of asceticism and had found that ascetic practices were, of themselves, by no means instrumental in bringing about development of vision, yet he was aware that a person adopting such practices might improve or might not improve. Concerning the use of current terminology, it is often remarked that the Buddha took over the beliefs in the Brahman *devas*, gods, devils, and other features. In the sense that he made use of the range of worlds as commonly accepted in his day, the statement contains an element of truth, but that either the worlds or the *devas* furnishing them formed an integral and indispensable part of his teaching is not correct since he made it clear that beings superior to men were still subject to birth and death and therefore to a measure of suffering. The Four Noble Truths were therefore unaffected by either the presence or absence of *devas* and contingent worlds. That the *devas* were instrumental, or the worlds applicable, in regard to the fact that better conditions of life awaited persons who maintained a high morality and developed their insight in the present life accordingly, is a logical enough outcome of the karma doctrine, but that the *devas* and worlds contributed to the question of the final state of excellence of the Tathāgata after death was clearly impossible. They were therefore unavailing in the actual developing of the main Buddhist theme, and it was with this development and the expounding thereof that the Buddha naturally concerned himself to the exclusion of all other themes. Throughout his teaching there holds good the dictum: 'But these are only designations, figures of speech,

[1] D.. I. 161 f.

concepts, belonging to the world, and the Tathāgata makes use of them without being bound to, or holding on to, any of them.'[1]

Similarly with the Jhānic states. These were of extreme use and provided a valuable practice; the Buddha quoted them on many occasions. But he also names them amongst the theories which, if adhered to, would help to constitute the Net of Opinions tying one to the round of rebirths.[2] We get moreover, his definite pronouncement on his two early teachers, Ārāda Kālāma and Udraka Rāmaputra, that their teachings, culminating in the third and fourth *arūpajhānas* respectively, did not satisfy him.[3] He does not mention the Jhānic states in the course of his description of his attainment to Enlightenment under the Bodhi tree, but states definitely that he and all the Buddhas came to their Enlightenment by way of the reasoning of the *Paṭiccasamuppāda*.[4] It may be that the *arūpāvacara jhānas*, being held in such high regard by the brahmans themselves, were interpolated on many occasions, suitable and unsuitable, by ex-brahman converts to Buddhism when engaged in compiling or commenting on Buddhist texts, and here the case of the *Vimokkhas* immediately suggests itself by reason of the types of phraseology employed. It is noteworthy that the Jhānic states are not mentioned explicity in the *Dhammapada*, nor, as far as is known at present, in any other of the *Dharmapadas*.

Further concerning the use of current terminology, perhaps the most difficult case to appreciate is that of the word '*Brahman*' in the sense employed by the Buddha in the famous set of *gāthās* in the *Brāhmaṇavagga* of the *Dhammapada* and in the *Mahāvagga* of *Sutta Nipāta*. Here each *gāthā* ends with the sentence: '*Tam ahaṃ brūmi brāhmaṇaṃ*': That one I call a brahman. If, as is often intimated, the brahmans as a class were the natural antagonists of the Buddha, why should he employ such a sentence in recounting, as he does in the *gāthās*, the salient qualities of the Buddhist of the highest attainments? One may infer that in the general course of events it would have been a brahman by caste who would have been the seeker after truth, but whether he ranked as '*Brāhmana*', '*Samaṇa*',

[1] D. I. 202.
[2] *Ibid.* I. 45.
[3] See p. 35, note 1
[4] D. II. 30, 33, 35.

or was known by any other title, he must, as a genuine seeker after truth, fulfil certain conditions. The technical title must be immaterial. Since the conditions cover the Buddhist teaching we consider them in detail, taking the block in the *Sutta Nipāta*[1] as being entirely representative of the particular *gāthās* and the most conveniently arranged for the present purpose.

620. I do not call a man a brahman because of his ancestry; if he is with possessions he is a *bhovādi*.[2] He who is without possessions and does not seize any, that one I call a brahman.

621. Having cut all fetters, he who has no longing for anything, does not cling to anything, is detached, that one I call a brahman.

622. Having cut off pleasure, the strap and chains and all that goes with them, lifted up the cross-bar, become enlightened, that one I call a brahman.

623. He who, though guiltless, strongly equipped with the power of patience, endures insults, ill-treatment and bonds, that one I call a brahman.

624. He who is observant of religious duties and the moralities who is without attributes, is controlled, bearing his final body, that one I call a brahman.

625. As water does not smear a lotus leaf, or a mustard seed the point of an awl, he who similarly is not smeared by lusts that one I call a brahman.

626. He who comes to know, here in the present existence, destruction of suffering, who has put down the burden of self, who is unyoked from the world, that one I call a brahman.

627. A man of profound insight, with possession of right wisdom regarding the Path and Not-Path, a man who has attained to the topmost height, that one I call a brahman.

628. One who does not associate with either householders

[1] Sn. vv. 620–47. The verses in the following translation are numbered accordingly.

[2] *'bho'* is the vocative form of *bhavant* (Cf. Skt. *bhoḥ*, the shortened voc. of *bhagoḥ*, of Vedic *bhagavant*): Sir, friend, my dear or you. A familiar term of address in speaking to equals or inferiors. *bhovādi:* A person who addresses others as 'bho', so assuming familiarity. If this familiarity is not justified, the speaker is implying his superiority. From *'bhovādi'* was inferred a brahman by caste as contrasted with a 'true' brahman.

or non-householders, is houseless and is satisfied with little, that one I call a brahman.

629. One who, having laid aside the stick, does not injure or destroy living beings, movable or immovable, that one I call a brahman.

630. One who amongst hostility is not hostile, who is peaceful in the midst of violence, who amongst people attached to the world is not grasping, that one I call a brahman.

631. One whose greed, hatred, pride, depreciation of others, fall off like a mustard seed from the point of an awl, that one I call a brahman.

632. One who does not speak harshly, speaks clearly and truthfully, by whose speech no one is offended, that one I call a brahman.

633. One who does not take that which in this world is not given, whether long or short, fine or coarse, pleasant or unpleasant, that one I call a brahman.

634. One who has no wishes in this or any other world, who does not rely on outward things, is detached, that one I call a brahman.

635. One of whom through understanding there does not exist any resting-place for doubt or uncertainty, who has attained to the deep conception of Immortality, that one I call a brahman.

636. One who in this present existence has overcome attachment both to merit and evil, is without grief, stainless and pure, that one I call a brahman.

637. One who is unstained, clean, bright as the moon, undisturbed, who has surmounted the state of existence dominated by lust, that one I call a brahman.

638. One who, from the passing away of the delusion of repeated existences, has crossed over this path beset with obstacles, difficult of access, has reached to the end, who meditates, is free from lusts, is without doubts, without grasping, and who has finished with movement, that one I call a brahman.

639. One who in this world, having beaten down lusts, is homeless, having in a wanderer's life surmounted the plane of sensuous existence, that one I call a brahman.

640. One who in this world having overcome craving, is

homeless, having in a wanderer's life surmounted the plane of existence where is craving, that one I call a brahman.

641. One who, having cast off human bonds, having overcome celestial bonds, is detached from all bonds, that one I call a brahman.

642. One who, having cast off attachment and lack of attachment, is calmed, without substratum for further rebirth, conqueror of all the worlds, a hero, that one I call a brahman.

643. One who has found out in every respect the passing-away and uprising of beings, is non-attached, happy, enlightened, that one I call a brahman.

644. The one whose way neither gods nor *gandhabbas*[1] nor men know, who has destroyed the *āsavas*, the arahant, that one I call a brahman.

645. One to whom 'before', 'afterwards', 'between', do not exist, are nothing, who does not take anything on to himself, that one I call a brahman.

646. The man of great strength, noble, heroic, a great sage, one who has conquered, who is free from lusts not a slave to them, that one I call a brahman.

647. He who recognizes his former abodes, perceiving happiness and misery therein, and has attained to destruction of birth, that one I call a brahman.

The above *gāthās* show the 'brahman' at various stages along his path. In *gāthās* of the nature of 629, 632, 633, he is shown as keeping the precepts of non-injury (629), speaking truthfully (632), and not taking that which is not given (633). He is patient (623) and is peaceful in the midst of violence (630). He overcomes greed, hatred, pride (631), and is unaffected by lusts (625). He attains to a state of no longing (621), no doubts (635), no craving (640), has no bonds of any kind, human or otherwise (641), even attachment to merit or evil (631), and he suffers no delusion about repeated existences (638). Here his achievements approach their highest, for he comes to know the destruction of suffering (626). He has put down the burden of self (626), has no attributes (624), and for

[1] *gandhabba:* a heavenly musician belonging to the *Cātummahārājika* realm; a being ready to take a new existence is also called *gandhabba*. In this context it is of the former sense.

him time does not exist (643). Having attained to the conception of no-change, with no attachment or lack of attachment he is entirely calm (642).

In conclusion we draw attention to two remarks made by the Buddha concerning his own teaching. At the outset, as has been referred to in the case of Vipassi Buddha, he refused to preach the Dhamma for the sake of the few but consented to do so for the sake of mankind at large.[1] The second allusion concerns the Buddha's conversation with Venerable Ānanda when he was recovering from his last illness. The circumstances were as follows. Venerable Ānanda, distraught with anxiety, had tried to comfort himself with the thought: The Exalted One will not go to his *Parinibbāna* until he has spoken something about the Saṅgha of bhikkhus. The Buddha replied: 'But what, then, does the Saṅgha expect of me? I have expounded the Dhamma throughout, in entirety; the Tathāgata has not the closed fist of a teacher who holds back something of his doctrine. If there is anyone who thinks: "I should look after the Saṅgha", "It is mine to arrange a programme for the Saṅgha", he it is who should speak something.'[2] But the Buddha had already taught his Dhamma in full, to mankind at large, as he had promised he would. It began with the most elementary of the Moralities, and proceeded without a break to the realization of the Ultimate Goal: the attainment of Nibbāna with the Realization of the Four Noble Truths.

[1] D. II. 37, 39.

[2] *Ibid.* II. 100: *Kim pan'Ānanda bhikkhu-saṅgho mayi paccāsiṃsati? Desito Ānanda mayā dhammo anantaraṃ abāhiraṃ karitvā, na tatth'Ānanda Tathāgatassa dhammesu ācariya-muṭṭhi. Yassa nūna Ānanda evam assa ahaṃ bhikkhu-saṅghaṃ pariharissāmīti vā mam'uddesiko bhikkhu-saṅgho ti vā, so nūna Ānanda bhikkhu-saṅghaṃ ārabbha kiñcid eva udāhareyya.* See also p. 33, note 2.

SELECTED BIBLIOGRAPHY

(Primary sources were given under the abbreviations.)

Arnold, Sir Edwin *The Light of Asia*, many editions.

Basham, A. L. *The Wonder that was India*, Sidgwick & Jackson, London, 1954.

Bendall, C., and Rouse, W. H. D. (trs.) *Śikṣāsamuccaya* (Compendium of Training) of Sāntideva, London, 1922.

Bhargava, Dayanand *Jain Ethics*, Motilal Banarasidass, Delhi, 1968.

Brahmacari, Situl Prasad *A Comparative Study of Jainism and Buddhism*, Madras, 1929.

Burtt, Edwin A. *The Teaching of the Compassionate Buddha*, New York, 1955.

Conze, Edward *Buddhism*, 3rd edition, Faber, London, 1957.

Conze, Horner, Snellgrove, Waley *Buddhist Texts through the Ages*, Faber, London, 1957.

Coomaraswamy, Ananda K. *Buddha and the Gospel of Buddhism*, New York, 1964.

Time and Eternity (Chapter on Buddhism), Ascona, 1947.

Coomaraswamy, Ananda K., and I. B. Horner *Introduction to Living Thoughts of Gotama the Buddha*, London, 1948; India edition, Bombay, 1956.

Eliot, Sir Charles *Hinduism and Buddhism*, 3 vols., Routledge, London, 1922.

Evola, J. *Doctrine of Awakening*, trs. H. E. Musson, Luzac & Co., London, 1951.

Floyd Ross, H. *The Meaning of Life in Hinduism and Buddhism*, London, 1952.

Foucher, A. *La Vie du Bouddha d'après les Textes et les Monuments de l'Inde*, Paris, 1949.

Hare, E. M. *Woven Cadences* (Suttanipāta), PTS, London, 1948.

The Book of the Gradual Sayings, vol. III, 1953, IV, 1954 (trs. *Aṅguttaranikāya*) PTS, London.

Hastings, James (ed.) *Encyclopaedia of Religion and Ethics*, New York, 1955.

Horner, I. B. (trs.) *Middle Length Sayings*, vol. I, 1954, II, 1957, III, 1959 (*Majjhimanikāya*), PTS, London.

Milinda's Questions, 2 vols. (*Milindapañha*), PTS, London.

Humphreys, Christmas *Buddhism*, Pelican Series.

Jayasuriya, W. F. *The Psychology and Philosophy of Buddhism* (being an introduction of Abhidhamma), Y.M.B.A. Press, Colombo, 1963.

Jayatilleke, K. N. *Early Buddhist Theory of Knowledge*, London, 1963.

Kashyap, Bhikkhu J. *The Abhidhamma Philosophy*, 2 vols., Nalanda, Patna, 1954.

Khantipālo, Phra *Tolerance*, a Study from Buddhist Sources, Rider & Co., London, 1964.

What is Buddhism, Social Science Association, Press of Thailand, 1965.

Law, B. C. *History of Pali Literature*, 2 vols., London, 1933.

Mackenzie, John S. *A Manual of Ethics*, Univ. Tut., London, 1929.

Hindu Ethics, London, 1922.

Macnicol, N. *Living Religions of the Indian People*, London, 1934.

Morgan, Kenneth W. *The Path of Buddhism*, Ronald Press, New York, 1956.

Muirhead, John H. *The Elements of Ethics*, London, 1910.

Murti, T. R. *The Central Philosophy of Buddhism*, Allen & Unwin, London, 1955.

Ñāṇamoli, Bhikkhu (trs.) *The Path of Purification* (*Visuddhimagga*), Lake House, Colombo, 1956.

Nārada, Thera (trs.) *The Dhammapada*, London, 1954.

The Buddha and His Teachings, Saigon, 1964.

Nyāṇatiloka, Mahāthera *Fundamentals of Buddhism*, Colombo, 1949.

Guide through the Abhidhamma-Piṭaka and essay on *Paṭiccasamuppáda*, Colombo, 1957.

Buddhist Dictionary (A Manual of Buddhist Terms and Doctrines), Colombo, 1956.

The Word of the Buddha, Buddhist Publication Society, Kandy, 1959.

Nyāṇaponika, Thera *The Heart of Buddhist Meditation*, Colombo, 1954.

Radhakrishnan, S. *Indian Philosophy*, 2 vols., Allen & Unwin, London, 1929.

Introduction to Dhammapada, O.U.P., Oxford, 1950.

Rāhula, Walpola Sri *What the Buddha Taught*, Second and enlarged edition, Gordon Fraser, Bedford, 1967.

Rhys Davids, C. A. F. *The Book of Kindred Sayings*, Vol. I, 1950, II, 1952 (*Saṃyuttanikāya*), PTS, London.

Rhys Davids, T. W. *Buddhist India*, 3rd India edition, Calcutta, 1957.

Rhys Davids, T. W., and C. A. F. *Dialogues of the Buddha*, 3 vols. (trs.) *Dīghanikāya*), PTS, London, 1951.

Rogers, A. P. *A Short History of Ethics*, London, 1913.

Saddhatissa, H. *Handbook of Buddhists*, Mahabodhi Society, Sarnath, Banaras, 1956.

Upāsakajanālaṅkāra, A Critical Edition and Study, PTS, London, 1965.

Stcherbatsky, Th. *The Conception of Buddhist Nirvāṇa*, Leningrad, 1927.

The Central Conception of Buddhism, Calcutta, 1961.

Tachibana, S. *The Ethics of Buddhism*, Oxford University Press, London, 1926.

Takakusu, Junjiro *The Essentials of Buddhist Philosophy*, University of Hawaii, Honolulu, 1947.

SELECTED BIBLIOGRAPHY

Thomas, E. J. *The Road to Nirvana,* A Selection of the Buddhist Scriptures, Murray, London, 1950.

Early Buddhist Scriptures, a selection, trs. and ed., K. Paul, Trench, Trubner & Co., London, 1935.

History of Buddhist Thought, Routledge, London, 1933.

Life of Buddha as Legend and History, 3rd edition, Routledge, London, 1949.

Warren, Henry Clark *Buddhism in Translation,* Harvard University Press, 1947.

Winternitz, Maurice *A History of Indian Literature,* Vol. II, Calcutta, 1933.

Woodward, F. L. *Some Sayings of the Buddha,* World's Classics, Oxford, 1938.

The Book of Gradual Sayings, Vol. I, 1961, II, 1963, V, 1961 (trs. *Aṅguttaranikāya*), PTS, London.

The Book of Kindred Sayings, Vo. III, 1954, IV, V, 1956 (trs. *Saṃyuttanikāya*), PTS, London.

Zaehner, R. C. (ed.) *The Concise Encyclopaedia of Living Faiths,* New York, 1967.

Zimmer, H. *Philosophy of India,* ed. J. Campbell, Bollingen Series, XXVI, New York, 1951.

INDEX

INDEX

son 142
Soṇadaṇḍa 68
soul (*jīva*) 27
śraddhā (confidence) 54, 58
stages 183 f.
State 151 ff., 159
Stcherbatsky, Th. 36, 45
stealing 100 ff.
stupas 122 f.
Subha 68; *Subha Sutta* 67
suddas 117
Suddhodana 120
Sujātā 136
Sumer 157 f.
Sumerian 157
supramundane (*lokuttara*) 19, 21, 84
Sutta 74, 76; *-vibhaṅga* 75
Svetaketu 142
symbol 57

taṇhā (desire) 38
Tapassu 79 f.
Tathāgata 33, 41, 47, 57, 61 f., 117, 135, 167, 178, 188, 193
Tathatā (Thusness) 46
Tattvasaṅgraha 36, 54
teacher 141
Ten Precepts (*Dasa Sīla*) 111 f.
ten questions 63 f.
tevācika 80
Tevijja Sutta 181, 183
theft 156
Theravāda 75
thieving 16
thīna-middha (sloth and torpor) 24
thirst (*taṇhā*) 179
Tisaraṇa 53
trades 144
Tudi 68

Udayana 162
Udāyi 169
uddhacca-kukkucca (restlessness and worry) 24
Udraka Rāmaputra 35, 172, 189
Ugga 148
Ujuññā 124
Ukkala 79
ultimate aim 18 f.; truth 29
upādāna (attachment) 38
Upaniṣad 8, 20 f., 26, 29, 131, 142, 165, 172 f.
upāsakas and *upāsikās* 80 f., 115 ff., 119 f., 123
upasampadā 84
Upatissa 75, 177
upekkhā (equanimity) 24, 182
Uposatha 76, 110 f., 116
Ur 157
Uruvelā 70

vaikhānasas 30, 115
Vajjians 162 f.
Vakkali 58
vānaprastha (forest-dweller) 30
Vāseṭṭha 182 ff.
vedanā (feeling)
Vedic 8, 22 f., 26, 53, 110, 126, 165
vicikicchā (doubt) 24
vigilance 69
vijjā (knowledge) 37
Vijñānavāda 45, 78, 167
Vijñaptimātravāda 45 f.
Vikhanas 30
vīmaṃsā 185 f.
vimokkhas 184, 189
Vimokṣamārgaśāstra 75
vimutti 64, 75
Vimuttimagga 75
Vinaya 74 f., 79
viññāṇa (consciousness) 38
viññāṇañcāyatana (Infinity of Consciousness) 25
vipassanā 73; *-dhura* 85
Vipassi 48 ff., 114, 158, 178, 193
virtue 16 f.
Visuddhimagga 75
vyāpāda (ill-will) 24

wealth 143 ff., 146
wheel 154 ff.
wife 133 ff.
Williams, H. H. 15
wisdom 123 f.
Wolf, A. 18
workpeople 142

yaj 23
Yajurveda 23
Yasa 115
yathābhūta 25, 33, 44
yoga 172
Yogācāra 45

Zoroastrians 43, 153